Microsoft
Excel 2019
Step by Step

By Curtis Frye

Microsoft Excel 2019 Step by Step
Published with the authorization of Microsoft Corporation by:
Pearson Education, Inc.

ISBN-13: 978-1-5093-0767-8
ISBN-10: 1-5093-0767-2

Library of Congress Control Number: 2018959691

1 18

Trademarks
Microsoft and the trademarks listed at http://www.microsoft.com on the "Trademarks" webpage are trademarks of the Microsoft group of companies. All other marks are property of their respective owners.

Warning and Disclaimer
Every effort has been made to make this book as complete and as accurate as possible, but no warranty or fitness is implied. The information provided is on an "as is" basis. The author, the publisher, and Microsoft Corporation shall have neither liability nor responsibility to any person or entity with respect to any loss or damages arising from the information contained in this book or from the use of the CD or programs accompanying it.

Special Sales
For information about buying this title in bulk quantities, or for special sales opportunities (which may include electronic versions; custom cover designs; and content particular to your business, training goals, marketing focus, or branding interests), please contact our corporate sales department at corpsales@ pearsoned.com or (800) 382-3419.

For government sales inquiries, please contact governmentsales@pearsoned.com. For questions about sales outside the U.S., please contact intlcs@pearson.com.

Editor-in-Chief
Brett Bartow

Executive Editor
Loretta Yates

Assistant Sponsoring Editor
Charvi Arora

Development Editor
Songlin Qiu

Managing Editor
Sandra Schroeder

Senior Project Editor
Tracey Croom

Copy Editor
Kate Shoup

Indexer
Valerie Haynes Perry

Proofreader
Dan Foster

Technical Editor
Laura Acklen

Editorial Assistant
Cindy Teeters

Cover Designer
Twist Creative, Seattle

Compositor
Danielle Foster

Contents

Part 1: Create and format workbooks

Part 2: Analyze and present data

Part 3: Collaborate and share in Excel

11   Print worksheets and charts 293

Part 4: Perform advanced analysis

16   Create forecasts and visualizations. **409**

Acknowledgments

Books are team efforts. I'd like to thank Loretta Yates, who invited me to write *Microsoft Excel 2019 Step by Step*, and my agent Sherry Rogelberg of Studio B for arranging the contract. Thanks also to Tracey Croom for taking on the book as its production editor and Charvi Arora who joined the project as assistant sponsoring editor. Thanks to Songlin Qiu for her work as developmental editor, Laura Acklen for providing a thorough technical edit, and Kate Shoup for making the text better with an insightful copy edit. Thanks also to Danielle Foster for layout and graphic design, Dan Foster for serving as production editor, and to Valerie Haynes Perry for producing the index. Finally, heartfelt thanks and love to my wife, Virginia Belt, who makes it all worthwhile.

About the Author

Curt Frye is the author of more than 30 books, including *Microsoft Excel 2016 Step by Step* and *Microsoft OneNote Step by Step* for Microsoft Press. He has also created and recorded more than 60 online training courses for lynda.com and LinkedIn Learning, including *Office 365 for Mac: Excel Essential Training, Excel: Scenario Planning and Analysis, Excel: Statistical Process Control*, and *Microsoft Excel: Using Solver for Decision Analysis*.

Curt is a popular conference speaker, offering his *Improspectives*® program on applying the techniques of improvisational theater to business and life as well as *Which Game Are You Playing?*, which applies lessons from the strategies and tactics of popular games to business. He earned his undergraduate degree in political science from Syracuse University in 1990 and will receive his MBA from the University of Illinois in December 2018.

Curt lives in Portland, Oregon with his wife Virginia.

Introduction

Welcome! This *Step by Step* book has been designed so you can read it from the beginning to learn about Microsoft Excel 2019 and then build your skills as you learn to perform increasingly specialized procedures. Or, if you prefer, you can jump in wherever you need guidance for performing tasks. The how-to steps are delivered crisply and concisely—just the facts. You'll also find informative graphics that support the instructional content.

Who this book is for

Microsoft Excel 2019 Step by Step is designed for use as a learning and reference resource by home and business users of Microsoft Office apps who want to use Excel to manage their data, create useful analyses and visualizations, and discover insights into their operations. The content of the book is designed to be useful for people who have previously used earlier versions of Excel as well as for people who are discovering Excel for the first time.

The Step by Step approach

The book's coverage is divided into parts representing general Excel skill sets. Each part is divided into chapters representing skill set areas, and each chapter is divided into topics that group related skills. Each topic includes expository information followed by generic procedures. At the end of the chapter, you'll find a series of practice tasks you can complete on your own by using the skills taught in the chapter. You can use the practice files available from this book's website to work through the practice tasks, or you can use your own files.

Download the practice files

Before you can complete the practice tasks in this book, you need to download the book's practice files to your computer from microsoftpressstore.com/Excel2019SBS/ downloads. Follow the instructions on the webpage.

 IMPORTANT Excel 2019 is not available from the book's website. You should install that app before working through the procedures and practice tasks in this book.

You can open the supplied files for the practice tasks and save the finished versions of each file. If you later want to repeat practice tasks, you can download the original practice files again.

 SEE ALSO For information about opening and saving files, see "Create workbooks" in Chapter 1, "Set up a workbook."

The following table lists the practice files for this book.

Chapter	Folder	File
1: Set up a workbook	Excel2019SBS\Ch01	CreateWorkbooks.xlsx CustomizeRibbonTabs.xlsx MergeCells.xlsx ModifyWorkbooks.xlsx ModifyWorksheets.xlsx
2: Work with data and Excel tables	Excel2019SBS\Ch02	CompleteFlashFill.xlsx CreateExcelTables.xlsx EnterData.xlsx FindValues.xlsx MoveData.xlsx ResearchItems.xlsx
3: Perform calculations on data	Excel2019SBS\Ch03	AuditFormulas.xlsx BuildFormulas.xlsx CreateArrayFormulas.xlsx CreateConditonalFormulas.xlsx CreateNames.xlsx SetIterativeOptions.xlsx

Chapter	Folder	File
4: Change workbook appearance	Excel2019SBS\Ch04	AddImages.xlsx ApplyStyles.xlsx CreateConditionalFormats.xlsx DefineStyles.xlsx FormatCells.xlsx FormatNumbers.xlsx phone.jpg texture.jpg
5: Manage worksheet data	Excel2019SBS\Ch05	LimitData.xlsx SummarizeValues.xlsx ValidateData.xlsx
6: Reorder and summarize data	Excel2019SBS\Ch06	LookupData.xlsx OrganizeData.xlsx SortCustomData.xlsx SortData.xlsx
7: Combine data from multiple sources	Excel2019SBS\Ch07	ConsolidateData.xlsx CreateDataLinks.xlsx CreateTemplate.xlsx FebruaryCalls.xlsx FleetOperatingCosts.xlsx JanuaryCalls.xlsx
8: Analyze alternative data sets	Excel2019SBS\Ch08	BuildSolverModel.xlsx CreateScenarios.xlsx DefineDataTables.xlsx ManageMultipleScenarios.xlsx PerformGoalSeekAnalysis.xlsx PerformQuickAnalysis.xlsx UseDescriptiveStatistics.xlsx
9: Create charts and graphics	Excel2019SBS\Ch09	CreateCharts.xlsx CreateNewCharts.xlsx CreateShapes.xlsx CreateSparklines.xlsx CustomizeCharts.xlsx IdentifyTrends.xlsx MakeComboCharts.xlsx MakeSmartArt.xls

Chapter	Folder	File
10: Create dynamic worksheets by using PivotTables and PivotCharts	Excel2019SBS\Ch10	CreatePivotCharts.xlsx CreatePivotTables.xlsx EditPivotTables.xlsx FilterPivotTables.xlsx FormatPivotTables.xlsx ImportData.txt ImportPivotData.xlsx
11: Print worksheets and charts	Excel2019SBS\Ch11	AddHeaders.xlsx ConsolidatedMessenger.png PrepareWorksheets.xlsx PrintCharts.xlsx PrintParts.xlsx PrintWorksheets.xlsx
12: Automate repetitive tasks by using macros	Excel2019SBS\Ch12	AssignMacros.xlsm ExamineMacros.xlsm InsertFormControls.xlsm RecordMacros.xlsm RunOnOpen.xlsm
13: Work with other Microsoft Office apps	Excel2019SBS\Ch13	CreateHyperlinks.xlsx EmbedWorkbook.xlsx LevelDescriptions.xlsx LinkCharts.xlsx LinkFiles.xlsx LinkWorkbooks.pptx ReceiveLinks.pptx
14: Collaborate with colleagues	Excel2019SBS\Ch14	AuthenticateWorkbooks.xlsx DistributeFiles.xlsx ExceptionTracking.xml FinalizeWorkbooks.xlsx ImportXMLData.xlsx ManageComments.xlsx ManageOneDrive.xlsx ProtectWorkbooks.xlsx SaveForWeb.xlsx

Chapter	Folder	File
15: Perform business intelligence analysis	Excel2019SBS\Ch15	AnalyzePowerPivotData.xlsx DefineRelationships.xlsx EnableAddIns.xlsx ManagePowerQueryData.xlsx ViewUsingTimelines.xlsx
16. Create forecasts and visualizations	Excel2019SBS\Ch16	CreateForecastSheets.xlsx CreateKPIs.xlsx CreateMaps.xlsx DefineMeasures.xlsx

Ebook edition

If you're reading the ebook edition of this book, you can do the following:

- Search the full text

- Print

- Copy and paste

You can purchase and download the ebook edition from the Microsoft Press Store at microsoftpressstore.com/Excel2019SBS/detail.

Adapt exercise steps

This book contains many images of the Excel user interface elements (such as the ribbon and the app window) that you'll work with while performing tasks in Excel on a Windows computer. Unless we're demonstrating an alternative view of content, the screenshots shown in this book were captured on a horizontally oriented display at a screen resolution of 1920 × 1080 and a magnification of 100 percent. If your settings are different, the ribbon on your screen might not look the same as the one shown in this book. As a result, exercise instructions that involve the ribbon might require a little adaptation.

Simple procedural instructions use this format:

1. On the **Insert** tab, in the **Illustrations** group, click the **Chart** button.

If the command is in a list, our instructions use this format:

1. On the **Home** tab, in the **Editing** group, click the **Find** arrow and then, in the **Find** list, click **Go To**.

If differences between your display settings and ours cause a button to appear differently on your screen than it does in this book, you can easily adapt the steps to locate the command. First click the specified tab, and then locate the specified group. If a group has been collapsed into a group list or under a group button, click the list or button to display the group's commands. If you can't immediately identify the button you want, point to likely candidates to display their names in ScreenTips.

Multistep procedural instructions use this format:

1. To select the paragraph that you want to format in columns, triple-click the paragraph.

2. On the **Layout** tab, in the **Page Setup** group, click the **Columns** button to display a menu of column layout options.

3. On the **Columns** menu, click **Three**.

On subsequent instances of instructions that require you to follow the same process, the instructions might be simplified in this format because the working location has already been established:

1. Select the paragraph that you want to format in columns.

2. On the **Columns** menu, click **Three**.

The instructions in this book assume that you're interacting with on-screen elements on your computer by clicking (with a mouse, touchpad, or other hardware device). If you're using a different method—for example, if your computer has a touchscreen interface and you're tapping the screen (with your finger or a stylus)—substitute the applicable tapping action when you interact with a user interface element.

Instructions in this book refer to Excel user interface elements that you click or tap on the screen as *buttons*, and to physical buttons that you press on a keyboard as *keys*, to conform to the standard terminology used in documentation for these products.

When the instructions tell you to enter information, you can do so by typing on a connected external keyboard, tapping an on-screen keyboard, or even speaking aloud, depending on your computer setup and your personal preferences.

Get support and give feedback

This topic provides information about getting help with this book and contacting us to provide feedback or report errors.

Errata and support

We've made every effort to ensure the accuracy of this book and its companion content. If you discover an error, please submit it to us at microsoftpressstore.com/Excel2019SBS/errata.

If you need to contact the Microsoft Press Support team, please send an email to microsoftpresscs@pearson.com.

For help with Microsoft software and hardware, go to *http://support.microsoft.com*.

Stay in touch

Let's keep the conversation going! We're on Twitter at twitter.com/MicrosoftPress.

Part 1

Create and format workbooks

Set up a workbook

When you create a new Excel 2019 workbook, the app presents a blank workbook that contains one worksheet. You can add or delete worksheets, hide worksheets within the workbook without deleting them, and change the order of your worksheets within the workbook. You can also copy a worksheet to another workbook or move the worksheet without leaving a copy of the worksheet in the first workbook. If you and your colleagues work with a large number of documents, you can define property values to make your workbooks easier to find when you and your colleagues attempt to locate them by using the Windows search box.

Another way to make Excel easier to use is by customizing the Excel app window to fit your work style. If you find that you use a command frequently, you can add it to the Quick Access Toolbar so it's never more than one click away. If you use a set of commands frequently, you can create a custom ribbon tab, so they appear in one place. You can also hide, display, or change the order of the tabs on the ribbon.

This chapter guides you through procedures related to creating and modifying workbooks, creating and modifying worksheets, merging and unmerging cells, and customizing the Excel 2019 app window. First, however, it introduces you to the various editions of Excel 2019, and new features of the software.

In this chapter

- Explore the editions of Excel 2019
- Become familiar with new features in Excel 2019
- Create workbooks
- Modify workbooks
- Modify worksheets
- Merge and unmerge cells
- Customize the Excel 2019 app window

Practice files

For this chapter, use the practice files from the Excel2019SBS\Ch01 folder. For practice file download instructions, see the introduction.

Explore the editions of Excel 2019

The Microsoft Office 2019 suite includes apps that give you the ability to create and manage every type of file you need to work effectively at home, work, or school. The apps include Microsoft Word, Excel, Outlook, PowerPoint, Access, OneNote, and Publisher. You can purchase the apps as part of a package that includes multiple apps or purchase most of the apps individually.

Using the Office 2019 apps, you can find the tools you need quickly. Moreover, because they were designed as an integrated package, you'll find that the skills you learn in one app transfer readily to the others. That flexibility extends well beyond your personal computer. In addition to the traditional desktop edition of Excel, you can also use Excel Online in combination with Microsoft OneDrive (formerly called SkyDrive).

Excel 2019

The click-to-run version of Excel 2019 is installed directly on your computer. The desktop version of the app includes all the capabilities built into Excel 2019. You can purchase Excel 2019 as part of an Office app suite or as a separate app.

> **TIP** Office 365 is a cloud-based subscription licensing solution that provides access to a continually updated version of Excel, which adds new capabilities on a regular basis. Excel 2019 receives security updates but not feature updates.

Excel Online

Information workers require their data to be available to them at all times, not just when they're using their personal computers. To provide mobile workers with access to their data, Microsoft developed Office Online, which includes online versions of Excel, Word, PowerPoint, Outlook, and OneNote. Office Online is available as part of an Office 365 subscription or for free as part of the OneDrive cloud service.

You can use Excel Online to edit files stored in your OneDrive account or on a Microsoft SharePoint site. Excel Online displays your Excel files (version 2010 and later) as they appear in the desktop version of the app and includes all the functions you use to summarize your data. You can also view and manipulate PivotTables, add charts, and format your data to communicate its meaning clearly.

You can also use Excel Online to share your workbooks online, embed them as part of another webpage, and create web-accessible surveys that save user responses directly to an Excel workbook in your OneDrive account.

After you open a file by using Excel Online, you can choose to continue editing the file in your browser or open the file in the desktop app. When you open the file in your desktop app, any changes you save are written to the version of the file on your OneDrive account. This means that you will always have access to the most recent version of your file, regardless of where and how you access it.

At the time of this writing, Excel Online is compatible with the most recent versions of Microsoft Edge, Internet Explorer 11 and later, Mozilla Firefox, and Google Chrome for Windows. You can also use Excel Online on a Mac if you have the most recent version of Safari or Chrome, as well as on Linux with Firefox or Chrome, although some features might not be available. Most Office Online features are also supported in Microsoft Edge for HoloLens and Xbox One.

You can use Excel Online on Apple devices running iOS versions earlier than 10.0. For iOS 10.0 or later, it's recommended that you use the Office for iPad or Office for iPhone app. There are no officially supported Android browsers for Office Online, but you can use the Office for Android apps instead.

Excel Mobile Apps

Office for iPad and Office for iPhone require iOS 10.0 or later. If you own an Android device, Office for Android can be installed on tablets and phones that are running Android KitKat 4.4 or later and that have an ARM-based or Intel x86 processor.

Become familiar with new features in Excel 2019

Excel 2019 includes all the most useful capabilities included in previous versions of the app. If you've used an earlier version of Excel, you probably want to know about the new features introduced in Excel 2019. These include the following:

- Funnel charts and 2D maps, which let users visualize data more effectively
- New worksheet functions and data connectors for importing and summarizing data

- The capability to publish Excel data to Power BI, the data visualization and dashboarding app from Microsoft

- Enhancements to PowerPivot and Power Query, which enable users to import, process, and summarize millions of rows of data

Create workbooks

Any time you want to gather and store data that isn't closely related to any of your other existing data, you should create a new workbook. A workbook is the basic Excel file, comparable to a Microsoft Word document or Microsoft PowerPoint presentation. The default new workbook in Excel has one worksheet, which is like a page in a Word document or a slide in a PowerPoint presentation. You can add more worksheets to help organize your data more effectively. When you start Excel, the app displays the Start screen.

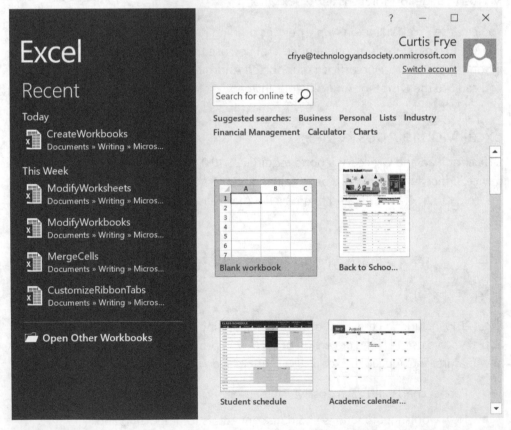

Create new workbooks from the Start screen, which is part of the Backstage view.

The Start screen is part of the Backstage view, (which you can display from an open workbook by clicking the File tab on the ribbon) where you can manage your Excel workbooks and account settings and perform operations such as printing. You can click one of the built-in templates available in Excel 2019 or create a blank workbook. You can then begin to enter data into the worksheet's cells or open an existing workbook. After you start entering workbook values, you can save your work.

 TIP To save your workbook by using a keyboard shortcut, press Ctrl+S. For more information about keyboard shortcuts, see "Keyboard shortcuts" at the end of this book.

 IMPORTANT Readers frequently ask, "How often should I save my files?" You might save your changes every half hour or even every five minutes, but the best time to save a file is whenever you make a change that you would hate to have to make again.

When you save a file, you overwrite the previous copy of the file. If you have made changes that you want to save, but you also want to keep a copy of the file as it was when you saved it previously, you can save your file under a new name or in a new folder.

 TIP To open the Save As dialog box by using a keyboard shortcut, press F12.

You also can use the controls in the Save As dialog box to specify a different format for the new file and a different location in which to save the new version of the file. For example, if you work with a colleague who requires data saved in the Excel 97–2003 file format, you can save a file in that format from within the Save As dialog box.

If you want to work with a file you created previously, you can open it by displaying the Open page of the Backstage view.

 TIP To display the Open page of the Backstage view by using a keyboard shortcut, press Ctrl+O.

After you create a file, you can add information to make the file easier to find. Each category of information, or property, stores specific information about your file. In Windows, you can search for files based on the author or title, or by keywords associated with the file.

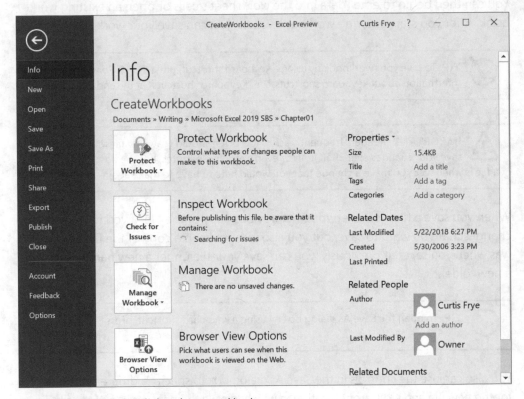

Assign properties to help Windows locate workbooks.

In addition to setting property values on the Info page of the Backstage view, you can display the Properties dialog box to select one of the existing custom categories or create your own. You can also edit your properties or delete any that you no longer want to use.

When you're finished modifying a workbook, you should save your changes and then close the file.

 TIP To close a workbook by using a keyboard shortcut, press Ctrl+W.

To create a new workbook

1. Do any of the following:

   - If Excel is not running, start Excel. Then, on the **Start** screen, double-click **Blank workbook**.

   - If Excel is already running, click the **File** tab of the ribbon, click **New** to display the New page of the Backstage view, and then double-click **Blank workbook**.

   - If Excel is already running, press **Ctrl+N**.

To save a workbook under a new name or in a new location

1. Click the **File** tab, and then click **Save As**.

2. On the **Save As** page of the Backstage view, navigate to the folder where you want to save the workbook.

3. In the **Save As** dialog box, in the **File name** box, enter a new name for the workbook.

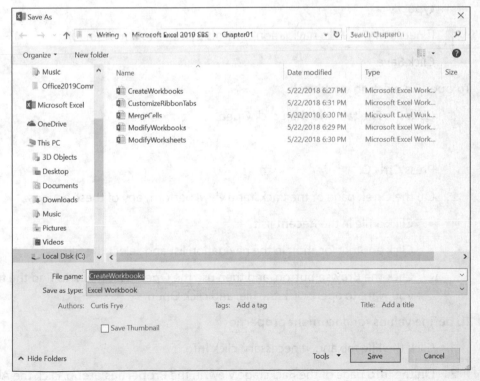

Save a new version of your file using the Save As dialog box.

4. To save the file in a different format, in the **Save as type** list, click a new file type.

> **TIP** The Save as type list contains an extensive list of file formats, including older Excel formats used in Excel 97–2003, macro-enabled workbooks, Comma Separated Value (CSV), and XML Spreadsheet 2003. Not all Excel 2019 features are available in other formats, so be sure your workbook only uses capabilities available in other file formats if you need to use them.

5. If necessary, use the navigation controls to move to a new folder.

6. Click **Save**.

Or

1. Press **F12**.

2. In the **Save As** dialog box, in the **File name** box, enter a new name for the workbook.

3. To save the file in a different format, in the **Save as type** list, click a new file type.

4. If necessary, use the navigation controls to move to a new folder.

5. Click **Save**.

To open an existing workbook

1. Click the **File** tab, and then click **Open**.

   Or

   Press **Ctrl+O**.

2. On the **Open** page of the Backstage view, perform any of these actions:

   - Click a file in the **Recent** list.

   - Click another location in the navigation list and select the file.

   - Click the **Browse** button, and then use the **Open** dialog box to find the file you want to open, click the file, and click **Open**.

To define values for document properties

1. Click the **File** tab and, if necessary, click **Info**.

2. On the **Info** page of the Backstage view, in the **Properties** group, click the **Add a *property*** text next to a label.

3. Enter a value or series of values (separated by commas) for the property.

4. Click a blank space on the **Info** page to finish adding properties.

To create a custom property

1. Click the **File** tab and then, if necessary, click **Info**.

2. In the **Properties** group, click **Properties**, and then click **Advanced Properties**.

3. In the *filename* **Properties** dialog box, click the **Custom** tab.

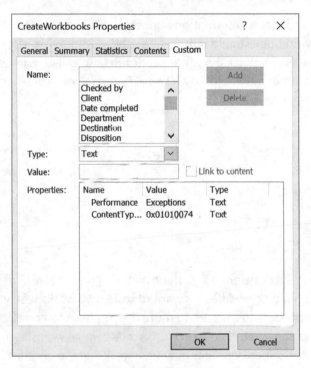

Define custom properties for your workbooks.

4. In the **Name** list, click an existing property name.

   Or

   In the **Name** box, enter a name for the new property.

5. Click the **Type** control's arrow, and then click a data type.

6. In the **Value** box, enter a value for the property.

7. Click **Add**.

8. Repeat steps 4–7 to add more properties. When you are finished, click **OK**.

To close a workbook

1. Do either of the following:

    - Display the Backstage view, and then click **Close**.

    - Press **Ctrl+W**.

Modify workbooks

You can use Excel workbooks to record information about specific business activities. Each worksheet within that workbook should represent a subdivision of that activity. To display a particular worksheet, just click the worksheet's tab (also called a sheet tab) on the tab bar (just below the grid of cells). You can also create new worksheets when you need them.

Display and create worksheets without leaving the main program window.

When you create a worksheet, Excel assigns it a generic name such as *Sheet2*, *Sheet3*, or *Sheet4*. After you decide what type of data you want to store on a worksheet, you should change the worksheet's name to something more descriptive. You can also move and copy worksheets within and between workbooks. Moving a worksheet within a workbook changes its position, whereas moving a worksheet to another workbook removes it from the original workbook. Copying a worksheet keeps the original in its position and creates a second copy in the new location, whether within the same workbook or in another workbook.

> **TIP** Selecting the Create A Copy check box in the Move or Copy dialog box leaves the copied worksheet in its original workbook, whereas clearing the check box causes Excel to delete the worksheet from its original workbook.

1

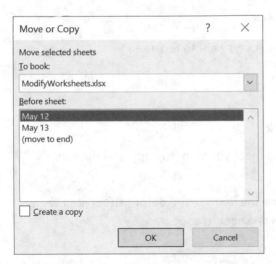

Move or copy worksheets within and among workbooks.

> **TIP** You can also copy a worksheet within a workbook by holding down the Ctrl key while dragging the worksheet's tab to a new position in the workbook.

After the worksheet is in the target workbook, you can change the worksheet's position within the workbook, hide its tab on the tab bar without deleting the worksheet, unhide its tab, or change the sheet tab's color.

> **TIP** If you copy a worksheet to another workbook and the destination workbook has the same Office theme applied as the active workbook, the worksheet retains its tab color. If the destination workbook has another theme applied, the worksheet's tab color changes to reflect that theme. For more information about Office themes, see Chapter 4, "Change workbook appearance."

If you determine that you no longer need a particular worksheet, such as one you created to store some figures temporarily, you can delete the worksheet quickly.

To display a worksheet

1. On the tab bar in the lower-left corner of the app window, click the tab of the worksheet you want to display.

To create a new worksheet

1. Next to the tab bar in the lower-left corner of the app window, click the **New Sheet** button (the plus sign).

To rename a worksheet

1. Double-click the tab of the worksheet you want to rename.

2. Enter a new name for the worksheet.

3. Press **Enter**.

To move a worksheet within a workbook

1. Right-click the sheet tab of the worksheet you want to copy, and then click **Move or Copy**.

2. In the **Move or Copy** dialog box, use the items in the **Before sheet** area to indicate where you want the new worksheet to appear.

3. Click **OK**.

Or

1. On the tab bar in the lower-left corner of the app window, drag the sheet tab to the new position in the worksheet order.

To move a worksheet to another workbook

1. Open the workbook to which you want to move a worksheet from another workbook.

2. In the source workbook, right-click the sheet tab of the worksheet you want to move, and then click **Move or Copy**.

3. In the **Move or Copy** dialog box, click the **To book** arrow and select the open workbook to which you want to move the worksheet.

4. In the **Before sheet** area, indicate where you want the moved worksheet to appear.

5. Click **OK**.

To copy a worksheet within a workbook

1. Right-click the sheet tab of the worksheet you want to copy, and then click **Move or Copy**.

2. In the **Move or Copy** dialog box, select the **Create a copy** check box.

3. In the **Before sheet** area, indicate where you want the new worksheet to appear.

4. Click **OK**.

Or

1. Hold down the **Ctrl** key and drag the worksheet's tab to the desired position in the worksheet order.

To copy a worksheet to another workbook

1. Open the workbook to which you want to add a copy of a worksheet from another workbook.

2. In the source workbook, right-click the sheet tab of the worksheet you want to copy, and then click **Move or Copy**.

3. In the **Move or Copy** dialog box, select the **Create a copy** check box.

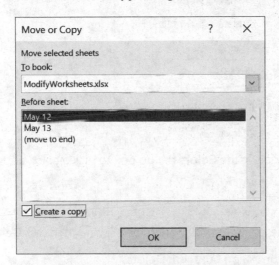

Copy worksheets to other workbooks without deleting the original sheet.

4. Click the **To book** arrow and select the open workbook in which you want to create a copy of the worksheet.

5. In the **Before sheet** area, indicate where you want the new worksheet to appear.

6. Click **OK**.

To hide a worksheet

1. Right-click the sheet tab of the worksheet you want to hide, and then click **Hide**.

To unhide a worksheet

1. Right-click any visible sheet tab, and then click **Unhide**.

2. In the **Unhide** dialog box, click the worksheet you want to redisplay.

3. Click **OK**.

To change a sheet tab's color

1. Right-click the sheet tab whose color you want to change and point to **Tab Color**.

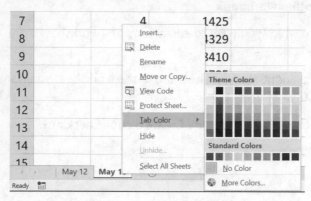

Change a sheet tab's color to make it stand out.

2. Click a color from the color palette.

    Or

    Click **More Colors**, use the tools in the **Colors** dialog box to pick a color, and then click **OK**.

To delete a worksheet

1. Right-click the sheet tab of the worksheet you want to delete, and then click **Delete**.

2. If Excel displays a confirmation dialog box, click **Delete**.

> **TIP** Excel displays a confirmation dialog box when you attempt to delete a worksheet that contains data.

Modify worksheets

After you put up the signposts that make your data easy to find, you can take other steps to make the data in your workbooks easier to work with. Excel helps by identifying worksheet rows by number, and columns by one or more letters. Each row has a header at the left edge of the worksheet and each column has a header at the top of the worksheet. You can change the width of a column or the height of a row in a worksheet by dragging the column header's right edge or the row header's bottom edge to the position you want. Increasing a column's width or a row's height increases the space between cell contents, making your data easier to read and work with.

 TIP You can apply the same change to more than one row or column by selecting the rows or columns you want to change and then dragging the border of one of the selected rows or columns to the location you want. When you release the mouse button, all the selected rows or columns change to the new height or width.

Modifying column width and row height can make a workbook's contents easier to work with, but you can also insert a row or column between cells that contain data to make your data easier to read. Adding space between the edge of a worksheet and cells that contain data, or perhaps between a label and the data to which it refers, makes the workbook's contents less crowded.

TIP Inserting a column adds a column to the left of the selected column or columns. Inserting a row adds a row above the selected row or rows.

When you insert a row, column, or cell in a worksheet that has had formatting applied, the Insert Options button appears. Clicking this button displays a list of choices you can make about how the inserted row or column should be formatted. The following table summarizes these options.

Option	Action
Format Same As Above	Applies the formatting of the row above the inserted row to the new row
Format Same As Below	Applies the formatting of the row below the inserted row to the new row
Format Same As Left	Applies the formatting of the column to the left of the inserted column to the new column
Format Same As Right	Applies the formatting of the column to the right of the inserted column to the new column
Clear Formatting	Applies the default format to the new row or column

You can also delete, hide, and unhide columns and rows. Deleting a column or row removes it and its contents from the worksheet entirely, whereas hiding a column or row removes it from the display without deleting its contents.

 IMPORTANT If you hide the first row or column in a worksheet and then want to unhide it, you must click the Select All button in the upper-left corner of the worksheet (above the first row header and to the left of the first column header) or press Ctrl+A to select the entire worksheet. Then, on the Home tab, in the Cells group, click Format, point to Hide & Unhide, and click either Unhide Rows or Unhide Columns to make the hidden data visible again.

Just as you can insert rows or columns, you can insert individual cells into a worksheet. After you insert cells, you can use the Insert dialog box to choose whether to shift the cells surrounding the inserted cell down (if your data is arranged as a column) or to the right (if your data is arranged as a row).

TIP The Insert dialog box also includes options to insert a new row or column; the Delete dialog box has similar options for deleting an entire row or column.

If you want to move the data in a group of cells to another location in your worksheet, select the cells you want to move and then point to the selection's border. When the pointer changes to a four-pointed arrow, you can drag the selected cells to the target location on the worksheet. If the destination cells contain data, Excel displays a dialog box asking whether you want to overwrite the destination cells' contents. You can choose to overwrite the data or cancel the move.

To change row height

1. Select the row headers for the rows you want to resize.

2. Point to the bottom border of a selected row header.

3. When the pointer changes to a double-headed vertical arrow, drag the border until the row is the height you want.

Or

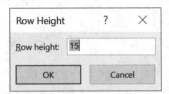

1. Select the row headers for the rows you want to resize.

2. Right-click any of the selected row headers, and then click **Row Height**.

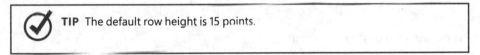

*The Row Height dialog box displaying
the default row height.*

3. In the **Row Height** dialog box, enter a new height for the selected rows.

> ✓ **TIP** The default row height is 15 points.

4. Click **OK**.

To change column width

1. Select the column headers for the columns you want to resize.

2. Point to the right border of a selected column header.

3. When the pointer changes to a double-headed horizontal arrow, drag the border until the column is the width you want.

Or

1. Select the column headers for the columns you want to resize.

2. Right-click any of the selected column headers, and then click **Column Width**.

3. In the **Column Width** dialog box, enter a new width for the selected columns.

> ✓ **TIP** The default column width is 8.09 standard characters.

4. Click **OK**.

To insert a column

1. Right-click a column header, and then click **Insert**.

To insert multiple columns

1. Select a number of column headers equal to the number of columns you want to insert.

2. Right-click any selected column header, and then click **Insert**.

To insert a row

1. Right-click a row header, and then click **Insert**.

To insert multiple rows

1. Select a number of row headers equal to the number of rows you want to insert.

2. Right-click any selected row header, and then click **Insert**.

To delete one or more columns

1. Select the column headers of the columns you want to delete.

2. Right-click any selected column header, and then click **Delete**.

To delete one or more rows

1. Select the row headers of the rows you want to delete.

2. Right-click any selected row header, and then click **Delete**.

To hide one or more columns

1. Select the column headers of the columns you want to hide.

2. Right-click any selected column header, and then click **Hide**.

To hide one or more rows

1. Select the row headers of the rows you want to hide.

2. Right-click any selected row header, and then click **Hide**.

To unhide one or more columns

1. Select the column headers to the immediate left and right of the column or columns you want to unhide.

2. Right-click either selected column header, and then click **Unhide**.

Or

1. Press **Ctrl+A** to select the entire worksheet.

2. Right-click anywhere in the worksheet, and then click **Unhide**.

To unhide one or more rows

1. Select the row headers immediately above and below the row or rows you want to unhide.

2. Right-click any selected column header, and then click **Unhide**.

Or

1. Press **Ctrl+A** to select the entire worksheet.

2. Right-click anywhere in the worksheet, and then click **Unhide**.

To insert one or more cells

1. Select a cell range the same size as the range you want to insert.

2. On the **Home** tab of the ribbon, in the **Cells** group, click **Insert**.

   Or

   Right-click a cell in the selected range, and then click **Insert**.

3. If necessary, use the controls in the **Insert** dialog box to tell Excel how to shift the existing cells.

Indicate how Excel should move existing cells when you insert new cells into a worksheet.

4. Click **OK**.

To move one or more cells within a worksheet

1. Select the cell range you want to move.

2. Point to the edge of the selected range.

3. When the pointer changes to a four-headed arrow, drag the cell range to its new position.

4. If necessary, click **OK** to confirm that you want to delete data in the target cells.

Merge and unmerge cells

Most Excel worksheets contain data about a specific subject. One of the best ways to communicate the contents of a worksheet is to use a label.

	A	B	C	D
1				
2		**Distribution Center Hubs**		
3		Listed by region name and city		
4		Northeast	Boston	
5		Atlantic	Baltimore	
6		Southeast	Atlanta	
7		North Central	Cleveland	
8		Midwest	St. Louis	
9		Southwest	Albuquerque	
10		Mountain West	Denver	
11		Northwest	Portland	
12		Central	Omaha	
13				

Labels provide important context to worksheet data.

For example, consider a worksheet in which the label text *Distribution Center Hubs* appears to span three cells, B2:D2, but is in fact contained within cell B2. If you select cell B2, Excel highlights the cell's border, which obscures the text. You can solve this problem by merging cells B2:D2 into a single cell.

	A	B	C	D	Formula Bar E
1					
2		**Distribution Center Hubs**			
3		Listed by region name and city			
4		Northeast	Boston		
5		Atlantic	Baltimore		
6		Southeast	Atlanta		
7		North Central	Cleveland		
8		Midwest	St. Louis		
9		Southwest	Albuquerque		
10		Mountain West	Denver		
11		Northwest	Portland		
12		Central	Omaha		
13					

A worksheet with the label contained within a merged cell.

IMPORTANT When you merge two or more cells, Excel retains just the text in the range's upper-left cell. All other text is deleted.

In addition to merging cells, you can click Merge & Center to combine the selected cells into a single cell and center the text within the merged cell. You should consider using the Merge & Center option for label text, such as above a list of data where the title spans more than one column. You can also merge the cells in multiple rows at the same time by using Merge Across.

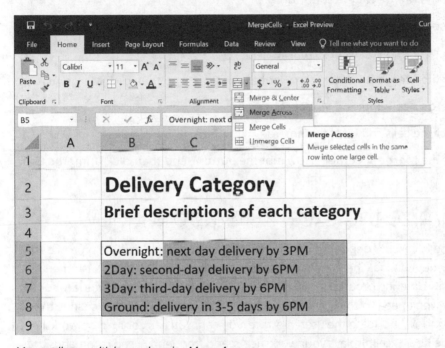

Merge cells on multiple rows by using Merge Across.

 IMPORTANT Selecting the header cells, clicking the Home tab, clicking Merge & Center, and then clicking either Merge & Center or Merge Cells will delete any text that is not in the upper-left cell of the selected range.

If you want to split merged cells into their individual cells, you can always unmerge them.

To merge cells

1. Select the cells you want to merge.

2. On the **Home** tab, in the **Alignment** group, click the **Merge & Center** arrow (not the button), and then click **Merge Cells**.

To merge and center cells

1. Select the cells you want to merge.

2. Click the **Merge & Center** button.

To merge cells in multiple rows by using Merge Across

1. Select the cells you want to merge.

2. Click the **Merge & Center** arrow (not the button), and then click **Merge Across**.

To split merged cells into individual cells

1. Select the cells you want to unmerge.

2. Click the **Merge & Center** arrow (not the button), and then click **Unmerge Cells**.

Customize the Excel 2019 app window

How you use Excel 2019 depends on your personal working style and the type of data collections you manage. The Excel product team at Microsoft interviews customers, observes how differing organizations use the app, and sets up the user interface so that many users won't need to change it to work effectively. If you do want to change the Excel app window, including the user interface, you can. You can zoom in on worksheet data; change how Excel displays your worksheets; add frequently used commands to the Quick Access Toolbar; hide, display, and reorder ribbon tabs; and create custom ribbon tabs to make groups of commands you commonly use readily accessible.

Zoom in on a worksheet

One way to make Excel easier to work with is to change the app's zoom level. Just as you can zoom in with a camera to increase the size of an object in the camera's viewer, you can use the zoom setting in Excel 2019 to change the size of objects in the app window. You can change the zoom level from the ribbon or by using the Zoom control in the lower-right corner of the Excel 2019 window. The minimum zoom level in Excel 2019 is 10 percent; the maximum is 400 percent.

Change worksheet magnification using the Zoom control.

To zoom in on a worksheet

1. Using the **Zoom** control in the lower-right corner of the app window, click the **Zoom In** button (the plus sign).

To zoom out on a worksheet

1. Using the **Zoom** control in the lower-right corner of the app window, click the **Zoom Out** button (the minus sign).

To set the zoom level to 100 percent

1. On the **View** tab of the ribbon, in the **Zoom** group, click the **100%** button.

To set a specific zoom level

1. In the **Zoom** group, click the **Zoom** button.

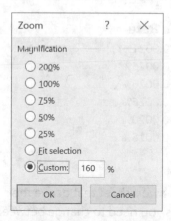

Set a magnification level by using the Zoom dialog box.

2. In the **Zoom** dialog box, enter a value in the **Custom** box.

3. Click **OK**.

To zoom in on specific worksheet highlights

1. Select the cells you want to zoom in on.

2. In the **Zoom** group, click the **Zoom to Selection** button.

Arrange multiple workbook windows

As you work with Excel, you might need to have more than one workbook open at a time. For example, you might open a workbook that contains customer contact information and copy it into another workbook to be used as the source data for a mass mailing you create in Word 2019. When you have multiple workbooks open simultaneously, you can switch between them or arrange your workbooks on the desktop so that most of the active workbook is shown prominently but the others are easily accessible.

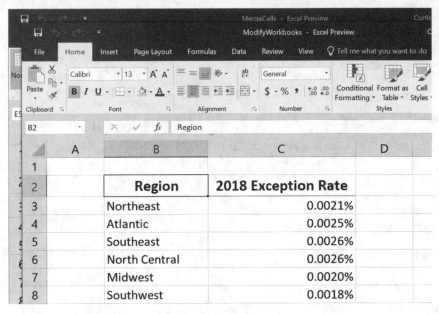

Arrange multiple Excel windows to make them easier to access.

Many Excel 2019 workbooks contain formulas on one worksheet that derive their value from data on another worksheet, which means you need to change between two worksheets every time you want to see how modifying your data changes the formula's result. To facilitate this, you can display two copies of the same workbook simultaneously, with the worksheet that contains the data in the original window and the worksheet with the formula in a new window. When you change the data in either copy of the workbook, Excel updates the other copy.

1

If the original workbook's name is *Merge Cells*, Excel 2019 displays the name *Merge Cells:1* on the original workbook's title bar and *Merge Cells:2* on the second workbook's title bar.

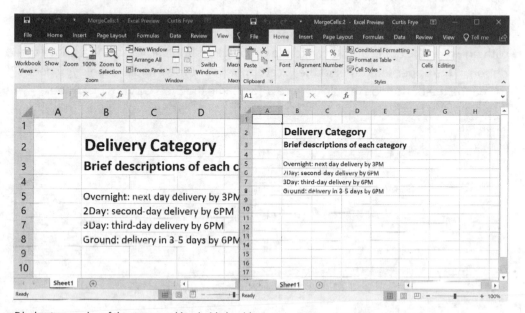

Display two copies of the same workbook side by side.

To switch to another open workbook

1. On the **View** tab, in the **Window** group, click **Switch Windows**.

2. In the **Switch Windows** list, click the workbook you want to display.

To display two copies of the same workbook

1. In the **Window** group, click **New Window**.

To change how Excel displays multiple open workbooks

1. In the **Window** group, click **Arrange All**.

2. In the **Arrange Windows** dialog box, click the windows arrangement you want.

3. If necessary, select the **Windows of active workbook** check box.

4. Click **OK**.

Add buttons to the Quick Access Toolbar

As you continue to work with Excel 2019, you might discover that you use certain commands much more frequently than others. If your workbooks draw data from external sources, for example, you might find yourself using certain ribbon buttons more often than the app's designers might have expected. You can make any button accessible with one click by adding the button to the Quick Access Toolbar, located just above the ribbon in the upper-left corner of the Excel app window. You'll find the tools you need to change the buttons on the Quick Access Toolbar in the Excel Options dialog box.

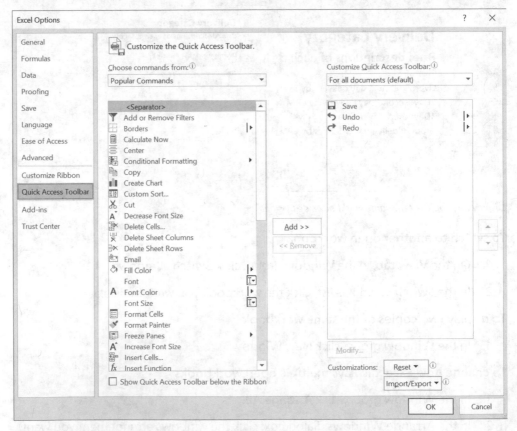

Control which buttons appear on the Quick Access Toolbar.

You can add buttons to the Quick Access Toolbar, change their positions, and remove them when you no longer need them. Later, if you want to return the Quick Access Toolbar to its original state, you can reset it.

You can also choose whether your Quick Access Toolbar changes affect all your workbooks or just the active workbook. If you'd like to export your Quick Access Toolbar customizations to a file that can be used to apply those changes to another Excel 2019 installation, you can do so quickly.

To add a button to the Quick Access Toolbar

1. Display the Backstage view, and then click **Options**.

2. In the **Excel Options** dialog box, click **Quick Access Toolbar**.

3. If necessary, click the **Customize Quick Access Toolbar** arrow and select whether to apply the change to all workbooks or just the current workbook.

4. If necessary, click the **Choose commands from** arrow and click the category of commands from which you want to choose.

5. Click the command you want to add to the **Quick Access Toolbar**.

6. Click **Add**.

7. Click **OK**.

To change the order of buttons on the Quick Access Toolbar

1. Open the **Excel Options** dialog box, and then click **Quick Access Toolbar**.

2. In the right pane, which contains the buttons on the **Quick Access Toolbar**, click the button you want to move.

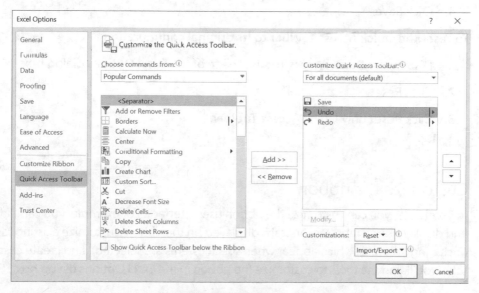

Change the order of buttons on the Quick Access Toolbar.

3. Click the **Move Up** button (the upward-pointing triangle on the far right) to move the button higher in the list and to the left on the **Quick Access Toolbar**.

   Or

   Click the **Move Down** button (the downward-pointing triangle on the far right) to move the button lower in the list and to the right on the **Quick Access Toolbar**.

4. Click **OK**.

To delete a button from the Quick Access Toolbar

1. Open the **Excel Options** dialog box, and then click **Quick Access Toolbar**.

2. In the right pane, click the button you want to delete.

3. Click **Remove**.

To export your Quick Access Toolbar settings to a file

1. Display the **Quick Access Toolbar** page of the **Excel Options** dialog box.

2. Click **Import/Export**, and then click **Export all customizations**.

3. In the **File Save** dialog box, in the **File name** box, enter a name for the settings file.

4. Click **Save**.

To reset the Quick Access Toolbar to its original configuration

1. Display the **Quick Access Toolbar** page of the **Excel Options** dialog box.

2. Click **Reset**.

3. Click **Reset only Quick Access Toolbar**.

4. Click **OK**.

Customize the ribbon

In Excel 2019, you can customize the ribbon user interface. For example, you can hide and display ribbon tabs, reorder tabs displayed on the ribbon, customize existing tabs (including tool tabs, which appear when specific items are selected), and create custom tabs. You'll find the tools to customize the ribbon in the Excel Options dialog box.

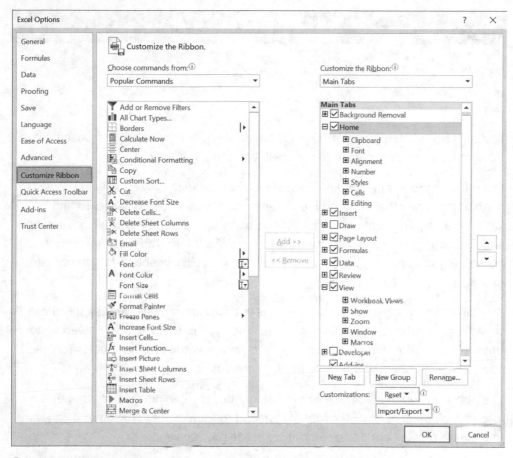

Control which items appear on the ribbon by using the Excel Options dialog box.

From the Customize Ribbon page of the Excel Options dialog box, you can select which tabs appear on the ribbon and in what order. Each ribbon tab's name has a check box next to it. If a tab's check box is selected, that tab appears on the ribbon.

Just as you can change the order of the tabs on the ribbon, with Excel 2019 you can change the order in which groups of commands appear on a tab. For example, the Page Layout tab contains five groups: Themes, Page Setup, Scale to Fit, Sheet Options, and Arrange. If you use the Themes group less frequently than the other groups, you could move the group to the right end of the tab.

Change the order of tabs on the ribbon.

You can also remove groups from a ribbon tab. If you remove a group from a built-in tab and later decide you want to restore it, you can put it back.

The built-in ribbon tabs are designed efficiently, so adding new command groups might crowd the other items on the tab and make those controls harder to find. Rather than adding controls to an existing ribbon tab, you can create a custom tab and then add groups and commands to it. The default New Tab (Custom) name doesn't tell you anything about the commands on your new ribbon tab, so you can rename it to reflect its contents.

You can export your ribbon customizations to a file that can be used to apply those changes to another Excel 2019 installation. When you're ready to apply saved customizations to Excel, import the file and apply it. And, as with the Quick Access Toolbar, you can always reset the ribbon to its original state.

The ribbon is designed to use space efficiently, but you can hide it and other user interface elements such as the formula bar and row and column headings if you want to increase the amount of space available inside the app window.

 TIP Press Ctrl+F1 to hide and unhide the ribbon.

To display a ribbon tab

1. Display the Backstage view, and then click **Options**.

2. In the **Excel Options** dialog box, click **Customize Ribbon**.

3. In the tab list on the right side of the dialog box, select the check box next to the name of the tab you want to display.

1

Select the check box next to the tab you want to appear on the ribbon.

4. Click **OK**.

To hide a ribbon tab

1. In the **Excel Options** dialog box, click **Customize Ribbon**.

2. In the tab list on the right side of the dialog box, clear the check box next to the name of the tab you want to hide.

3. Click **OK**.

To reorder ribbon elements

1. In the **Excel Options** dialog box, click **Customize Ribbon**.

2. In the tab list on the right side of the dialog box, click the name of the button or group you want to move.

3. Click the **Move Up** button (the upward-pointing triangle on the far right) to move the button or group higher in the list and to the left on the ribbon tab.

    Or

    Click the **Move Down** button (the downward-pointing triangle on the far right) to move the button or group lower in the list and to the right on the ribbon tab.

4. Click **OK**.

To create a custom ribbon tab

1. On the **Customize Ribbon** page of the **Excel Options** dialog box, click **New Tab**.

To create a custom group on a ribbon tab

1. On the **Customize Ribbon** page of the **Excel Options** dialog box, click the ribbon tab on which you want to create the custom group.

2. Click **New Group**.

To add a button to the ribbon

1. On the **Customize Ribbon** page of the **Excel Options** dialog box, click the ribbon tab or group to which you want to add a button.

2. If necessary, click the **Customize the Ribbon** arrow and select **Main Tabs** or **Tool Tabs**.

> **TIP** Tool tabs are contextual tabs that appear when you work with workbook elements such as shapes, images, or PivotTables.

3. If necessary, click the **Choose commands from** arrow on the left side of the Customize Ribbon dialog box and click the category of commands from which you want to choose.

4. Click the command to add to the ribbon.

5. Click **Add**.

6. Click **OK**.

To rename a ribbon element

1. On the **Customize Ribbon** page of the **Excel Options** dialog box, click the ribbon tab or group you want to rename.

2. Click **Rename**.

3. In the **Rename** dialog box, enter a new name for the ribbon element.

4. Click **OK**.

To remove an element from the ribbon

1. On the **Customize Ribbon** page of the **Excel Options** dialog box, click the ribbon tab or group you want to remove.

2. Click the **Remove** button in the middle of the dialog box.

To export your ribbon customizations to a file

1. On the **Customize Ribbon** page of the **Excel Options** dialog box, click **Import/Export**, and then click **Export all customizations**.

2. In the **File Save** dialog box, in the **File name** box, enter a name for the settings file.

3. Click **Save**.

To import ribbon customizations from a file

1. On the **Customize Ribbon** page of the **Excel Options** dialog box, click **Import/Export**, and then click **Import customization file**.

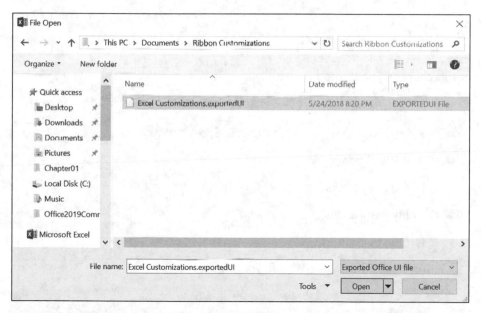

Import ribbon settings saved from another Office installation.

2. In the **File Open** dialog box, navigate to and select the configuration file.

3. Click **Open**.

To reset the ribbon to its original configuration

1. On the **Customize Ribbon** page of the **Excel Options** dialog box, click **Reset**, and then click **Reset all customizations**.

2. In the dialog box that appears, click **Yes**.

To hide or unhide the ribbon

1. Press **Ctrl+F1**.

To hide or unhide the formula bar

1. On the **View** tab, in the **Show** group, select or clear the **Formula Bar** check box.

To hide or unhide the row and column headings

1. In the **Show** group, select or clear the **Headings** check box.

To hide or unhide gridlines

1. In the **Show** group, select or clear the **Gridlines** check box.

Skills review

In this chapter, you learned how to:

- Explore the editions of Excel 2019
- Become familiar with new features in Excel 2019
- Create workbooks
- Modify workbooks
- Modify worksheets
- Merge and unmerge cells
- Customize the Excel 2019 app window

Practice tasks

The practice files for these tasks are located in the Excel2019SBS\Ch01 folder. You can save the results of the tasks in the same folder.

Create workbooks

Open the CreateWorkbooks workbook in Excel, and then perform the following tasks:

1. Close the **CreateWorkbooks** file, and then create a new, blank workbook.

2. Save the new workbook as Exceptions2018.

3. Add the following tags to the file's properties: exceptions, regional, and percentage.

4. Add a tag to the **Category** property called performance.

5. Create a custom property called Performance, leave the value of the **Type** field as **Text**, and assign the new property the value Exceptions.

6. Save your work.

Modify workbooks

Open the ModifyWorkbooks workbook in Excel, and then perform the following tasks:

1. Create a new worksheet named 2019.

2. Rename the **Sheet1** worksheet to 2018 and change its tab color to green.

3. Delete the **ScratchPad** worksheet.

4. Copy the **2018** worksheet to a new workbook, and then save the new workbook under the name Archive2018.

5. In the **ModifyWorkbooks** workbook, hide the **2018** worksheet.

Modify worksheets

Open the ModifyWorksheets workbook in Excel, and then perform the following tasks:

1. On the **May 12** worksheet, insert a new column **A** and a new row **1**.

2. After you insert the new row **1**, click the **Insert Options** button, and then click **Clear Formatting**.

3. Hide column **E**.

4. On the **May 13** worksheet, delete cell **B6**, shifting the remaining cells up.

5. Click cell **C6**, and then insert a cell, shifting the other cells down. Enter the value 4499 in the new cell **C6**.

6. Select cells **E13:F13** and move them to cells **B13:C13**.

Merge and unmerge cells

Open the MergeCells workbook in Excel, and then perform the following tasks:

1. Merge cells **B2:D2**.

2. Merge and center cells **B3:F3**.

3. Merge the cell range **B5:E8** by using **Merge Across**.

4. Unmerge cell **B2**.

Customize the Excel 2019 app window

Open the CustomizeRibbonTabs workbook in Excel, and then perform the following tasks:

1. Add the **Spelling** button to the **Quick Access Toolbar**.

2. Move the **Review** ribbon tab so it is positioned between the **Insert** and **Page Layout** tabs.

3. Create a new ribbon tab named **My Commands**.

4. Rename the **New Group (Custom)** group to **Formatting**.

5. In the list on the left side of the Excel Options dialog box, display the main tabs.

6. From the buttons on the **Home** tab, add the **Styles** group to the **My Commands** ribbon tab you created earlier.

7. Again using the buttons available on the **Home** tab, add the **Number** group to the **Formatting** group on your custom ribbon tab.

8. Save your ribbon changes and click the **My Commands** tab on the ribbon.

Work with data and Excel tables

2

With Excel 2019, you can visualize and present information effectively by using charts, graphics, and formatting, but the data is the most important part of any workbook. By learning to enter data efficiently, you will make fewer data-entry errors and give yourself more time to analyze your data, so you can make decisions about your organization's performance and direction.

Excel provides a wide variety of tools you can use to enter and manage worksheet data effectively. For example, you can organize your data into Excel tables so that you can store and analyze your data quickly and efficiently. You can also quickly enter a data series, repeat one or more values, and control how Excel formats cells, columns, and rows that you move from one part of a worksheet to another, all with minimal effort. Finally, with Excel, you can check the spelling of worksheet text, use the thesaurus to look up alternative words, and translate words to foreign languages.

This chapter guides you through procedures related to entering and revising Excel data, moving data within a workbook, finding and replacing existing data, using proofing and reference tools to enhance your data, and organizing your data by using Excel tables.

In this chapter

- Enter and revise data
- Manage data by using Flash Fill
- Move data within a workbook
- Find and replace data
- Correct and expand upon data
- Define Excel tables

Practice files

For this chapter, use the practice files from the Excel2019SBS\Ch02 folder. For practice file download instructions, see the introduction.

Enter and revise data

After you create a workbook, you can begin entering data. The simplest way to enter data is to click a cell and type a value. This method works very well when you're entering a few pieces of data, but it is less than ideal when you're entering long sequences or series of values.

	A	B	C	D	E
1					
2		**Customer**	**Month**	**Program Savings**	
3		Contoso	January	$ 182,423	
4		Contoso	February	$ 173,486	
5		Contoso	March	$ 88,027	
6		Fabrikam	January	$ 139,434	
7		Fabrikam	February	$ 29,461	
8		Fabrikam	March	$ 91,295	
9		Lucerne Publishing	January	$ 136,922	
10		Lucerne Publishing	February	$ 151,370	
11		Lucerne Publishing	March	$ 160,250	
12		Wide World Importers	January	$ 109,903	
13		Wide World Importers	February	$ 102,243	
14		Wide World Importers	March	$ 105,077	

Store important business data in your worksheets.

 TIP To cancel data entry and return a cell to its previous state, press Esc.

For example, suppose you are creating a worksheet tracking each customer's monthly program savings. You could repeatedly enter the sequence *January, February, March*, and so on by copying and pasting the first occurrence of the sequence, but there's an easier way to do it: by using AutoFill. With AutoFill, you enter the first element in a recognized series, and then drag the fill handle in the lower-right corner of the cell until the series extends far enough to accommodate your data. By using a similar tool, FillSeries, you can enter two values in a series and use the fill handle to extend the series in your worksheet.

2

You do have some control over how Excel extends the values in a series when you drag the fill handle. If you drag the fill handle up or to the left, Excel extends the series to include previous values. For example, if you enter *January* in a cell and then drag that cell's fill handle up or to the left, Excel places *December* in the first cell, *November* in the second cell, and so on.

Another way to control how Excel extends a data series is by holding down the Ctrl key while you drag the fill handle. If you select a cell that contains the value *January* and then drag the fill handle down, Excel extends the series by placing *February* in the next cell, *March* in the cell after that, and so on. If you hold down the Ctrl key while you drag the fill handle, however, Excel repeats the value *January* in each cell you add to the series.

> **TIP** Experiment with how the fill handle extends your series and how pressing the Ctrl key changes that behavior. Using the fill handle can save you a lot of time entering data.

Other data-entry techniques you'll learn about in this section include the following:

- **AutoComplete** This detects when a value you're entering is similar to previously entered values.

- **Pick from Drop-Down List** You can use this to choose a value from among the existing values in a column.

- **Ctrl+Enter** Use this to enter a value in multiple cells simultaneously.

> **TIP** If an AutoComplete suggestion doesn't appear as you begin entering a cell value, the option might be turned off. To turn on AutoComplete, display the Backstage view, and then click Options. In the Excel Options dialog box, display the Advanced page. In the Editing Options section, select the Enable AutoComplete For Cell Values check box, and then click OK.

The following table summarizes these data-entry techniques.

Method	Action
AutoFill	Enter the first value in a recognized series and drag the fill handle to extend the series.
FillSeries	Enter the first two values in a series and drag the fill handle to extend the series.
AutoComplete	Enter the first few letters in a cell. If a similar value exists in the same column, Excel suggests the existing value.
Pick from Drop-Down List	Right-click a cell, and then click Pick from Drop-Down List. A list of existing values in the cell's column is displayed. Click the value you want to enter into the cell.
Ctrl+Enter	When you want several cells to all contain the same data, select the range, enter the data in the active cell, and press Ctrl+Enter.

Another handy feature in Excel is the AutoFill Options button that appears next to data you add to a worksheet by using the fill handle.

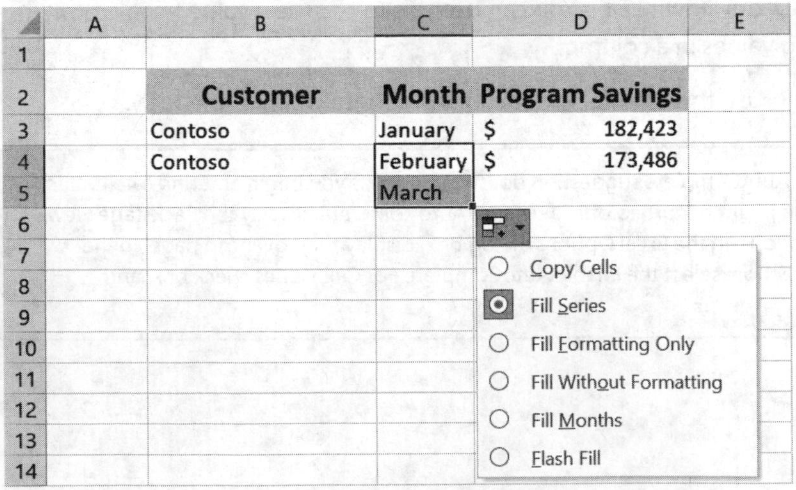

Use AutoFill options to control how the fill handle affects your data.

Clicking the AutoFill Options button displays a menu of actions Excel can take regarding the cells affected by your fill operation. The options on the menu are summarized in the following table.

2

Option	Action
Copy Cells	Copies the contents of the selected cells to the cells indicated by the fill operation.
Fill Series	Fills the cells indicated by the fill operation with the next items in the series.
Fill Formatting Only	Copies the format of the selected cells to the cells indicated by the fill operation, but does not place any values in the target cells.
Fill Without Formatting	Fills the cells indicated by the fill operation with the next items in the series, but ignores any formatting applied to the source cells.
Fill Days, Weekdays, and so on	The appearance of this option changes according to the series you extend. For example, if you extend the values *Wed*, *Thu*, and *Fri*, Excel presents two options: Fill Days and Fill Weekdays. You can then select which one you intended. If you do not use a recognized sequence, this option does not appear.
Flash Fill	Enters values based on patterns established in other cells in the column.

 SEE ALSO For more information about Flash Fill, see "Manage data by using Flash Fill" later in this chapter.

To enter values into a cell

1. Click the cell into which you want to enter the value.

2. Type the value by using the keyboard.

3. Press **Enter** to enter the value and move one cell down.

   Or

   Press **Tab** to enter the value and move one cell to the right.

To extend a series of values by using the fill handle

1. Select the cells that contain the series values.

2. Drag the fill handle to cover the cells where you want the new values to appear.

To enter a value into multiple cells at the same time

1. Select the cells into which you want to enter the value.

2. Enter the value.

3. Press **Ctrl+Enter**.

To enter cell data by using AutoComplete

1. Start entering a value into a cell.

2. Use the arrow keys or the mouse to highlight a suggested AutoComplete value.

3. Press **Tab**.

To enter cell data by picking from a list

1. Right-click the cell below a list of data.

2. Click **Pick from Drop-down List**.

3. Click the value you want to enter.

To control AutoFill options

1. Create an AutoFill sequence.

2. Click the **AutoFill Options** button.

3. Click the option you want to apply.

Manage data by using Flash Fill

When you manage data in Excel, you will often find that you want to combine values from several cells into a single value. For example, one common data configuration is to have a customer's first name, last name, and middle initial in separate cells.

	A	B	C	D
1	**LastName**	**FirstName**	**Initial**	**FullName**
2	Hassall	Mark		
3	Harrison	Justin	K	
4	Plonsky	Idan	L	
5	Preston	Chris		
6				

Fill in data according to a pattern by using Flash Fill.

You could combine this data into a separate cell to show each customer's full name manually or by creating a formula. Alternatively, you can use Flash Fill. Flash Fill can figure out the pattern if you give it a few examples.

	A	B	C	D
1	**LastName**	**FirstName**	**Initial**	**FullName**
2	Hassall	Mark		Mark Hassall
3	Harrison	Justin	K	Justin Harrison
4	Plonsky	Idan	L	Idan Plonsky
5	Preston	Chris		Chris Preston
6				

Flash Fill suggests values if it detects a pattern in your data.

Note that in this example, Flash Fill did not include middle initials in the FullName column. This was because some rows did not contain a middle initial. If you click in the FullName cell next to a row that contains an Initial value and edit the name as you would like it to appear, Flash Fill recognizes the new pattern for this subset of the data and offers to fill in the values. Press Enter to accept the values Flash Fill suggests.

	A	B	C	D
1	**LastName**	**FirstName**	**Initial**	**FullName**
2	Hassall	Mark		Mark Hassall
3	Harrison	Justin	K	Justin K. Harrison
4	Plonsky	Idan	L	Idan L. Plonsky
5	Preston	Chris		Chris Preston
6				

Edit a Flash Fill value to add data to the pattern.

Flash Fill also lets you fix errors in your data. One common issue occurs when you try to enter numbers with leading zeros, such as United States postal codes, into cells formatted as General or with a number format. If you enter a zero-leading number into such a cell, Excel removes the zero.

	A	B	C	D	E
1	**Name**	**Address**	**City**	**State**	**PostalCode**
2	Mark Hassall	123 Maple St.	Bangor	ME	3214
3	Justin K. Harrison	234 Oak Ave.	Boston	MA	7921
4	Idan L. Plonsky	345 Willow Cr.	Seattle	WA	98012
5	Chris Preston	456 Larkspur Ln.	Providence	RI	6999
6					

Use Flash Fill to correct common data-entry issues.

To fix this error, select the cells that contain the postal codes and format those cells and the cells in the next column as text. Then, in the blank cell next to the first postal code that should have a leading zero, enter the postal code as it should appear, and press Enter. When you start entering the postal code into the second cell, Flash Fill offers to change the data by adding a zero to every value in the list.

	A	B	C	D	E	F
1	**Name**	**Address**	**City**	**State**	**PostalCode**	
2	Mark Hassall	123 Maple St.	Bangor	ME	3214	03214
3	Justin K. Harrison	234 Oak Ave.	Boston	MA	7921	07921
4	Idan L. Plonsky	345 Willow Cr.	Seattle	WA	98012	098012
5	Chris Preston	456 Larkspur Ln.	Providence	RI	6999	06999
6						

Flash Fill can overgeneralize the rule it applies to your data.

Flash Fill guessed that you wanted to add a zero to every postal code, but this change is incorrect for any value that should start with a number other than zero. To correct this, after you accept the values Flash Fill suggests, move to a blank cell next to a postal code that shouldn't start with a zero and enter the correct value. When you do, Flash Fill updates its logic to suggest the correct values.

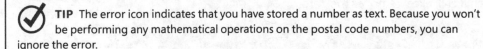

	A	B	C	D	E	F
1	**Name**	**Address**	**City**	**State**	**PostalCode**	
2	Mark Hassall	123 Maple St.	Bangor	ME	3214	03214
3	Justin K. Harrison	234 Oak Ave.	Boston	MA	7921	07921
4	Idan L. Plonsky	345 Willow Cr.	Seattle	WA	98012	98012
5	Chris Preston	456 Larkspur Ln.	Providence	RI	6999	06999
6						

Correct Flash Fill changes to fix your data.

> ✓ **TIP** The error icon indicates that you have stored a number as text. Because you won't be performing any mathematical operations on the postal code numbers, you can ignore the error.

To enter data by using Flash Fill

1. In a cell on the same row as data you're working with, enter the desired value based on data in that row, and press **Enter**.

2. In the cell directly below the first cell into which you entered data, start entering a new value based on data in that row.

3. Press **Enter** to accept the suggested value.

To correct a Flash Fill entry

1. Create a series of Flash Fill values in a worksheet.

2. Edit a cell that contains an incorrect Flash Fill value so that it contains the correct value.

3. Press **Enter**.

Move data within a workbook

You can move and copy data in lots of ways. First, though, you must select the data. The most direct method of selecting data is to click the cell that contains it. The cell you click will be outlined in black, and its contents, if any, will appear in the formula bar. When a cell is outlined, it is the active cell. You can cut, copy, delete, or change the format of the contents of a selected cell.

You're not limited to selecting cells individually. You can also select cells that are a part of a range. Alternatively, you can select an entire column or row. For example, you might need to move a column of price data one column to the right to make room for a column of headings that indicate to which category a set of numbers belongs. To move an entire column (or columns) of data at a time, you first click the column's header, located at the top of the worksheet, to select it. Clicking a column header highlights every cell in that column so that you can copy or cut the column and paste it elsewhere in the workbook. Similarly, clicking a row's header highlights every cell in that row, so that you can copy or cut the row and paste it elsewhere in the workbook.

 IMPORTANT When you select a group of cells, the first cell you click is designated as the active cell.

When you copy a cell, cell range, row, or column, Excel copies the cells' contents and formatting. The Paste Live Preview capability in Excel displays what your pasted data will look like without forcing you to commit to the paste operation.

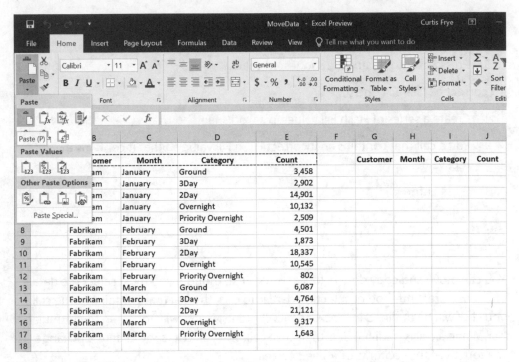

View live previews of your pasted data.

If you point to one icon in the Paste gallery and then point to another icon without clicking, Excel will update the preview to reflect the new option. Depending on the cells' contents, two or more of the paste options might lead to the same result.

> **TIP** If pointing to an icon in the Paste gallery doesn't result in a live preview, that option might be turned off. To turn Paste Live Preview on, in the Backstage view, click Options to open the Excel Options dialog box. Then click General, select the Enable Live Preview check box, and click OK.

After you click an icon to complete the paste operation, Excel displays the Paste Options button next to the pasted cells. Clicking the Paste Options button displays the Paste Options palette. Pointing to one of the options in the palette doesn't generate a preview, however. If you want to display Paste Live Preview again, you will need to press Ctrl+Z to undo the paste operation and, if necessary, cut or copy the data again with the icons in the Clipboard group of the Home tab.

> **TIP** If the Paste Options button doesn't appear, you can turn the feature on by clicking Options in the Backstage view to open the Excel Options dialog box. In the Excel Options dialog box, display the Advanced page. Then, in the Cut, Copy, And Paste area, select the Show Paste Options Button When Content Is Pasted check box. Finally, click OK to close the dialog box and save your setting.

After cutting or copying data to the Clipboard, you can access additional paste options from the Paste gallery and from the Paste Special dialog box.

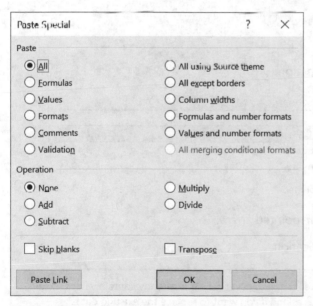

Use the Paste Special dialog box for uncommon paste operations.

In the Paste Special dialog box, you can specify which aspect of the Clipboard contents you want to paste, restricting the pasted data to values, formats, comments, or one of several other options. You can also perform mathematical operations involving the cut or copied data and the existing data in the cells you paste the content into, and you can transpose data—that is, change rows to columns and columns to rows—when you paste it.

To select a cell or cell range

1. Click the first cell you want to select, and then drag to highlight the other cells you want to select.

To select disconnected groups of cells

1. Click the first cell you want to select.

2. Hold down the **Ctrl** key and select additional cells you want to include in the selection.

To move a cell range

1. Select a cell range.

2. Point to the edge of the selection.

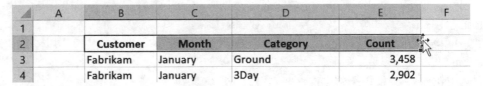

Move a cell range by dragging its border.

The cursor changes to a four-pointed arrow.

3. Drag the range to its new location.

> **TIP** If you move the cell range to cover cells that already contain values, Excel displays a message box asking if you want to replace the existing data.

To select one or more rows

1. Do any of the following:

   - At the left edge of the worksheet, click the row's header.

   - Click a row header and drag to select other row headers.

   - Click a row header, press and hold the **Ctrl** key, and click the headers of other rows you want to copy. The rows do not need to be adjacent to each other.

To select one or more columns

1. Do any of the following:

   - At the top edge of the worksheet, click the column's header.

   - Click a column header and drag to select other column headers.

   - Click a column header, press and hold the **Ctrl** key, and click the column headers of other columns you want to copy. The columns do not need to be adjacent to each other.

To copy a cell range

1. Select the cell range you want to copy.

2. On the **Home** tab of the ribbon, in the **Clipboard** group, click **Copy**.

   Or

   Press **Ctrl+C**.

To cut or move a cell range

1. Select the cell range you want to cut or move.

2. In the **Clipboard** group, click **Cut**.

   Or

   Press **Ctrl+X**.

To paste a cell range

1. Copy or cut a cell range.

2. Click the cell in the upper-left corner of the range where you want the pasted range to appear.

3. In the **Clipboard** group, click **Paste**.

   Or

   Press **Ctrl+V**.

To paste a cell range by using paste options

1. Copy a cell range.

2. Click the cell in the upper-left corner of the range where you want the pasted range to appear.

3. In the **Clipboard** group, click the **Paste** arrow (not the button).

4. Click the icon representing the paste operation you want to use.

To display a preview of a cell range you want to paste

1. Copy or cut a cell range.

2. Click the cell in the upper-left corner of the range where you want the pasted range to appear.

3. Click the **Paste** arrow (not the button).

4. Point to the paste operation for which you want to see a preview.

To paste a cell range by using the Paste Special dialog box controls

1. Copy a cell range.

2. Click the cell in the upper-left corner of the range where you want the pasted range to appear.

3. Click the **Paste** arrow (not the button), and then click **Paste Special** (scroll down if necessary).

4. Select the options you want for the paste operation.

5. Click **OK**.

Find and replace data

Excel worksheets can hold more than one million rows of data. With a large data collection, it's unlikely you would have the time to move through a worksheet one row at a time to locate the data you want to find.

You can locate specific data in an Excel worksheet by using the Find and Replace dialog box. It contains two tabs—one named Find, the other named Replace—that you can use to search for cells that contain particular values. Using the controls on the Find tab, you can identify cells that contain the data you specify; using the controls on the Replace tab, you can substitute one value for another.

 TIP To display the Find tab of the Find and Replace dialog box by using a keyboard shortcut, press Ctrl+F. Press Ctrl+H to display the Replace tab of the Find and Replace dialog box.

When you need more control over the data that you find and replace—for instance, if you want to find cells in which the entire cell value matches the value you're searching for—you can expand the Find and Replace dialog box to display more options.

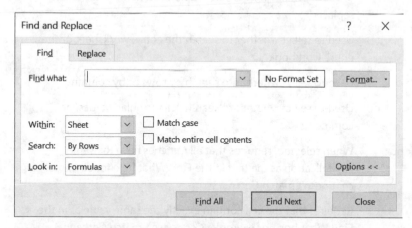

Expand the Find and Replace dialog box for more options.

 TIP By default, Excel looks in formulas, not cell values. To change that option, open the Look In drop-down list and click Values.

The following table summarizes the elements of the Find and Replace dialog box.

Element	Function
Find What box	Contains the value you want to find or replace
Find All button	Locates and selects every cell that contains the value in the Find What field
Find Next button	Locates and selects the next cell that contains the value in the Find What field
Replace With box	Contains the value to overwrite the value in the Find What box
Replace All button	Replaces every instance of the value in the Find What box with the value in the Replace With box
Replace button	Replaces the highlighted occurrence of the value in the Find What box and highlights the next cell that contains that value
Options button	Expands the Find and Replace dialog box to display additional capabilities
Format button	Displays the Find Format dialog box, which you can use to specify the format of values to be found or values to be replaced
Within box	Used to select whether to search the active worksheet or the entire workbook
Search box	Used to select whether to search by rows or by columns
Look In box	Used to select whether to search cell formulas, values, or comments
Match Case check box	When selected, requires that all matches have the same capitalization as the text in the Find What box (for example, *cat* doesn't match *Cat*)
Match Entire Cell Contents check box	Requires that the cell contain exactly the same value as in the Find What box (for example, *Cat* doesn't match *Catherine*)
Close button	Closes the Find and Replace dialog box

To edit a cell's contents

1. Do any of the following:

   - Click the cell, enter a new value, and press **Enter**.

   - Click the cell, edit the value on the formula bar, and press **Enter**.

   - Double-click the cell, edit the value in the body of the cell, and press **Enter**.

To edit part of a cell's contents

1. Click the cell.

2. Edit the part of the cell's value that you want to change on the formula bar.

3. Press **Enter**.

Or

1. Double-click the cell.

2. Edit the part of the cell's value that you want to change in the body of the cell.

3. Press **Enter**.

To find the next occurrence of a value in a worksheet

1. On the **Home** tab, in the **Editing** group, click the **Find & Select** button to display a menu of choices, and then click **Find**.

2. In the **Find what** box, enter the value you want to find.

3. Click **Find Next**.

To find all instances of a value in a worksheet

1. On the **Find & Select** menu, click **Find**.

2. In the **Find what** box, enter the value you want to find.

3. Click **Find All**.

To replace a value with another value

1. On the **Find & Select** menu, click **Replace**.

2. In the **Find what** box, enter the value you want to change.

3. In the **Replace with** box, enter the value you want to replace the value from the **Find what** box.

4. Click the **Replace** button to replace the next occurrence of the value.

   Or

   Click the **Replace All** button to replace all occurrences of the value.

To require find or replace to match an entire cell's contents

1. On the **Find & Select** menu, click either **Find** or **Replace**.

2. Set your **Find what** and, if applicable, **Replace with** values.

3. Click **Options**.

4. Select the **Match entire cell contents** check box.

5. Complete the find or replace operation.

To require find or replace to match cell contents, including uppercase and lowercase letters

1. On the **Find & Select** menu, click either **Find** or **Replace**.

2. Set your **Find what** and, if applicable, **Replace with** values.

3. Click **Options**.

4. Select the **Match case** check box.

5. Complete the find or replace operation.

To find or replace formats

1. On the **Find & Select** menu, click either **Find** or **Replace**.

2. Click **Options**.

3. Click the **Find what** row's **Format** button, set a format by using the **Find Format** dialog box, and click **OK**.

4. If you want to perform a Replace operation, click the **Replace with** row's **Format** button, set a format by using the **Find Format** dialog box, and click **OK**.

5. Complete the find or replace operation.

Correct and expand upon data

After you make a change in a workbook, you can usually remove the change as long as you haven't closed the workbook. You can even change your mind again if you decide you want to restore your change.

 TIP To undo an action by using a keyboard shortcut, press Ctrl+Z. To redo an action, press Ctrl+Y.

After you enter your data, you should check and correct it. You don't need to verify visually that each piece of numeric data is correct, but you can make sure that your worksheet's text is spelled correctly by using the Excel spelling checker. When the spelling checker encounters a word it doesn't recognize, it highlights the word and offers suggestions representing its best guess of the correct word. You can then edit the word directly, pick the proper word from the list of suggestions, or have the spelling checker ignore the misspelling. You can also use the spelling checker to add new words to a custom dictionary so that Excel will recognize them later, saving you time by not requiring you to identify the words as correct every time they occur in your worksheets.

 TIP To start checking spelling by using a keyboard shortcut, press F7.

If you're not sure of your word choice, or if you use a word that is almost but not quite right for your intended meaning, you can check for alternative words by using the thesaurus included with Excel 2019.

Get suggestions for alternative words by using the thesaurus.

Excel 2019 includes a new capability called Smart Lookup, which lets you use the Bing search engine to find information related to a highlighted word. When you use Smart Lookup, Excel displays the Insights task pane, which has two tabs: Explore and Define. The Explore tab displays search results from Wikipedia and other web resources. The Define tab displays definitions provided by Oxford Dictionaries from Oxford University Press.

 IMPORTANT If you are asked if you want to use Intelligent Services, click Turn on. Intelligent Services are the backbone of Microsoft's Smart Lookup and Translator tools.

Finally, if you want to translate a word from one language to another, you can do so by selecting the cell that contains the value you want to translate and clicking the Translate button on the Review tab. The Translator task pane opens and displays tools you can use to select the original and destination languages.

 IMPORTANT The Smart Lookup and Translator tools require an Internet connection.

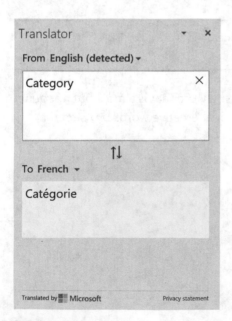

Translate words to other languages.

> **IMPORTANT** Excel translates a sentence by using word substitutions, which means that the translation routine doesn't always pick the best word for a particular context. In other words, the translated sentence might not capture your exact meaning.

To undo or redo an action

1. Do either of the following:

   - Click the **Undo** button on the Quick Access Toolbar to undo the action.

   - Click the **Redo** button on the Quick Access Toolbar to restore the change.

To check spelling in a worksheet

1. On the **Review** tab, in the **Proofing** group, click **Spelling**.

2. For the first misspelled word, do one of the following:

   - Click **Change** to accept the first suggested replacement for this occurrence of the misspelled word.

   - Click **Change All** to accept the first suggested replacement for all occurrences of the misspelled word in the worksheet.

   - Click a different word from the **Suggestions** list to replace the misspelled word and click **Change** or **Change All**.

   - Enter the spelling you want in the **Not in Dictionary** box and click **Change** or **Change All**.

   - Click **Ignore Once** to ignore this occurrence of the word and move to the next misspelled word.

   - Click **Ignore All** to ignore all occurrences of the word.

3. Repeat step 2 until you have checked spelling for the entire worksheet.

4. Click **Close**.

> **TIP** Excel starts checking spelling with the active cell. If that cell isn't A1, Excel asks if you want to continue checking spelling from the beginning of the worksheet.

To add a word to the main dictionary

1. Click **Spelling**.

2. When the word you want to add appears in the **Not in Dictionary** box, click **Add to Dictionary**.

3. Finish checking spelling and click **Close**.

To change the dictionary used to check spelling

1. Click **Spelling**.

2. Click the arrow next to the **Dictionary language** box, and click the dictionary you want to use.

To look up word alternatives by using the thesaurus

1. Select the cell that contains the word for which you want to find alternatives.

2. On the **Review** tab, in the **Proofing** group, click **Thesaurus**.

3. Use the tools in the **Thesaurus** task pane to find alternative words.

4. On the title bar of the **Thesaurus** task pane, click the **Close** button to close the task pane.

To research a word by using Smart Lookup

1. Select the cell that contains the word you want to research.

2. On the **Review** tab, in the **Insights** group, click the **Smart Lookup** button.

3. On the **Explore** tab of the **Insights** task pane, use the resources in the **Explore with Wikipedia** and other web resources lists.

   Or

   On the **Define** tab of the task pane, look up definitions of the selected word.

4. On the title bar of the **Insights** task pane, click the **Close** button to close the task pane.

To translate a word from one language to another

1. Click the cell that contains the word you want to translate.

2. On the **Review** tab, in the **Language** group, click **Translate**.

3. If necessary, click **Yes** to send the text over the Internet.

2

4. Review the results.

5. Click the **Close** button to close the task pane.

Define Excel tables

With Excel, you've always been able to manage lists of data effectively, so that you can sort your worksheet data based on the values in one or more columns, limit the data displayed by using criteria (for example, show only routes with fewer than 100 stops), and create formulas that summarize the values in visible (that is, unfiltered) cells. Excel 2019 provides those capabilities, and more, through Excel tables.

	A	B	C	D
1				
2		Driver	Sorting Minutes	
3		D101	102	
4		D102	102	
5		D103	165	
6		D104	91	
7		D105	103	
8		D106	127	
9		D107	112	
10		D108	137	
11		D109	102	
12		D110	147	
13		D111	163	
14		D112	109	
15		D113	91	
16		D114	107	
17		D115	93	

Manage data by using an Excel table.

 TIP Sorting, filtering, and summarizing data are all covered elsewhere in this book.

Excel can also create an Excel table from an existing cell range, as long as the range has no blank rows or columns within the data, and there is no extraneous data in cells immediately below or next to the list. If your existing data has formatting applied to it, that formatting remains applied to those cells when you create the Excel table, but you can have Excel replace the existing formatting with the Excel table's formatting.

 TIP To create an Excel table by using a keyboard shortcut, press Ctrl+L, specify the range that contains the data, and then click OK.

Entering values into a cell below or to the right of an Excel table adds a row or column to the table. After you enter the value and move out of the cell, the AutoCorrect Options button appears. If you didn't mean to include the data in the Excel table, you can click Undo Table AutoExpansion to exclude the cells from the Excel table. If you never want Excel to include adjacent data in an Excel table again, click Stop Automatically Expanding Tables.

> **TIP** To stop Table AutoExpansion before it starts, click Options in the Backstage view. In the Excel Options dialog box, click Proofing, and then click the AutoCorrect Options button to open the AutoCorrect dialog box. Click the AutoFormat As You Type tab, clear the Include New Rows and Columns in Table check box, and then click OK twice.

You can resize an Excel table manually by using your mouse. If your Excel table's headers contain a recognizable series of values (such as *Region1*, *Region2*, and *Region3*), and you drag the resize handle to create a fourth column, Excel creates the column with a label that is the next value in the series—in this example, *Region4*.

Excel tables often contain data you can summarize by calculating a sum or average, or by finding the maximum or minimum value in a column. To summarize one or more columns of data, you can add a *Total* row to your Excel table.

	A	B	C	D
1				
2		Driver	Sorting Minutes	
3		D101	102	
4		D102	162	
5		D103	165	
6		D104	91	
7		D105	103	
8		D106	127	
9		D107	112	
10		D108	137	
11		D109	102	
12		D110	147	
13		D111	163	
14		D112	109	
15		D113	91	
16		D114	107	
17		D115	93	
18		Total	1811	

An Excel table with a Total row.

When you add the *Total* row, Excel creates a formula that summarizes the values in the rightmost Excel table column. You can change the summary function by picking a new one from the partial list displayed in the Excel table or by selecting a function from the full set.

Much as it does when you create a new worksheet, Excel gives your Excel tables generic names such as *Table1* and *Table2*. You can change an Excel table's name to something easier to recognize in your formulas. Changing an Excel table name might not seem important, but it helps make formulas that summarize Excel table data much easier to understand. You should make a habit of renaming your Excel tables, so you can recognize the data they contain.

If for any reason you want to convert your Excel table back to a normal range of cells, you can do so quickly.

To create an Excel table

1. Click a cell in the list of data you want to make into an Excel table.

2. On the **Home** tab, in the **Styles** group, click **Format as Table**.

3. In the gallery that appears, click the style you want to apply to the table.

4. In the Format As Table dialog box, verify that the cell range is correct.

5. If necessary, select or clear the **My table has headers** check box, and then click **OK**.

To create an Excel table with default formatting

1. Click a cell in the range that you want to make into an Excel table.

2. Press **Ctrl+L**.

3. In the Format As Table dialog box, verify that the cell range is correct.

4. Click **OK**.

To add a column or row to an Excel table

1. Click a cell in the row below or the column to the right of the Excel table.

2. Enter the desired data and press **Enter**.

To expand or contract an Excel table

1. Click any cell in the Excel table.

2. Point to the lower-right corner of the Excel table.

3. When the mouse pointer changes to a diagonal arrow, drag the Excel table's outline to redefine the table.

To add a Total row to an Excel table

1. Click any cell in the Excel table.

2. On the **Design** tool tab in the ribbon, in the **Table Style Options** group, select the **Total Row** check box.

To change the calculation used in a Total row cell

1. Click any **Total** row cell that contains a calculation.

2. Click the cell's arrow.

3. Select a summary function.

   Or

   Click **More Functions**, use the **Insert Function** dialog box to create the formula, and click **OK**.

> **SEE ALSO** For more information about using the Insert Function dialog box and about referring to tables in formulas, see "Create formulas to calculate values" in Chapter 3, "Perform calculations on data."

To rename an Excel table

1. Click any cell in the Excel table.

2. On the **Design** tool tab, in the **Properties** group, enter a new name for the Excel table in the **Table Name** box.

3. Press **Enter**.

To convert an Excel table to a cell range

1. Click any cell in the Excel table.

2. On the **Design** tool tab, in the **Tools** group, click **Convert to Range**.

3. In the confirmation dialog box that appears, click **Yes**.

Skills review

In this chapter, you learned how to:

- Enter and revise data
- Manage data by using Flash Fill
- Move data within a workbook
- Find and replace data
- Correct and expand upon data
- Define Excel tables

Practice tasks

The practice files for these tasks are located in the Excel2019SBS\Ch02 folder. You can save the results of the tasks in the same folder.

Enter and revise data

Open the EnterData workbook in Excel, and then perform the following tasks:

1. Use the fill handle to copy the value from cell **B3**, *Fabrikam*, to cells **B4:B7**.

2. Extend the series of months starting in cell **C3** to cell **C7**, and then use the **Auto Fill Options** button to copy the cell's value instead of extending the series.

3. In cell **B8**, enter the letters Fa and accept the AutoComplete value *Fabrikam*.

4. In cell **C8**, enter **February**.

5. Enter the value **Ground** in cell **D8** by using **Pick from Drop-down List**.

6. Edit the value in cell **E5** to $6,591.30.

Manage data by using Flash Fill

Open the CompleteFlashFill workbook in Excel, and then perform the following tasks:

1. On the **Names** worksheet, in cell **D2**, enter Mark Hassall and press **Enter**.

2. In cell **D3**, enter J and, when Excel displays a series of names in column **D**, press **Enter** to accept the Flash Fill suggestions.

3. Edit the value in cell **D3** to include the middle initial found in cell **C3**, and press **Enter**.

4. Click the **Addresses** sheet tab.

5. Select cells **F2:F5** and then, on the **Home** tab, in the **Number** group, click the arrow next to the **Number Format** button and click **Text**.

6. In cell **F2**, enter 03214 and press **Enter**.

7. In cell **F3**, enter 0 and then press **Enter** to accept the Flash Fill suggestions.

8. Edit the value in cell **F4** to read 98012.

Move data within a workbook

Open the MoveData workbook in Excel, and then perform the following tasks:

1. On the **Count** worksheet, copy the values in cells **B2:D2**.

2. Display the **Sales** worksheet, preview what the data would look like if pasted as values only, and paste the contents you just copied into cells **B2:D2**.

3. On the **Sales** worksheet, cut column **I** and paste it into the space currently occupied by column **E**.

Find and replace data

Open the FindValues workbook in Excel, and then perform the following tasks:

1. On the **Time Summary** worksheet, find the cell that contains the value *114*.

2. On the **Time Summary** worksheet, find all cells with contents formatted as italic type.

3. Click the **Customer Summary** sheet tab.

4. Replace all instances of the value *Contoso* with the value *Northwind Traders*.

Correct and expand upon data

Open the ResearchItems workbook in Excel, and then perform the following tasks:

1. Check spelling in the file and accept the suggested changes for *shipped* and *within*.

2. Ignore the suggestion for *TwoDay*.

3. Add the word *ThreeDay* to the main dictionary.

4. Use the thesaurus to find alternate words for the word *Overnight* in cell **B6**, then translate the same word to French.

5. Click cell **B2** and use Smart Lookup to find more information about the word *level*.

Define Excel tables

Open the CreateExcelTables workbook in Excel, and then perform the following tasks:

1. Create an Excel table from the list of data on the **Sort Times** worksheet.

2. Add a row of data to the Excel table for driver **D116** and assign a value of 100 sorting minutes.

3. Add a **Total** row to the Excel table, and then change the summary function to **Average**.

4. Rename the Excel table to SortTimes.

Perform calculations on data

Excel 2019 workbooks give you a handy place to store and organize your data, but you can do a lot more with your data in Excel than just store it. One important task you can perform is to calculate totals for values in a series of related cells. You can also use Excel to discover other information about data you select, such as the maximum or minimum value in a group of cells. And if you make an error, you can find the cause and correct it quickly.

Often, you can't access the information you want without referencing more than one cell, and it's also often true that you'll use the data in the same group of cells for more than one calculation. Excel makes it easy to reference several cells at the same time, so you can define your calculations quickly.

This chapter guides you through procedures related to streamlining references to groups of data on your worksheets and creating and correcting formulas that summarize an organization's business operations.

In this chapter

- Name groups of data
- Create formulas to calculate values
- Summarize data that meets specific conditions
- Set iterative calculation options and enable or disable automatic calculation
- Use array formulas
- Find and correct errors in calculations

Practice files

For this chapter, use the practice files from the Excel2019SBS\Ch03 folder. For practice file download instructions, see the introduction.

Name groups of data

When you work with large amounts of data, it's often useful to identify groups of cells that contain related data. For example, you can create a worksheet in which columns of cells contain data summarizing the number of packages handled during a specific time period and each row represents a region.

	A	B	C	D	E	F	G	H	I	J
1										
2										
3			5:00 PM	6:00 PM	7:00 PM	8:00 PM	9:00 PM	10:00 PM	11:00 PM	
4		Northeast	53,587	41,438	36,599	43,023	37,664	44,030	36,930	
5		Atlantic	8,896	14,467	9,209	10,767	11,277	10,786	14,838	
6		Southeast	7,207	13,475	13,589	14,702	7,769	10,979	10,919	
7		North Central	9,829	9,959	10,367	8,962	14,847	12,085	8,015	
8		Midwest	7,397	7,811	10,292	7,776	14,805	8,777	14,480	
9		Southwest	7,735	11,352	7,222	11,412	14,948	10,686	14,741	
10		Mountain West	9,721	8,404	11,944	8,162	14,531	11,348	8,559	
11		Northwest	9,240	10,995	7,836	9,702	9,265	14,240	9,798	
12		Central	11,810	13,625	8,921	13,593	11,042	10,223	13,338	
13										

Worksheets often contain logical groups of data.

Instead of specifying the cells individually every time you want to use the data they contain, you can define those cells as a *range* (also called a *named range*). For example, you could group the hourly packages handled in the Northeast region shown in the preceding image into a group called *NortheastVolume*. Whenever you want to use the contents of that range in a calculation, you can use the name of the range instead of specifying the range's address.

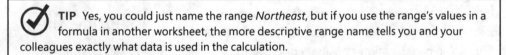

> **TIP** Yes, you could just name the range *Northeast*, but if you use the range's values in a formula in another worksheet, the more descriptive range name tells you and your colleagues exactly what data is used in the calculation.

If the cells you want to define as a named range have labels in a row or column that's part of the cell group, you can use those labels as the names of the named ranges. For example, if your data appears in worksheet cells B4:I12 and the values in column B are the row labels, you can make each row its own named range.

	A	B	C
1			
2			
3			5:00 PM
4		**Northeast**	53,587
5		**Atlantic**	8,896
6		**Southeast**	7,207
7		**North Central**	9,829
8		**Midwest**	7,397
9		**Southwest**	7,735
10		**Mountain West**	9,721
11		**Northwest**	9,240
12		**Central**	11,810

Select a group of cells to create a named range.

If you want to manage the named ranges in your workbook—for example, to edit a range's settings or delete a range you no longer need—you can do so in the Name Manager dialog box.

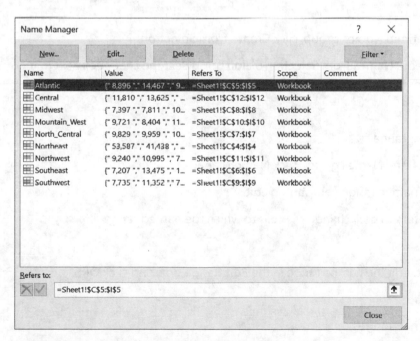

Manage named ranges in the Name Manager dialog box.

> ✓ **TIP** If your workbook contains a lot of named ranges, you can click the Filter button in the Name Manager dialog box and select a criterion to limit the names displayed in the dialog box.

71

To create a named range

1. Select the cells you want to include in the named range.

2. In the **Name Box**, next to the formula bar, enter a name for your named range.

Or

1. Select the cells you want to include in the named range.

2. On the **Formulas** tab of the ribbon, in the **Defined Names** group, click **Define Name**.

3. In the **New Name** dialog box, enter a name for the named range.

4. Verify that the named range includes the cells you want.

5. Click **OK**.

To create a series of named ranges from worksheet data with headings

1. Select the cells that contain the headings and data you want to include in the named ranges.

2. In the **Defined Names** group, click **Create from Selection**.

3. In the **Create Names from Selection** dialog box, select the check box next to the location of the heading text from which you want to create the range names.

4. Click **OK**.

To edit a named range

1. In the **Defined Names** group, click **Name Manager**.

2. Click the named range you want to edit.

3. In the **Refers to** box, change the cells to which the named range refers.

   Or

   Click **Edit**, edit the named range in the **Edit Range** box, and click **OK**.

4. Click **Close**.

To delete a named range

1. Click **Name Manager**.

2. Click the named range you want to delete.

3. Click **Delete**.

4. Click **Close**.

Create formulas to calculate values

After you add your data to a worksheet and define ranges to simplify data references, you can create a formula, which is an expression that performs calculations on your data. For example, you can calculate the total cost of a customer's shipments, figure the average number of packages for all Wednesdays in the month of January, or find the highest and lowest daily package volumes for a week, month, or year.

To enter an Excel formula into a cell, you start with an equal (=) sign. Excel then knows that the expression that follows should be interpreted as a calculation, not text. After the equal sign, you enter the formula. For example, you can find the sum of the numbers in cells C2 and C3 by using the formula =C2+C3. After you have entered a formula into a cell, you can revise it by clicking the cell and then editing the formula in the formula bar. For example, you can change the preceding formula to =C3-C2, which calculates the difference between the contents of cells C2 and C3.

> ⚠️ **IMPORTANT** If Excel treats your formula as text, make sure you haven't accidentally put a space before the equal sign. Remember, the equal sign must be the first character!

Entering the cell references for 15 or 20 cells in a calculation would be tedious, but in Excel you can easily enter complex calculations by using the Insert Function dialog box. The Insert Function dialog box includes a list of functions, or predefined formulas, from which you can choose.

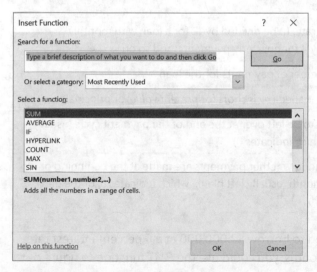

Create formulas in the Insert Function dialog box.

The following table describes some of the most useful functions in the list.

Function	Description
SUM	Finds the sum of the numbers in the specified cells
AVERAGE	Finds the average of the numbers in the specified cells
COUNT	Finds the number of entries in the specified cells
MAX	Finds the largest value in the specified cells
MIN	Finds the smallest value in the specified cells

Two other functions you might use are the *NOW* and *PMT* functions. The *NOW* function displays the time at which Excel updated the workbook's formulas, so the value will change every time the workbook recalculates. The proper form for this function is =*NOW()*. You could, for example, use the *NOW* function to calculate the elapsed time from when you started a process to the present time.

The *PMT* function is a bit more complex. It calculates payments due on a loan, assuming a constant interest rate and constant payments. To perform its calculations, the *PMT* function requires an interest rate, the number of payments, and the starting balance. The elements to be entered into the function are called *arguments* and must be entered in a certain order. That order is written as *PMT(rate, nper, pv, fv, type)*. The following table summarizes the arguments in the *PMT* function.

Argument	Description
rate	The interest rate, to be divided by 12 for a loan with monthly payments, by 4 for quarterly payments, and so on
nper	The total number of payments for the loan
pv	The amount loaned (*pv* is short for *present value*, or principal)
fv	The amount to be left over at the end of the payment cycle (usually left blank, which indicates 0)
type	0 or 1, indicating whether payments are made at the beginning or end of the month (usually left blank, which indicates 0, or the end of the month)

For example, if a company wanted to borrow $2,000,000 at a 6 percent interest rate and pay the loan back over 24 months, you could use the *PMT* function to figure out the monthly payments. In this case, you would write the function =*PMT(6%/12, 24, 2000000)*, which calculates a monthly payment of $88,641.22.

 TIP The 6-percent interest rate is divided by 12 because the loan's interest is compounded monthly.

3

You can also use the names of any ranges you have defined to supply values for a formula. For example, if the named range *NortheastLastDay* refers to cells C4:I4, you can calculate the average of cells C4:I4 with the formula =*AVERAGE(NortheastLastDay)*.

With Excel, you can add functions, named ranges, and table references to your formulas more efficiently by using the application's Formula AutoComplete capability. Just as AutoComplete offers to fill in a cell's text value when Excel recognizes that the value you're typing matches a previous entry, Formula AutoComplete offers to help you fill in a function, named range, or table reference while you create a formula.

As an example, consider a worksheet that contains a two-column Excel table named *Exceptions*. The first column is labeled *Route*; the second is labeled *Count*. You refer to the table by typing the table name, followed by the column or row name in brackets. For example, the table reference *Exceptions[Count]* would refer to the *Count* column in the *Exceptions* table.

	A	B
1	Route	Count
2	101	4
3	102	9
4	103	12
5	104	8
6	105	5
7	106	6
8	107	6
9	108	5
10	109	14
11	110	7
12		

Excel tables track data in a structured format.

To create a formula that finds the total number of exceptions by using the *SUM* function, you begin by typing =*SU*. When you enter the letter *S*, Formula AutoComplete lists functions that begin with the letter *S*; when you enter the letter *U*, it narrows the list down to the functions that start with the letters *SU*.

	A	B	C	D	E	F	G	H	I
1	Route	Count		=SU					
2	101	4		*fx* SUBSTITUTE		Replaces existing text with new text in a text string			
3	102	9		*fx* SUBTOTAL					
4	103	12		*fx* SUM					
5	104	8		*fx* SUMIF					
6	105	5		*fx* SUMIFS					
7	106	6		*fx* SUMPRODUCT					
8	107	6		*fx* SUMSQ					
9	108	5		*fx* SUMX2MY2					
10	109	14		*fx* SUMX2PY2					
11	110	7		*fx* SUMXMY2					
12									

Excel displays Formula AutoComplete suggestions to help with formula creation.

To add the *SUM* function to the formula, click *SUM* and then press Tab. The function appears in the formula bar followed by an open parenthesis. To begin adding the table reference, enter the letter *E*. Excel displays a list of available functions, tables, and named ranges that start with the letter *E*. Click *Exceptions*, and press Tab to add the table reference to the formula. Then, because you want to summarize the values in the table's *Count* column, enter an opening bracket, and, in the list of available table items, click *Count*. Finally, enter a closing bracket followed by a closing parenthesis to finish creating the formula =*SUM(Exceptions[Count])*.

If you want to include a series of contiguous cells in a formula, but you haven't defined the cells as a named range, you can click the first cell in the range and drag to the last cell. If the cells aren't contiguous, hold down the Ctrl key and select all the cells to be included. In both cases, when you release the mouse button, references to the cells you selected appear in the formula.

	A	B	C	D	E	F	G	H	I	J	K
1											
2		Conveyer									
3		350' track	$ 14,012.00								
4		Catch bin	$ 895.00								
5		Motor	$ 1,249.00			=SUM(C3,C6,C14,C17					
6		Chain drive	$ 1,495.00			SUM(number1, [number2], [number3], **[number4]**, [number5], ...)					
7		Sorting table	$ 675.00								
8		*Subtotal*		$ 18,326.00							
9											
10		**Loading Dock**									
11		Concrete	$ 2,169.00								
12		Labor	$ 4,500.00								
13		Posts	$ 300.00								
14		Excavation	$ 2,500.00								
15		Drain	$ 1,800.00								
16		Rails	$ 495.00								
17		Stairs	$ 1,295.00								
18		*Subtotal*		$ 13,059.00							
19											
20		**Build Total**		$ 31,385.00							
21		**Labor Percentage**		#DIV/0!							
22											

A SUM formula that adds individual cells instead of a continuous range.

In addition to using the Ctrl key to add cells to a selection, you can expand a selection by using a wide range of keyboard shortcuts. The following table summarizes many of these shortcuts.

Key sequence	Description
Shift+Right Arrow	Extend the selection one cell to the right.
Shift+Left Arrow	Extend the selection one cell to the left.
Shift+Up Arrow	Extend the selection up one cell.
Shift+Down Arrow	Extend the selection down one cell.
Ctrl+Shift+Right Arrow	Extend the selection to the last non-blank cell in the row.
Ctrl+Shift+Left Arrow	Extend the selection to the first non-blank cell in the row.
Ctrl+Shift+Up Arrow	Extend the selection to the first non-blank cell in the column.
Ctrl+Shift+Down Arrow	Extend the selection to the last non-blank cell in the column.
Ctrl+Shift+8 (Ctrl+*)	Select the entire active region.
Shift+Home	Extend the selection to the beginning of the row.
Ctrl+Shift+Home	Extend the selection to the beginning of the worksheet.
Ctrl+Shift+End	Extend the selection to the end of the worksheet.
Shift+PageDown	Extend the selection down one screen.
Shift+PageUp	Extend the selection up one screen.
Alt+;	Select the visible cells in the current selection.

After you create a formula, you can copy it and paste it into another cell. When you do, Excel changes the formula to work in the new cells. For instance, suppose you have a worksheet in which cell D8 contains the formula *=SUM(C2:C6)*. If you click cell D8, copy the cell's contents, and then paste the result into cell D16, Excel writes *=SUM(C10:C14)* into cell D16. In other words, it reinterprets the formula so it fits the surrounding cells! Excel knows to reinterpret the cells used in the formula because the formula uses a relative reference, or a reference that can change if the formula is copied to another cell. Relative references are written with just the cell row and column—for example, *C14*.

Relative references are useful when you summarize rows of data and want to use the same formula for each row. As an example, suppose you have a worksheet with two columns of data, labeled *Sale Price* and *Rate*, and you want to calculate a sales representative's commission by multiplying the two values in a row. To calculate the commission for the first sale, you would enter the formula =A2*B2 in cell C2.

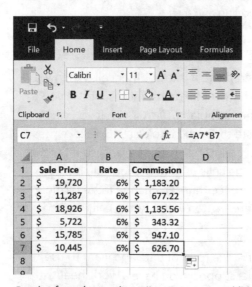

Use formulas to calculate values such as commissions.

Selecting cell C2 and dragging the fill handle until it covers cells C2:C7 copies the formula from cell C2 into each of the other cells. Because you created the formula by using relative references, Excel updates each cell's formula to reflect its position relative to the starting cell (in this case, cell C2.) The formula in cell C7, for example, is =A7*B7.

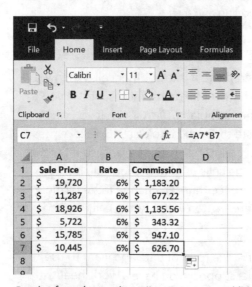

Copying formulas to other cells to summarize additional data.

You can use a similar technique when you add a formula to an Excel table column. For example, suppose the sale price and rate data were in an Excel table, and you created the formula =A2*B2 in cell C2. Excel would apply the formula to every other cell in the column. Because you used relative references in the formula, the formulas would change to reflect each cell's distance from the original cell.

	A	B	C	D
1	Sale Price ▾	Rate ▾	Commission ▾	
2	$ 19,720	6%	$ 1,183.20	
3	$ 11,287	6%	$ 677.22	
4	$ 18,926	6%	$ 1,135.56	
5	$ 5,722	6%	$ 343.32	
6	$ 15,785	6%	$ 947.10	
7	$ 10,445	6%	$ 626.70	
8				

Adding a formula to an Excel table cell to calculate values in a column.

If you want a cell reference to remain constant when you copy the formula that is using it to another cell, you can use an absolute reference. To write a cell reference as an absolute reference, you enter $ before the row letter and the column number. For example, if you want the formula in cell D16 to show the sum of values in cells C10 through C14 regardless of the cell into which it is pasted, you can write the formula as =SUM($C$10:$C$14).

TIP Another way to ensure that your cell references don't change when you copy a formula to another cell is to click the cell that contains the formula, copy the formula's text in the formula bar, press the Esc key to exit cut-and-copy mode, click the cell where you want to paste the formula, and press Ctrl+V. Excel doesn't change the cell references when you copy your formula to another cell in this manner.

One quick way to change a cell reference from relative to absolute is to select the cell reference in the formula bar and then press F4. Pressing F4 cycles a cell reference through the four possible types of references:

- Relative columns and rows (for example, C4)

- Absolute columns and rows (for example, $C$4)

- Relative columns and absolute rows (for example, C$4)

- Absolute columns and relative rows (for example, $C4)

To create a formula by entering it in a cell

1. Click the cell in which you want to create the formula.

2. Enter an equal sign (=).

3. Enter the remainder of the formula, and then press **Enter**.

To create a formula by using the Insert Function dialog box

1. On the **Formulas** tab, in the **Function Library** group, click the **Insert Function** button.

2. Click the function you want to use in your formula.

    Or

    Search for the function you want, and then click it.

3. Click **OK**.

4. In the **Function Arguments** dialog box, enter the function's arguments.

5. Click **OK**.

To display the current date and time by using a formula

1. Click the cell in which you want to display the current date and time.

2. Enter =**NOW()** into the cell.

3. Press **Enter**.

To update a NOW() formula

1. Press **F9**.

To calculate a payment by using a formula

1. Create a formula with the syntax =*PMT(rate, nper, pv, fv, type)*, where:

    • *rate* is the interest rate, to be divided by 12 for a loan with monthly payments, by 4 for quarterly payments, and so on.

    • *nper* is the total number of payments for the loan.

    • *pv* is the amount loaned.

    • *fv* is the amount to be left over at the end of the payment cycle.

    • *type* is 0 or 1, indicating whether payments are made at the beginning or at the end of the month.

2. Press **Enter**.

To refer to a named range in a formula

1. Click the cell where you want to create the formula.

2. Enter = to start the formula.

3. Enter the name of the named range in the part of the formula where you want to use its values.

4. Complete the formula.

5. Press **Enter**.

To refer to an Excel table column in a formula

1. Click the cell where you want to create the formula.

2. Enter = to start the formula.

3. At the point in the formula where you want to include the table's values, enter the name of the table.

   Or

   Use Formula AutoComplete to enter the table name.

4. Enter an opening bracket ([) followed by the column name.

   Or

   Enter [and use Formula AutoComplete to enter the column name.

5. Enter]) to close the table reference.

6. Press **Enter**.

To copy a formula without changing its cell references

1. Click the cell that contains the formula you want to copy.

2. Select the formula text in the formula bar.

3. Press **Ctrl+C**.

4. Click the cell where you want to paste the formula.

5. Press **Ctrl+V**.

6. Press **Enter**.

Operators and precedence

When you create an Excel formula, you use the built-in functions and arithmetic operators that define operations such as addition and multiplication. In Excel, mathematical operators are evaluated in the order listed in the following table.

Operator	Description
-	Negation
%	Percentage
^	Exponentiation
* and /	Multiplication and division
+ and −	Addition and subtraction
&	Concatenation (adding two strings together)

If two operators at the same level, such as + and −, occur in the same equation, Excel evaluates them in left-to-right order. For example, the operations in the formula = *4 + 8 * 3 − 6* would be evaluated in this order:

1. 8 * 3, with a result of 24
2. 4 + 24, with a result of 28
3. 28 − 6, with a final result of 22

You can control the order in which Excel evaluates operations by using parentheses. Excel always evaluates operations in parentheses first. For example, if the previous equation were rewritten as = *(4 + 8) * 3 − 6*, the operations would be evaluated in this order:

1. (4 + 8), with a result of 12
2. 12 * 3, with a result of 36
3. 36 − 6, with a final result of 30

If you have multiple levels of parentheses, Excel evaluates the expressions within the innermost set of parentheses first and works its way out. As with operations on the same level, such as + and –, expressions in the same parenthetical level are evaluated in left-to-right order. For example, the formula = *4 + (3 + 8 * (2 + 5)) – 7* would be evaluated in this order:

1. (2 + 5), with a result of 7

2. 7 * 8, with a result of 56

3. 56 + 3, with a result of 59

4. 4 + 59, with a result of 63

5. 63 – 7, with a final result of 56

To move a formula without changing its cell references

1. Click the cell that contains the formula you want to copy.

2. Point to the edge of the cell you selected.

3. Drag the outline to the cell where you want to move the formula.

To copy a formula while changing its cell references

1. Click the cell that contains the formula you want to copy.

2. Press **Ctrl+C**.

3. Click the cell where you want to paste the formula.

4. Press **Ctrl+V**.

To create relative and absolute cell references

1. Enter a cell reference into a formula.

2. Click within the cell reference.

3. Enter a $ in front of a row or column reference you want to make absolute.

   Or

   Press **F4** to advance through the four possible combinations of relative and absolute row and column references.

Summarize data that meets specific conditions

Another use for formulas is to display messages when certain conditions are met. This kind of formula is called a conditional formula. One way to create a conditional formula in Excel is to use the *IF* function. Clicking the Insert Function button next to the formula bar and then choosing the *IF* function displays the Function Arguments dialog box with the fields required to create an *IF* formula.

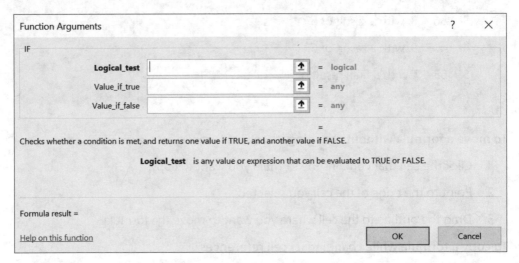

The Function Arguments dialog box for an IF formula.

When you work with an *IF* function, the Function Arguments dialog box has three boxes:

- **Logical_test**   This box holds the condition you want to check.

- **Value_if_true**   This box holds the message that will be displayed if the condition is met, enclosed in quotes. For example, in this case, you could type "High-volume shipper—evaluate for rate decrease."

- **Value_if_false**   This box holds the message that will be displayed if the condition is not met, enclosed in quotes. For example, in this case, you could type "Does not qualify at this time."

Excel also includes several other conditional functions you can use to summarize your data, as shown in the following table.

Function	Description
AVERAGEIF	Finds the average of values within a cell range that meet a specified criterion
AVERAGEIFS	Finds the average of values within a cell range that meet multiple criteria
COUNT	Counts the number of cells in a range that contain a numerical value
COUNTA	Counts the number of cells in a range that are not empty
COUNTBLANK	Counts the number of cells in a range that are empty
COUNTIF	Counts the number of cells in a range that meet a specified criterion
COUNTIFS	Counts the number of cells in a range that meet multiple criteria
IFERROR	Displays one value if a formula results in an error and another if it doesn't
SUMIF	Finds the sum of values in a range that meet a single criterion
SUMIFS	Finds the sum of values in a range that meet multiple criteria

As noted, the COUNTIF function counts the number of cells that meet a criterion, the SUMIF function finds the total of values in cells that meet a criterion, and the AVERAGEIF function finds the average of values in cells that meet a criterion. To create a formula that uses the AVERAGEIF function, you define the range to be examined for the criterion, the criterion, and, if required, the range from which to draw the values. As an example, consider a worksheet that lists each customer's ID number, name, state, and total monthly shipping bill. If you want to find the average order of customers from the state of Washington (abbreviated in the worksheet as WA), you can create the formula =AVERAGEIF(C3:C6, "WA", D3:D6).

	A	B	C	D
1	CustomerID	CustomerName	State	Total
2	CN100	Contoso	WA	$ 118,476.00
3	CN101	Fabrikam	WA	$ 125,511.00
4	CN102	Northwind Trade	OR	$ 103,228.00
5	CN103	Adventure Work:	WA	$ 86,552.00

A list of data that contains customer information.

The *AVERAGEIFS*, *SUMIFS*, and *COUNTIFS* functions extend the capabilities of the *AVERAGEIF*, *SUMIF*, and *COUNTIF* functions to allow for multiple criteria. For example, if you want to find the sum of all orders of at least $100,000 placed by companies in Washington, you can create the formula *=SUMIFS(D3:D6, C3:C6, "=WA", D3:D6, ">=100000")*.

The *AVERAGEIFS* and *SUMIFS* functions start with a data range that contains values that the formula summarizes. You then list the data ranges and the criteria to apply to that range. In generic terms, the syntax is *=AVERAGEIFS(data_range, criteria_range1, criteria1[,criteria_range2, criteria2...])*. The part of the syntax in brackets (which aren't used when you create the formula) is optional, so an *AVERAGEIFS* or *SUMIFS* formula that contains a single criterion will work. The *COUNTIFS* function, which doesn't perform any calculations, doesn't need a data range; you just provide the criteria ranges and criteria. For example, you could find the number of customers from Washington who were billed at least $100,000 by using the formula *=COUNTIFS(D3:D6, "=WA", E3:E6, ">=100000")*.

You can use the *IFERROR* function to display a custom error message instead of relying on the default Excel error messages to explain what happened. For example, you could create this type of formula to employ the *VLOOKUP* function to look up a customer's name in the second column of a table named *Customers* based on the customer identification number entered into cell G8. That formula might look like this: *=IFERROR(VLOOKUP(G8,Customers,2,FALSE),"Customer not found")*. If the function finds a match for the CustomerID in cell G8, it displays the customer's name; if not, it displays the text *Customer not found*.

> ✅ **TIP** The last two arguments in the *VLOOKUP* function tell the formula to look in the *Customers* table's second column and to require an exact match. For more information about the *VLOOKUP* function, see "Look up information in a worksheet" in Chapter 6, "Reorder and summarize data."

To summarize data by using the *IF* function

1. Click the cell in which you want to enter the formula.

2. Enter a formula with the syntax *=IF(Logical_test, Value_if_true, Value_if_false)* where:

   - *Logical_test* is the logical test to be performed.

   - *Value_if_true* is the value the formula returns if the test is true.

   - *Value_if_false* is the value the formula returns if the test is false.

To create a formula by using the Insert Function dialog box

1. To the left of the formula bar, click the **Insert Function** button.

2. In the **Insert Function** dialog box, click the function you want to use in your formula.

3. Click **OK**.

4. In the **Function Arguments** dialog box, define the arguments for the function you chose.

5. Click **OK**.

To count cells that contain numbers in a range

1. Click the cell in which you want to enter the formula.

2. Create a formula with the syntax =*COUNT(range)*, where *range* is the cell range in which you want to count cells.

To count cells that are non-blank

1. Click the cell in which you want to enter the formula.

2. Create a formula with the syntax =*COUNTA(range)*, where *range* is the cell range in which you want to count cells.

To count cells that contain a blank value

1. Click the cell in which you want to enter the formula.

2. Create a formula with the syntax =*COUNTBLANK(range)*, where *range* is the cell range in which you want to count cells.

To count cells that meet one condition

1. Click the cell in which you want to enter the formula.

2. Enter a formula of the form =*COUNTIF(range, criteria)* where:

   - *range* is the cell range that might contain the criteria value.

   - *criteria* is the logical test used to determine whether to count the cell.

3

To count cells that meet multiple conditions

1. Click the cell in which you want to enter the formula.

2. Enter a formula of the form *=COUNTIFS(criteria_range, criteria,...)* where for each *criteria_range* and *criteria* pair:

   - *criteria_range* is the cell range that might contain the *criteria* value.

   - *criteria* is the logical test used to determine whether to count the cell.

To find the sum of data that meets one condition

1. Click the cell in which you want to enter the formula.

2. Enter a formula of the form *=SUMIF(range, criteria, sum_range)* where:

   - *range* is the cell range that might contain the *criteria* value.

   - *criteria* is the logical test used to determine whether to include the cell.

   - *sum_range* is the range that contains the values to be included if the *range* cell in the same row meets the criterion.

To find the sum of data that meets multiple conditions

1. Click the cell in which you want to enter the formula.

2. Enter a formula of the form *=SUMIFS(sum_range, criteria_range, criteria,...)* where:

   - *sum_range* is the range that contains the values to be included if all *criteria_range* cells in the same row meet all criteria.

   - *criteria_range* is the cell range that might contain the *criteria* value.

   - *criteria* is the logical test used to determine whether to include the cell.

To find the average of data that meets one condition

1. Click the cell in which you want to enter the formula.

2. Enter a formula of the form *=AVERAGEIF(range, criteria, average_range)* where:

   - *range* is the cell range that might contain the *criteria* value.

   - *criteria* is the logical test used to determine whether to include the cell.

   - *average_range* is the range that contains the values to be included if the *range* cell in the same row meets the criterion.

To find the average of data that meets multiple conditions

1. Click the cell in which you want to enter the formula.

2. Enter a formula of the form =*AVERAGEIFS(average_range, criteria_range, criteria,...)* where:

   - *average_range* is the range that contains the values to be included if all *criteria_range* cells in the same row meet all criteria.

   - *criteria_range* is the cell range that might contain the *criteria* value.

   - *criteria* is the logical test used to determine whether to include the cell.

To display a custom message if a cell contains an error

1. Click the cell in which you want to enter the formula.

2. Enter a formula with the syntax =*IFERROR(value, value_if_error)* where:

   - *value* is a cell reference or formula.

   - *value_if_error* is the value to be displayed if the *value* argument returns an error.

Set iterative calculation options and enable or disable automatic calculation

Excel formulas use values in other cells to calculate their results. If you create a formula that refers to the cell that contains the formula, the result is a circular reference.

Under most circumstances, Excel treats a circular reference as a mistake for two reasons. First, the vast majority of Excel formulas don't refer to their own cell, so a circular reference is unusual enough to be identified as an error. The second, more serious consideration is that a formula with a circular reference can slow down your workbook. Because Excel repeats, or iterates, the calculation, you need to set limits on how many times the app repeats the operation.

You can control your workbook's calculation options by using the controls on the Formulas page of the Excel Options dialog box.

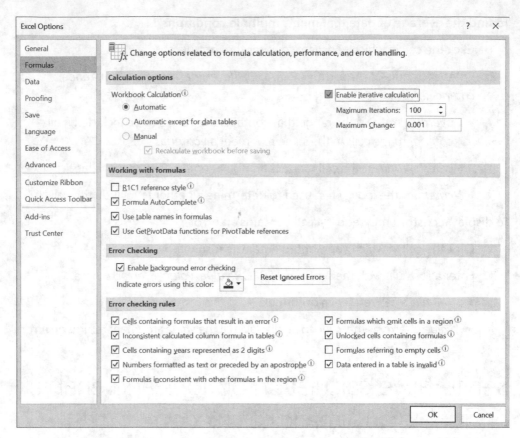

Set iterative calculation options on the Formulas page of the Excel Options dialog box.

The Calculation Options section of the Excel Options dialog box has three available settings:

- **Automatic** The default setting; recalculates a worksheet whenever a value affecting a formula changes

- **Automatic except for data tables** Recalculates a worksheet whenever a value changes, but doesn't recalculate data tables

- **Manual** Requires you to press F9 or, on the Formulas tab, in the Calculation group, click the Calculate Now button to recalculate your worksheet

You can also use options in the Calculation Options section to allow or disallow iterative calculations. If you select the Enable Iterative Calculation check box, Excel repeats calculations for cells that contain formulas with circular references. The default Maximum Iterations value of 100 and Maximum Change of 0.001 are appropriate for all but the most unusual circumstances.

> **TIP** You can also control when Excel recalculates its formulas by clicking the Formulas tab on the ribbon, clicking the Calculation Options button, and selecting the behavior you want.

3

To recalculate a workbook

1. Display the workbook you want to recalculate.

2. Press **F9**.

   Or

   On the **Formulas** tab, in the **Calculation** group, click **Calculate Now**.

To recalculate a worksheet

1. Display the worksheet you want to recalculate.

2. In the **Calculation** group, click the **Calculate Sheet** button.

To set worksheet calculation options

1. Display the worksheet whose calculation options you want to set.

2. In the **Calculation** group, click the **Calculate Options** button.

3. Click the calculation option you want in the list.

To set iterative calculation options

1. Display the Backstage view, and then click **Options**.

2. In the **Excel Options** dialog box, click **Formulas**.

3. In the **Calculation options** section, select or clear the **Enable iterative calculation** check box.

4. In the **Maximum Iterations** box, enter the maximum iterations allowed for a calculation.

5. In the **Maximum Change** box, enter the maximum change allowed for each iteration.

6. Click **OK**.

Use array formulas

Most Excel formulas calculate values to be displayed in a single cell. For example, you could add the formulas *=B1*B4*, *=B1*B5*, and *=B1*B6* to consecutive worksheet cells to calculate shipping insurance costs based on the value of a package's contents.

	A	B	C	D
1	**Insurance Rate**	2.25%		
2				
3	**PackageID**	**Value**	**Premium**	
4	PK101352	$ 591.00		
5	PK101353	$1,713.00		
6	PK101354	$3,039.00		
7				

A worksheet with data to be summarized by an array formula.

Rather than add the same formula to multiple cells one cell at a time, you can add a formula to every cell in the target range at the same time by creating an array formula. To create an array formula, you enter the formula's arguments and press Ctrl+Shift+Enter to identify the formula as an array formula. To calculate package insurance rates for values in the cell range B4:B6 and the rate in cell B1, you would select a range of cells with the same shape as the value range and enter the formula *=B1*B4:B6*. In this case, the values are in a three-cell column, so you must select a range of the same shape, such as C4:C6. When you press Ctrl+Shift+Enter, Excel creates an array formula in the selected cells. The formula appears within a pair of braces to indicate that it is an array formula.

C4		⋮	✕ ✓	*fx*	{=B1*B4:B6}	
	A		B	C	D	
1	**Insurance Rate**		2.25%			
2						
3	**PackageID**		**Value**	**Premium**		
4	PK101352		$ 591.00	13.2975		
5	PK101353		$1,713.00	38.5425		
6	PK101354		$3,039.00	68.3775		
7						
8						

A worksheet with an array formula ready to be entered.

IMPORTANT If you enter the array formula into a range of the wrong shape, Excel displays duplicate results, incomplete results, or error messages, depending on how the target range differs from the value range.

 IMPORTANT You can't add braces to a formula to make it an array formula. You must press Ctrl+Shift+Enter to create it.

In addition to creating an array formula that combines a single cell's value with an array, you can create array formulas that use two separate arrays. For example, a company might establish a goal to reduce sorting time in each of four distribution centers. This worksheet stores the previous sorting times in minutes in cells B2:B5, and the percentage targets in cells C2:C5. The array formula to calculate the targets for each of the four centers is *=B2:B5*C2:C5* which, when you enter it into cells D2:D5 by pressing Ctrl+Shift+Enter, would appear as *{= B2:B5*C2:C5}*.

	A	B	C	D
1	Center	Previous Time	Target Percentage	Target Time
2	North	145	85%	
3	South	180	90%	
4	East	195	75%	
5	West	205	70%	
6				

A worksheet with data for an array formula that multiplies two arrays.

To edit an array formula, you must select every cell that contains the array formula, click the formula bar to activate it, edit the formula in the formula bar, and then press Ctrl+Shift+Enter to re-enter the formula as an array formula.

 TIP Many operations that used to require an array formula can now be calculated by using functions such as *SUMIFS* and *COUNTIFS*.

To create or edit an array formula

1. Select the cells to include in the array formula.

2. Enter or edit your array formula.

3. Press **Ctrl+Shift+Enter.**

Find and correct errors in calculations

Including calculations in a worksheet gives you valuable answers to questions about your data. As is always true, however, it is possible for errors to creep into your formulas. With Excel, you can find the source of errors in your formulas by identifying the cells used in a specific calculation and describing any errors that have occurred. The process of examining a worksheet for errors is referred to as auditing.

Excel identifies errors in several ways. The first way is to display an error code in the cell holding the formula generating the error.

10	**Loading Dock**			
11	Concrete	$ 2,169.00		
12	Labor	$ 4,500.00		
13	Posts	$ 300.00		
14	Excavation	$ 2,500.00		
15	Drain	$ 1,800.00		
16	Rails	$ 495.00		
17	Stairs	$ 1,295.00		
18	*Subtotal*		$ 13,059.00	
19				
20	**Build Total**		$ 31,385.00	
21	**Labor Percentage**		#DIV/0!	
22				
23				

FirstBid ⊕

A worksheet with an error code displayed.

When a cell with an erroneous formula is the active cell, Excel displays an Error button next to it. If you point to the Error button, Excel displays an arrow on the button's right edge. Clicking the arrow displays a menu with options that provide information about the error and offer to help you fix it.

The following table lists the most common error codes and what they mean.

Error code	Description
#####	The column isn't wide enough to display the value.
#VALUE!	The formula has the wrong type of argument, such as text in a cell where a numerical value is required.
#NAME?	The formula contains text that Excel doesn't recognize, such as an unknown named range.
#REF!	The formula refers to a cell that doesn't exist, which can happen whenever cells are deleted.
#DIV/0!	The formula attempts to divide by zero.

Another technique you can use to find the source of formula errors is to ensure that the appropriate cells are providing values for the formula. You can identify the source of an error by having Excel trace a cell's precedents, which are the cells with values used in the active cell's formula. You can also audit your worksheet by identifying cells with formulas that use a value from a particular cell. Cells that use another cell's value in their calculations are known as dependents, meaning that they depend on the value in the other cell to derive their own value. They are identified in Excel by tracer arrows. If the cells identified by the tracer arrows aren't the correct cells, you can hide the arrows and correct the formula.

10	Loading Dock	
11	Concrete	$ 2,169.00
12	Labor	$ 4,500.00
13	Posts	$ 300.00
14	Excavation	$ 2,500.00
15	Drain	$ 1,800.00
16	Rails	$ 495.00
17	Stairs	$ 1,295.00
18	Subtotal	$ 13,059.00
19		
20	Build Total	$ 31,385.00
21	Labor Percentage	34%

A worksheet showing a cell's dependents.

If you prefer to have the elements of a formula error presented as text in a dialog box, you can use the Error Checking dialog box to locate errors one after the other, choose to ignore the selected error, or move to the next or the previous error.

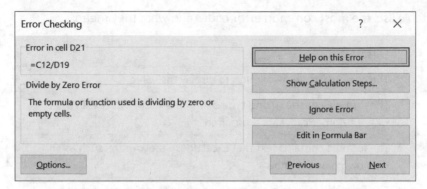

Identify and manage errors using the Error Checking dialog box.

> ✓ **TIP** You can have the Error Checking tool ignore formulas that don't use every cell in a region (such as a row or column). To do so, on the Formulas tab of the Excel Options dialog box, clear the Formulas Which Omit Cells in a Region check box. Excel will no longer mark these cells as an error.

When you just want to display the results of each step of a formula and don't need the full power of the Error Checking tool, you can use the Evaluate Formula dialog box to move through each element of the formula. The Evaluate Formula dialog box is particularly useful for examining formulas that don't produce an error but aren't generating the result you expect.

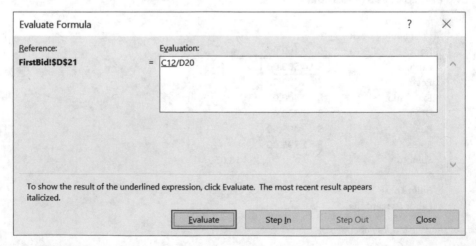

Step through formulas using the Evaluate Formula dialog box.

Finally, you can monitor the value in a cell regardless of where you are in your workbook by opening a Watch Window that displays the value in the cell. For example, if one of your formulas uses values from cells in other worksheets or even other workbooks, you can set a watch on the cell that contains the formula, and then change the values in the other cells. As soon as you enter the new value, the Watch Window displays the new result of the formula. When you're done watching the formula, you can delete the watch and hide the Watch Window.

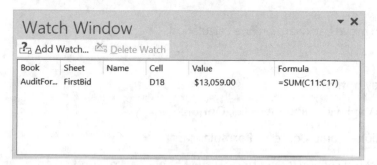

Follow cell values by using the Watch Window.

To display information about a formula error

1. Click the cell that contains the error.

2. Point to the error indicator next to the cell.

   Or

   Click the error indicator to display more information.

To display tracer arrows identifying formula precedents

1. On the **Formulas** tab, in the **Formula Auditing** group, click the **Trace Precedents** button.

To display tracer arrows identifying cell dependents

1. In the **Formula Auditing** group, click the **Trace Dependents** button.

To remove tracer arrows

1. Do either of the following:

   - In the **Formula Auditing** group, click the **Remove Arrows** button (not its arrow).

   - Click the **Remove Arrows** arrow and select the arrows you want to remove.

To evaluate a formula one calculation at a time

1. Click the cell that contains the formula you want to evaluate.

2. In the **Formula Auditing** group, click the **Evaluate Formula** button.

3. In the **Evaluate Formula** dialog box, click **Evaluate**.

4. Click **Step In** to move forward by one calculation.

   Or

   Click **Step Out** to move backward by one calculation.

5. Click **Close**.

To change error display options

1. Display the Backstage view, and then click **Options**.

2. In the **Excel Options** dialog box, click **Formulas**.

3. In the **Error Checking** section, select or clear the **Enable background error checking** check box.

4. Click the **Indicate errors using this color** button and select a color.

5. Click **Reset Ignored Errors** to return Excel to its default error indicators.

6. In the **Error checking rules** section, select or clear the check boxes next to errors you want to indicate or ignore, respectively.

To watch the values in a cell range

1. Click the cell range you want to watch.

2. In the **Formula Auditing** group, click the **Watch Window** button.

3. In the **Watch Window** dialog box, click **Add Watch**.

4. Click **Add**.

To delete a watch

1. Click the **Watch Window** button.

2. In the **Watch Window** dialog box, click the watch you want to delete.

3. Click **Delete Watch**.

Skills review

In this chapter, you learned how to:

- Name groups of data
- Create formulas to calculate values
- Summarize data that meets specific conditions
- Set iterative calculation options and enable or disable automatic calculation
- Use array formulas
- Find and correct errors in calculations

3

Practice tasks

The practice files for these tasks are located in the Excel2019SBS\Ch03 folder. You can save the results of the tasks in the same folder.

Name groups of data

Open the CreateNames workbook in Excel, and then perform the following tasks:

1. Create a named range named **Monday** for the V_101 through V_109 values (found in cells **C4:C12**) for that weekday.

2. Edit the **Monday** named range to include the V_110 value for that column.

3. Select cells **B4:H13** and create named ranges for V_101 through V_110, drawing the names from the row headings.

4. Delete the **Monday** named range.

Create formulas to calculate values

Open the BuildFormulas workbook in Excel, and then perform the following tasks:

1. On the **Summary** worksheet, in cell **F9**, create a formula that displays the value from cell **C4**.

2. Edit the formula in cell **F9** so it uses the *SUM* function to find the total of values in cells **C3:C8**.

3. In cell **F10**, create a formula that finds the total expenses for desktop software and server software.

4. Edit the formula in **F10** so the cell references are absolute references.

5. On the **JuneLabor** worksheet, in cell **F13**, create a *SUM* formula that finds the total of values in the **JuneSummary** table's **Labor Expense** column.

Summarize data that meets specific conditions

Open the CreateConditionalFormulas workbook in Excel, and then perform the following tasks:

1. In cell **G3**, create an *IF* formula that tests whether the value in **F3** is greater than or equal to 35,000. If it is, display **Request discount**; if not, display **No discount available**.

2. Copy the formula from cell **G3** to the range **G4:G14**.

3. In cell **I3**, create a formula that finds the average cost of all expenses in cells **F3:F14** where the **Type** column contains the value *Box*.

4. In cell **I6**, create a formula that finds the sum of all expenses in cells **F3:F14** where the **Type** column contains the value *Envelope* and the **Destination** column contains the value *International*.

Set iterative calculation options and enable or disable automatic calculation

Open the SetIterativeOptions workbook in Excel, and then perform the following tasks:

1. On the **Formulas** tab, in the **Calculation** group, click the **Calculation Options** button, and then click **Manual**.

2. In cell **B6**, enter the formula =B7*B9, and then press **Enter**.

   Note that this result is incorrect because the Gross Savings value minus the Savings Incentive value should equal the Net Savings value, which it does not.

3. Press **F9** to recalculate the workbook and read the message box indicating that you have created a circular reference.

4. Click **OK**.

5. Use options in the **Excel Options** dialog box to enable iterative calculation.

6. Close the **Excel Options** dialog box and recalculate the worksheet.

7. Change the workbook's calculation options to **Automatic**.

Use array formulas

Open the CreateArrayFormulas workbook in Excel, and then perform the following tasks:

1. On the **Fuel** worksheet, select cells **C11:F11**.

2. Enter the array formula =C3*C9:F9 in the selected cells.

3. Edit the array formula you just created to read =C3*C10:F10.

4. Display the **Volume** worksheet.

5. Select cells **D4:D7**.

6. Create the array formula =B4:B7*C4:C7.

Find and correct errors in calculations

Open the AuditFormulas workbook in Excel, and then perform the following tasks:

1. Create a watch that displays the value in cell **D20**.

2. Click cell **D8**, and then display the formula's precedents.

3. Remove the tracer arrows from the worksheet.

4. Click cell **A1**, and then use the **Error Checking** dialog box to identify the error in cell **D21**.

5. Show the tracer arrows for the error.

6. Remove the arrows, and then edit the formula in cell **D21** so it reads =C12/D20.

7. Use the **Evaluate Formula** dialog box to evaluate the formula in cell **D21**.

8. Delete the watch you created in step 1.

Change workbook appearance

Efficiently entering data into a workbook saves you time, but you must also ensure that your data is easy to read. Microsoft Excel 2019 gives you a wide variety of ways to make your data easier to understand. For example, you can change the font, character size, or color used to present a cell's contents. Changing how data appears on a worksheet helps set the contents of a cell apart from the contents of surrounding cells. To save time, you can define a number of custom formats and then apply them quickly to the cells you want to emphasize.

You might also want to specially format a cell's contents to reflect the value in that cell. For example, you could create a worksheet that displays the percentage of improperly delivered packages from each regional distribution center. If that percentage exceeds a threshold, Excel could display a red traffic light icon, indicating that the center's performance requires attention.

This chapter guides you through procedures related to changing the appearance of data, applying existing formats to data, making numbers easier to read, changing data's appearance based on its value, and adding images to worksheets.

In this chapter

- Format cells
- Define styles
- Apply workbook themes and Excel table styles
- Make numbers easier to read
- Change the appearance of data based on its value
- Add images to worksheets

Practice files

For this chapter, use the practice files from the Excel2019SBS\Ch04 folder. For practice file download instructions, see the introduction.

Format cells

Excel worksheets can hold and process lots of data, but when you manage numerous worksheets, it can be hard to remember from a worksheet's title exactly what data is kept in that worksheet. Data labels give you and your colleagues information about data in a worksheet, but it's important to format the labels so that they stand out visually. To make your data labels or any other data stand out, you can change the format of the cells that hold your data.

	A	B	C	D
1				
2		**Call Volume**		
3		Northeast	13,769	
4		Atlantic	19,511	
5		Southeast	11,111	
6		North Central	24,972	
7		Midwest	11,809	
8		Southwest	20,339	
9		Mountain West	20,127	
10		Northwest	12,137	
11		Central	20,047	

Use formatting to set labels apart from worksheet data.

 TIP Deleting a cell's contents doesn't delete the cell's formatting. To delete a selected cell's formatting, on the Home tab, in the Editing group, click the Clear button (which looks like an eraser), and then click Clear Formats. Clicking Clear All from the same list will remove the cell's contents and formatting.

Many of the formatting-related buttons on the ribbon have arrows at their right edges. Clicking the arrow displays a list of options for that button, such as the fonts available on your system or the colors you can assign to a cell.

TIP Clicking the body of the Border, Fill Color, or Font Color button applies the most recently applied formatting to the currently selected cells.

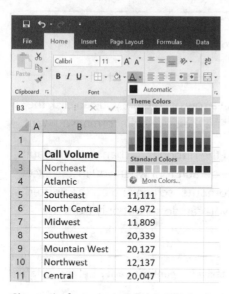

Change the font color to help labels and values stand out.

You can also make a cell stand apart from its neighbors by adding a border around the cell or changing the color or shading of the cell's interior.

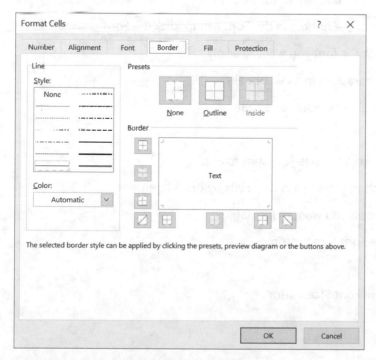

Add borders to set cells apart from their neighbors.

> ✓ **TIP** You can display the most commonly used formatting controls by right-clicking a selected range. When you do, a mini toolbar containing a subset of the Home tab formatting tools appears above the shortcut menu.

If you want to change the attributes of every cell in a row or column, you can click the header of the row or column you want to modify and then select the format you want.

One task you can't perform by using the tools on the ribbon is to change the default font for a workbook, used in the formula bar. The default font when you install Excel is Calibri, a simple font that is easy to read on a computer screen and on the printed page. If you'd prefer to change the default font, you can do so, but only from the Excel Options dialog box, not from the ribbon.

> ⚠ **IMPORTANT** The new standard font doesn't take effect until you exit Excel and restart the app.

To change the font used to display cell contents

1. Select the cell or cells you want to format.

2. On the **Home** tab of the ribbon, in the **Font** group, click the **Font** arrow.

3. In the font list, click the font you want to apply.

To change the size of characters in a cell or cells

1. Select the cell or cells you want to format.

2. Click the **Font Size** arrow.

3. In the list of sizes, click the size you want to apply.

To change the size of characters in a cell or cells by one increment

1. Select the cell or cells you want to format.

2. Click the **Increase Font Size** button.

    Or

    Click the **Decrease Font Size** button.

To change the color of a font

1. Select the cell or cells you want to format.

2. Click the **Font Color** arrow (not the button).

3. Click the color you want to apply.

   Or

   Click **More Colors**, select the color you want from the **Colors** dialog box, and then click **OK**.

To change the background color of a cell or cells

1. Select the cell or cells you want to format.

2. Click the **Fill Color** arrow (not the button).

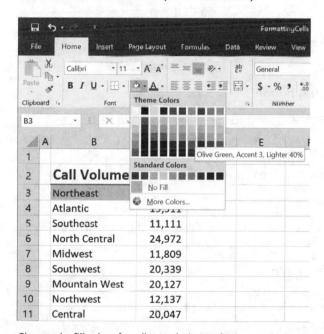

Change the fill color of a cell to make it stand out.

3. Click the color you want to apply.

   Or

   Click **More Colors**, select the color you want from the **Colors** dialog box, and click **OK**.

To add a border to a cell or cells

1. Select the cell or cells you want to format.

2. Click the **Border** arrow (not the button).

3. Click the border pattern you want to apply.

   Or

   Click **More Borders**, select the borders you want from the **Border** tab of the **Format Cells** dialog box, and click **OK**.

To change font appearance by using the controls on the Font tab of the Format Cells dialog box

1. Click the **Font** dialog box launcher.

2. Make the formatting changes you want, and then click **OK**.

To copy formatting between cells

1. Select the cell that contains the formatting you want to copy.

2. Click the **Format Painter** button.

3. Select the cells to which you want to apply the formatting.

Or

1. Select the cell that contains the formatting you want to copy.

2. Double-click the **Format Painter** button.

3. Select cells or groups of cells to which you want to apply the formatting.

4. Press the **Esc** key to turn off the Format Painter.

To delete cell formatting

1. Select the cell or cells from which you want to remove formatting.

2. In the **Editing** group, click the **Clear** button.

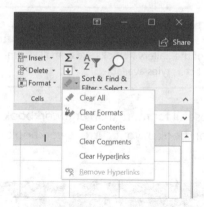

Use the Clear button to delete formats from a cell.

4

3. In the menu that appears, click **Clear Formats**.

To change the default font of a workbook

1. Display the Backstage view, and then click **Options**.

2. On the **General** page of the **Excel Options** dialog box, in the **Use this as the default font** list, click the font you want to use.

3. In the **Font size** list, click the font size you want.

4. Click **OK**.

5. Exit and restart Excel to complete the default font change.

Define styles

As you work with Excel, you will probably develop preferred formats for data labels, titles, and other worksheet elements. Instead of adding a format's characteristics one element at a time to the target cells, you can format the cell in one action by using a cell style. Excel comes with many built-in styles, which you can apply by using the Cell Style gallery. You can also create your own styles by using the Style dialog box, which will appear in a separate group at the top of the gallery when you open it. If you want to preview how the contents of your cell (or cells) will look when you apply the style, point to the style to get a live preview.

> **TIP** Depending on your screen's resolution, cell style options might be accessed via an in-ribbon gallery instead of a Cell Styles button. If you see an in-ribbon gallery, click the More button that appears in the lower-right corner of the gallery (it looks like a small, downward-pointing black triangle) to display the full set of cell styles available.

It's likely that any cell styles you create will be useful for more than one workbook. If you want to include cell styles from another workbook in your current workbook, you can merge the two workbooks' style collections.

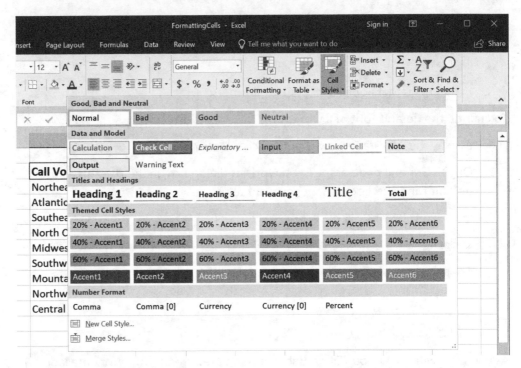

Apply styles from the Cell Styles gallery.

To apply a cell style to worksheet cells

1. Select the cells to which you want to apply the style.

2. On the **Home** tab, in the **Styles** group, click the **Cell Styles** button.

3. In the gallery that appears, click the style you want to apply.

To create a new cell style

1. Click the **Cell Styles** button, and then click **New Cell Style**.

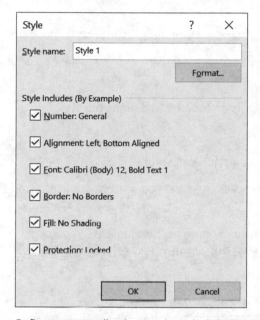

Define a custom cell style using the Style dialog box.

2. In the **Style** dialog box, enter a name for the new style.

3. Select the check boxes next to any elements you want to include in the style definition.

4. Click the **Format** button.

5. Use the controls in the **Format Cells** dialog box to define your style.

6. Click **OK**.

To create a cell style based on existing cell formatting

1. Select a cell that contains the formatting on which you want to base your new cell style.

2. Click the **Cell Styles** button, and then click **New Cell Style**.

   Excel displays the **Style** dialog box with the active cell's characteristics filled in.

3. Enter a name for the new style.

4. Click **OK**.

To modify an existing cell style

1. Click the **Cell Styles** button, right-click the style you want to modify, and then click **Modify**.

2. In the **Style** dialog box, make the necessary changes to your style name and style elements.

3. Click the **Format** button.

4. Use the controls in the **Format Cells** dialog box to define your style.

5. Click **OK**.

To create a new cell style based on an existing cell style

1. Click the **Cell Styles** button, right-click the style you want to duplicate, and then click **Duplicate**.

2. In the **Style** dialog box, type a distinct name for the duplicate version of the style and select the elements of the existing style to include in the duplicated one.

3. Click the **Format** button.

4. Use the controls in the **Format Cells** dialog box to make any other changes to the duplicate style.

5. Click **OK**.

To merge cell styles from another open workbook

1. Click the **Cell Styles** button, and then click **Merge Styles**.

2. In the **Merge Styles** dialog box, click the workbook from which you want to import cell styles.

3. Click **OK**.

To delete a custom cell style

1. Click the **Cell Styles** button, right-click the style you want to delete, and then click **Delete**.

Apply workbook themes and Excel table styles

Excel 2019 includes powerful design tools that you can use to quickly create workbooks and worksheets that look attractive and professional. These tools include workbook themes and table styles.

A theme is a way to specify the fonts, colors, and graphic effects that appear in a workbook. Excel comes with many themes.

4

*Change a workbook's overall appearance
by using a theme.*

When you start to format a workbook element, Excel displays a palette of colors with two sections: standard colors, which remain constant regardless of the workbook's theme, and colors that are available within the active theme. If you format workbook elements by using colors specific to a theme, applying a different theme changes the colors of those elements.

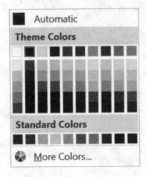

Select theme-specific or standard colors.

You can change a theme's colors, fonts, and graphic effects. If you like the combination you create, you can save your changes as a new theme that will appear at the top of the Themes gallery.

 TIP When you save a theme, you save it as an Office theme file. You can then apply the theme to other Office 2019 documents.

Just as you can define and apply themes to entire workbooks, you can apply and define Excel table styles. After you give your style a descriptive name, you can set the appearance for each Excel table element, decide whether to make your new style the default for the current document, and save your work.

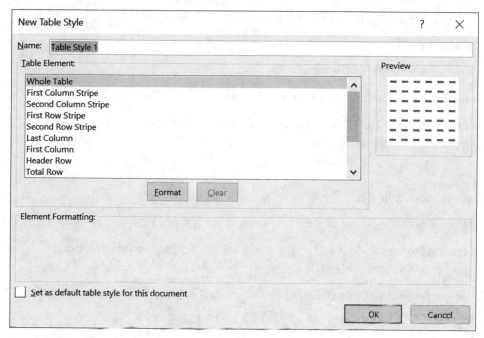

Define new Excel table styles in the New Table Style dialog box.

 TIP To remove formatting from a table element, click the name of the table element and then click the Clear button.

To apply an Office theme to a workbook

1. On the **Page Layout** tab of the ribbon, in the **Themes** group, click the **Themes** button.

2. Click the theme you want to apply.

To change the fonts, colors, and effects of an Office theme

1. In the **Themes** group, click the **Colors**, **Fonts**, or **Effects** button.

2. Click the set of colors, fonts, or effects you want to apply.

To create a new Office theme based on an existing theme

1. Use the controls in the **Themes** group to change the fonts, colors, or effects applied to the current theme.

2. Click the **Themes** button, and then click **Save Current Theme**.

3. Enter a name for your new theme.

4. Click **Save**.

To delete a custom Office theme

1. Click the **Themes** button, and then click **Save Current Theme**.

2. In the **Save Current Theme** dialog box, right-click the theme you want to delete, and then click **Delete**.

3. Click **Yes**.

To apply a table style

1. Click any cell in the list of data you want to format as a table.

2. On the **Home** tab, in the **Styles** group, click the **Format as Table** button, and then click the table style you want to apply.

3. In the **Format as Table** dialog box, verify that Excel has identified the data range correctly.

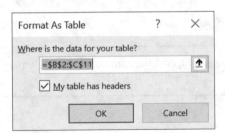

Verify that Excel has identified your table data correctly.

4. Select or clear the **My table has headers** check box to reflect whether or not your list of data has headers.

5. Click **OK**.

To apply a table style and overwrite existing formatting

1. Click any cell in the list of data you want to format as a table.

2. Click the **Format as Table** button, and right-click the table style you want to apply.

3. On the shortcut menu that appears, click **Apply and Clear Formatting**.

4. Click **OK**.

To create a new table style

1. Click the **Format as Table** button, and then click **New Table Style**.

2. In the **New Table Style** dialog box, enter a name for the new style.

3. Click the table element you want to format.

4. Click the **Format** button, change the element by using the controls in the **Format Cells** dialog box, and then click **OK**.

5. Repeat the previous step to change the format of other elements.

6. Click **OK** to close the **New Table Style** dialog box.

To modify an existing table style

1. Click the **Format as Table** button, right-click the table style you want to modify, and then click **Modify**.

 IMPORTANT You can't modify the built-in Excel table styles, just the ones you create.

2. In the **Modify Table Style** dialog box, edit style elements you want to modify.

3. Click **OK**.

To delete a table style

1. Click the **Format as Table** button, right-click the table style you want to delete, and then click **Delete**.

 IMPORTANT You can't delete the built-in Excel table styles, just the ones you create.

2. In the message box that appears, click **OK**.

Make numbers easier to read

Changing the format of the cells in your worksheet can make your data much easier to read, both by setting data labels apart from the actual data and by adding borders to define the boundaries between labels and data even more clearly.

You can also make idiosyncratic data types such as dates, phone numbers, or currency values easier to read by presenting them in a standardized way, regardless of how it was entered into Excel. As an example, consider US phone numbers. These numbers are 10 digits long and have a 3-digit area code, a 3-digit exchange, and a 4-digit line number written in the form *(###) ###-####*. Although it's certainly possible to enter a phone number with the expected formatting in a cell—that is, with the area code surrounded by parentheses and the exchange and digit values separated by a hyphen—it's much more straightforward to enter a sequence of 10 digits and have Excel add those formatting elements. To do so, you indicate to Excel that the contents of the cell will be a phone number.

Select built-in number formats from the Special category.

You can watch this format in operation if you compare the contents of the active cell and the contents of the formula box for a cell with the Phone Number formatting.

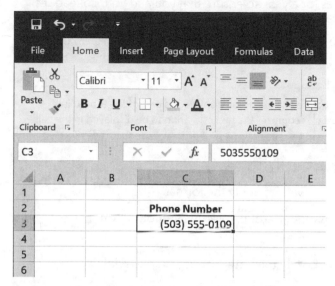

Chunge the appearance of data without affecting the underlying data.

> ⚠ **IMPORTANT** If you enter a 9-digit number in a field that expects a phone number, you won't get an error message. Instead, you'll get a 2-digit area code. For example, the number 425550012 would be displayed as (42) 555-0012. An 11-digit number would be displayed with a 4-digit area code. If the phone number doesn't look right, you probably left out a digit or included an extra one, so you should make sure your entry is correct.

Just as you can instruct Excel to expect a phone number in a cell, you can also inform Excel that a cell will contain a date or a currency amount. You can pick from a wide variety of date, currency, and other formats to best reflect your worksheet's contents, your company standards, and how you and your colleagues expect the data to appear.

> ✓ **TIP** You can make the most common format changes by displaying the Home tab and then, in the Number group, either clicking a button representing a built-in format or selecting a format from the Number Format list.

You can also create a custom numeric format to add a word or phrase to a number in a cell. For example, you can add the phrase *per month* to a cell with a formula that calculates average monthly sales for a year, to ensure that you and your colleagues will recognize the figure as a monthly average. If one of the built-in formats is close to the custom format you'd like to create, you can base your custom format on the one already included in Excel.

 IMPORTANT You must enclose any text to be displayed as part of the format in quotation marks so that Excel recognizes the text as a string to be displayed in the cell.

To apply a special number format

1. Select the cells to which you want to apply the format.

2. On the **Home** tab, in the **Number** group, click the **Number Format** arrow, and then click **More Number Formats**.

3. In the **Format Cells** dialog box, in the **Category** list, click **Special**.

4. In the **Type** list, click the format you want to apply.

5. Click **OK**.

To create a custom number format

1. On the **Number Format** menu, click **More Number Formats**.

2. In the **Format Cells** dialog box, in the **Category** list, click **Custom**.

3. Click the format you want to use as the base for your new format.

4. Edit the format in the **Type** box.

5. Click **OK**.

To add text to a number format

1. On the **Number Format** menu, click **More Number Formats**.

2. In the **Format Cells** dialog box, in the **Category** list, click **Custom**.

3. Click the format you want to use as the base for your new format.

4. In the **Type** box, after the format, enter the text you want to add, in quotation marks—for example, "**boxes**".

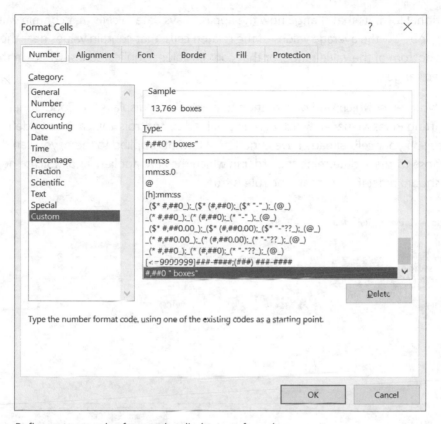

Define custom number formats that display text after values.

5. Click **OK**.

Change the appearance of data based on its value

Recording information such as package volumes, vehicle miles, and other business data in a worksheet enables you to make important decisions about your operations. And as you saw earlier in this chapter, you can change the appearance of data labels and the worksheet itself to make interpreting your data easier.

Another way you can make your data easier to interpret is to have Excel change the appearance of your data based on its value. The formats that make this possible are called conditional formats, because the data must meet certain conditions, defined in conditional formatting rules, to have a format applied to it. In Excel, you can define conditional formats that change how the app displays data in cells that contain values above or below the average values of the related cells, that contain values near the top or bottom of the value range, or that contain values duplicated elsewhere in the selected range.

When you select which kind of condition to create, Excel displays the Conditional Formatting Rules Manager, which contains fields and controls you can use to define your rule. If your cells already have conditional formats applied to them, you can display those formats, determine the order in which they are applied, and indicate how Excel should react if more than one rule is true.

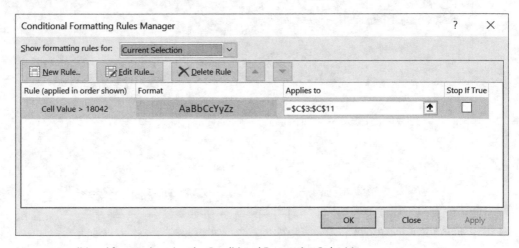

Manage conditional formats by using the Conditional Formatting Rules Manager.

You can control your conditional formats in the following ways:

- Create a new rule.

- Change a rule.

- Remove a rule.

- Move a rule up or down in the order.

- Control whether Excel continues evaluating conditional formats after it finds a rule to apply.

- Save any rule changes and stop editing rules.

- Save any rule changes and continue editing.

- Discard any unsaved changes.

Clicking the New Rule button in the Conditional Formatting Rules Manager opens the New Formatting Rule dialog box. The commands in the New Formatting Rule dialog box duplicate the options displayed when you click the Conditional Formatting button in the Styles group on the Home tab. You can use those controls to define your new rule and the format to be displayed if the rule is true.

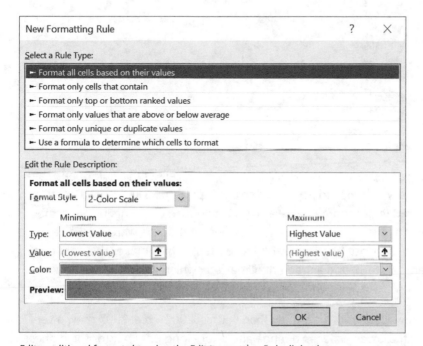

Edit conditional formats by using the Edit Formatting Rule dialog box.

 IMPORTANT Excel doesn't check to make sure that your conditions are logically consistent, so you need to be sure that you plan and enter your conditions correctly.

You can also create three other types of conditional formats in Excel: data bars, color scales, and icon sets.

Data bars summarize the relative magnitude of values in a cell range by extending a band of color across the cell.

Call Volume	
Northeast	13,769
Atlantic	19,511
Southeast	11,111
North Central	24,972
Midwest	11,809
Southwest	20,339
Mountain West	20,127
Northwest	12,137
Central	20,047

Apply data bars to view how values compare to one another.

When data bars were introduced in Excel 2007, they filled cells with a color band that decreased in intensity as it moved across the cell. This pattern, called a gradient fill, made it a bit difficult to determine the relative length of two data bars because the end points weren't as distinct as they would have been if the bars were a solid color. In Excel 2019 you can choose between a solid fill pattern, which makes the right edge of the bars easier to discern, and a gradient fill pattern, which you can use if you share your workbook with colleagues who use Excel 2007.

Excel 2019 also draws data bars differently than in Excel 2007. Excel 2007 drew a very short data bar for the lowest value in a range and a very long data bar for the highest value. The problem was that similar values could be represented by data bars of very different lengths if there wasn't much variance among the values in the conditionally formatted range. In Excel 2019, data bars compare values based on their distance from zero, so similar values are summarized by using data bars of similar lengths.

 TIP Excel 2019 data bars summarize negative values by using bars that extend to the left of a baseline that the app draws in a cell.

Color scales compare the relative magnitude of values in a cell range by applying colors from a two-color or three-color set to your cells. The intensity of a cell's color reflects the value's tendency toward the top or bottom of the values in the range.

Call Volume	
Northeast	13,769
Atlantic	19,511
Southeast	11,111
North Central	24,972
Midwest	11,809
Southwest	20,339
Mountain West	20,127
Northwest	12,137
Central	20,047

Apply a color scale to emphasize the magnitude of values within a cell range.

Finally, icon sets are collections of three, four, or five images that Excel displays when certain rules are met.

Call Volume		
Northeast	◼	13,769
Atlantic	◻	19,511
Southeast	◼	11,111
North Central	◒	24,972
Midwest	◼	11,809
Southwest	◻	20,339
Mountain West	◒	20,127
Northwest	◼	12,137
Central	◻	20,047

Icon sets show how values compare to a standard

When icon sets were introduced in Excel 2007, you could apply an icon set as a whole, but you couldn't create custom icon sets or choose to have Excel 2007 display no icon if the value in a cell met a criterion. In Excel 2019, you can display any icon from any set for any criterion or display no icon. Plus, you can edit the icon set in other ways so it summarizes your data exactly as you want it to.

When you click a color scale or icon set in the Conditional Formatting Rules Manager and then click the Edit Rule button, you can control when Excel applies a color or icon to your data.

> ⚠ **IMPORTANT** Do not include cells that contain summary formulas in your condition-ally formatted ranges. The values, which could be much higher or lower than your regular cell data, could throw off your comparisons.

To create a conditional formatting rule

1. Select the cells to which you want to apply a conditional formatting rule.

2. On the **Home** tab, in the **Styles** group, click the **Conditional Formatting** button, point to **Highlight Cells Rules**, and then click the type of rule you want to create.

3. In the **Conditional Formatting Rules Manager** that appears, set the rules for the condition.

4. Click the arrow next to the **with** box, and then click **Custom Format**.

5. Use the controls in the **Format Cells** dialog box to define the custom format.

6. Click **OK** to close the **Format Cells** dialog box.

7. Click **OK** to close the **Conditional Formatting Rules Manager**.

To edit a conditional formatting rule

1. Select the cells to which the conditional formatting rule is applied.

2. Click the **Conditional Formatting** button, and then click **Manage Rules**.

3. In the **Conditional Formatting Rules Manager**, click the rule you want to edit.

4. Click **Edit Rule**.

5. Use the controls in the **Edit Formatting Rule** dialog box to change the rule settings.

6. Click **OK** twice to close the **Edit Formatting Rule** dialog box and the **Conditional Formatting Rules Manager**.

To change the order of conditional formatting rules

1. Select the cells to which the conditional formatting rules are applied.

2. Click the **Conditional Formatting** button, and then click **Manage Rules**.

3. In the **Conditional Formatting Rules Manager**, click the rule you want to move.

4. Click the **Move Up** button to move the rule up in the order.

   Or

   Click the **Move Down** button to move the rule down in the order.

5. Click **OK**.

To stop applying conditional formatting rules when a condition is met

1. Select the cells to which the conditional formatting rules are applied.

2. Click the **Conditional Formatting** button, and then click **Manage Rules**.

3. In the **Conditional Formatting Rules Manager**, select the **Stop If True** check box next to the rule where you want Excel to stop.

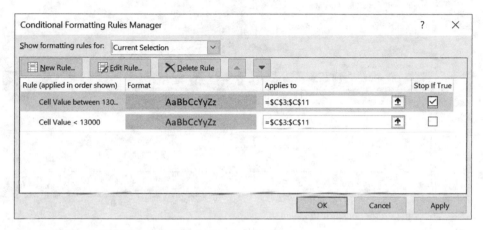

Stop checking conditional formats if a specific condition is met.

4. Click **OK**.

To create a data bar conditional format

1. Select the range to which you want to apply the conditional format.

2. Click the **Conditional Formatting** button, point to **Data Bars**, and then click the format you want to apply.

To create a color scale conditional format

1. Select the range to which you want to apply the conditional format.

2. Click the **Conditional Formatting** button, point to **Color Scales**, and then click the color scale you want to apply.

To create an icon set conditional format

1. Select the range to which you want to apply the conditional format.

2. Click the **Conditional Formatting** button, point to **Icon Sets**, and then click the icon set you want to apply.

To delete a conditional format

1. Select the cells to which the conditional formatting rule is applied.

2. Click the **Conditional Formatting** button, and then click **Manage Rules**.

3. In the **Conditional Formatting Rules Manager**, click the rule you want to delete.

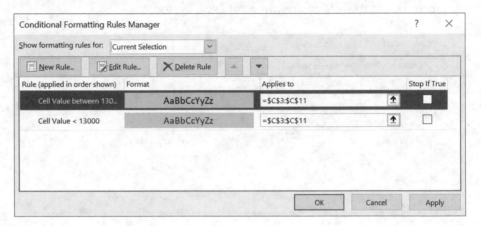

Delete a conditional format you no longer need.

4. Click **Delete Rule**.

5. Click **OK**.

To delete all conditional formats from a worksheet

1. Click the **Conditional Formatting** button, point to **Clear Rules**, and then click **Clear Rules from Entire Sheet**.

Add images to worksheets

Establishing a strong corporate identity helps you ensure that your customers remember your organization and the products and services you offer. Setting aside the obvious need for sound management, one important attribute of a strong business is an eye-catching, easy-to-remember logo. After you or your graphic artist creates a logo, you should add an image file containing the logo to all your documents, especially any that might be seen by your customers. Not only does the logo mark the documents as coming from your company, it also serves as an advertisement, encouraging anyone who sees your worksheets to call or visit your company.

One way to add a logo or any other type of image to a worksheet is to locate the picture you want to add from your hard disk, insert it, and then make any formatting changes you want. For example, you can rotate, reposition, and resize the picture.

◢	A	B	C	D	E	F	G	H	I
1									
2									
3									
4		**Call Volume**							
5		Northeast	13,769						
6		Atlantic	19,511						
7		Southeast	11,111						
8		North Central	24,972						
9		Midwest	11,809						
10		Southwest	20,339						
11		Mountain West	20,127						
12		Northwest	12,137						
13		Central	20,047						
14									

Insert images to enhance your data.

With Excel 2019, you can remove the background of an image you insert into a workbook. When you indicate that you want to remove an image's background, Excel guesses which aspects of the image are in the foreground and eliminates the rest.

An image just after the Remove Background tool has been applied.

You can drag the handles on the inner square of the background removal tool to change how the tool analyzes the image.

If you want to generate a repeating image in the background of a worksheet to form a tiled pattern or texture behind your worksheet's data, or perhaps add a single image that serves as a watermark, you can do so.

 TIP To remove a background image from a worksheet, display the Page Layout tab, and then in the Page Setup group, click Delete Background.

To add an image stored on your computer to a worksheet

1. On the **Insert** tab of the ribbon, in the **Illustrations** group, click **Pictures**.

2. In the **Insert Picture** dialog box, navigate to the folder that contains the image you want to add to your worksheet.

3. Click the image.

4. Click **Insert**.

To add an online image by using Bing Image Search

1. In the **Illustrations** group, click the **Online Pictures** button.

2. In the **Insert Pictures** dialog box, enter search terms identifying the type of image you want to find online.

3. Press **Enter**.

4. Click the image you want to add to your worksheet.

5. Click **Insert**.

To resize an image

1. Click the image.

Drag a handle to resize an image.

2. Drag one of the handles that appears on the image's border.

Or

On the **Format** tool tab of the ribbon, in the **Size** group, enter new values for the image's vertical and horizontal size in the **Height** and **Width** boxes.

To edit an image

1. Click the image.

2. Use the controls in the **Size** group to change your image's appearance.

To delete an image

1. Click the image.

2. Press the **Delete** key.

To remove the background from an image

1. Click the image.

2. Click the **Remove Background** button.

3. Drag the handles on the frame until the foreground of the image is defined correctly.

4. On the **Background Removal** tool tab of the ribbon, click the **Keep Changes** button.

To set an image as a repeating background

1. On the **Page Layout** tab, in the **Page Setup** group, click the **Background** button.

2. Click the **Browse** button and navigate to the folder that contains the file you want to use as your repeating background.

Or

Enter search terms in the **Search Bing** box, and then press **Enter**.

3. Click the image you want to set as your background.

4. Click **Insert**.

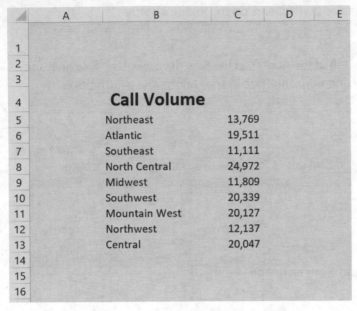

Add repeating images to enhance the background of a worksheet.

Skills review

In this chapter, you learned how to:

- Format cells
- Define styles
- Apply workbook themes and Excel table styles
- Make numbers easier to read
- Change the appearance of data based on its value
- Add images to worksheets

Practice tasks

The practice files for these tasks are located in the Excel2019SBS\Ch04 folder. You can save the results of the tasks in the same folder.

Format cells

Open the FormatCells workbook in Excel, and then perform the following tasks:

1. Change the formatting of cell **B4** so the text it contains appears in 14-point, bold type.

2. Center the text within cell **B4**.

3. Change the background fill color of cell **B4**.

4. Draw a border around the cell range **B4:C13**.

Define styles

Open the DefineStyles workbook in Excel, and then perform the following tasks:

1. Apply an existing cell style to the values in cells **B4** and **C3**.

2. Create a new cell style and apply it to the values in cell ranges **B5:B13** and **C4:N4**.

3. Edit the font size of the new cell style you just created and save it under a new name.

Apply workbook themes and Excel table styles

Open the ApplyStyles workbook in Excel, and then perform the following tasks:

1. Display the **MilesLastWeek** worksheet and change the theme applied to the workbook.

2. Change the colors used for the new theme.

3. Save a new theme based on the settings currently applied to the workbook.

4. On the **Summary** worksheet, create an Excel table from the list of data in the cell range **A1:B10**.

5. Define a new Excel table style and apply it to the same data.

Make numbers easier to read

Open the FormatNumbers workbook in Excel, and then perform the following tasks:

1. Apply a phone number format to the value in cell **G3**.

2. Apply a currency or accounting format to the value in cell **H3**.

3. For cell **H3**, create a custom number format that displays the value in that cell as *$255,000 plus benefits*.

Change the appearance of data based on its value

Open the CreateConditionalFormats workbook in Excel, and then perform the following tasks:

1. Apply a conditional format to cell **C15** that displays the cell's contents with a red background if the value the cell contains is less than 90 percent.

2. Apply a data bar conditional format to cells **C4:C12**.

3. Apply a color scale conditional format to cells **F4:F12**.

4. Apply an icon set conditional format to cells **I4:I12**.

5. Delete the conditional format from the cell range **C4:C12**.

6. Edit the data bar conditional format so the bars are a different color.

Add images to worksheets

Open the AddImages workbook in Excel, and then perform the following tasks:

1. Insert the **phone** image file from the Excel2019SBS\Ch04 folder.

2. Remove the background from the **phone** image.

3. Resize the **phone** image so it will fit between the **Call Volume** label in cell **B4** and the top of the worksheet.

4. Move the image to the upper-left corner of the worksheet, resizing it if necessary so it doesn't block any of the worksheet text.

5. Add a repeating background image by using the **texture** image from the Excel2019SBS\Ch04 folder.

Part 2

Analyze and present data

Manage worksheet data

With Excel 2019, you can manage huge data collections, but storing more than 1 million rows of data doesn't help you make business decisions unless you have the ability to focus on the most important data in a worksheet.

Excel includes many powerful and flexible tools with which you can limit the data displayed in your worksheet. When your worksheet displays the subset of data you need, you can perform calculations on that data. You can discover what percentage of monthly revenue was earned in the 10 best days in the month, find your total revenue for particular days of the week, or locate the slowest business day of the month.

Just as you can limit the data displayed by your worksheets, you can also create validation rules that limit the data entered into them. When you set rules for data entered into cells, you can catch many of the most common data-entry errors, such as entering values that are too small or too large or attempting to enter a word in a cell that requires a number. If you add a validation rule after data has been entered, Excel can circle any invalid data so that you know what to correct.

This chapter guides you through procedures related to limiting the data that appears on your screen, manipulating list data, and creating validation rules that limit data entry to appropriate values.

In this chapter

- Limit data that appears on your screen
- Manipulate worksheet data
- Define valid sets of values for ranges of cells

Practice files

For this chapter, use the practice files from the Excel2019SBS\Ch05 folder. For practice file download instructions, see the introduction.

Limit data that appears on your screen

Excel worksheets can hold as much data as you need them to, but you might not want to work with all the data in a worksheet at the same time. For example, you might want to look at the revenue figures for your company during the first third, second third, and final third of a month. You can limit the data shown on a worksheet by creating a filter, which is a rule that selects rows to be shown in a worksheet.

> ⚠️ **IMPORTANT** When you turn on filtering, Excel treats the cells in the active cell's column as a range. To ensure that the filtering works properly, you should always have a label at the top of the column you want to filter. If you don't, Excel treats the first value in the list as the label and doesn't include it in the list of values by which you can filter the data.

When you turn on filtering, a filter arrow appears to the right of each column label in the list of data. Clicking the filter arrow displays a menu of filtering options and a list of the unique values in the column. Each item has a check box next to it, which you can use to create a selection filter. Some of the commands vary depending on the type of data in the column. For example, if the column contains a set of dates, you will get a list of commands specific to that data type.

> ✓ **TIP** In Excel tables, filter arrows are turned on by default.

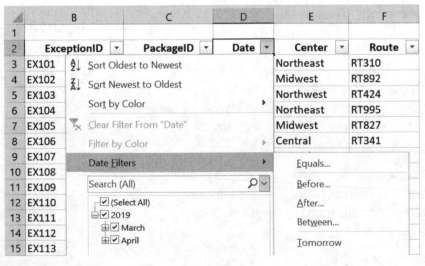

Use filters to limit the data that appears in a worksheet.

TIP When a column contains several types of data, the filter command Number Filters appears.

When you click a filtering option, Excel displays a dialog box in which you can define the filter's criteria. As an example, you could create a filter that displays only dates after 3/31/2019.

	B	C	D	E	F
2	ExceptionID ▾	PackageID ▾	Date ▾	Center ▾	Route ▾
16	EX114	PD132	4/1/2019	Midwest	RT436
17	EX115	PD133	4/1/2019	Midwest	RT758
18	EX116	PD134	4/1/2019	Midwest	RT529
19	EX117	PD135	4/1/2019	Northeast	RT243
20	EX118	PD136	4/1/2019	Northeast	RT189
21	EX119	PD137	4/1/2019	Northwest	RT714
22	EX120	PD138	4/2/2019	Central	RT151
23	EX121	PD139	4/2/2019	Midwest	RT543
24	EX122	PD140	4/2/2019	Southwest	RT208
25	EX123	PD141	4/2/2019	South	RT145
26	EX124	PD142	4/2/2019	Central	RT250
27	EX125	PD143	4/2/2019	Midwest	RT852
28					

Columns with a filter applied display a funnel icon on their filter arrows.

If you want to display the highest or lowest values in a data column, you can create a Top 10 filter. You can choose whether to show values from the top or bottom of the list, define the number of items you want to display, and choose whether that number indicates the actual number of items or the percentage of items to be shown when the filter is applied.

TIP Top 10 filters can be applied only to columns that contain number values.

Excel 2019 includes a capability called the search filter, which you can use to enter a search string that Excel uses to identify which items to display in an Excel table or a data list. Enter the character string you want to search for, and Excel limits your data to values that contain that string.

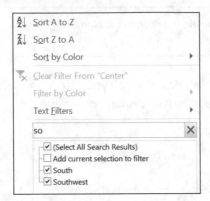

Applying a search filter limits the items that appear in the selection list.

When you create a custom filter, you can define a rule that Excel uses to decide which rows to show after the filter is applied. For instance, you can create a rule that determines that only days with package volumes of less than 100,000 should be shown in your worksheet. You might then be able to determine whether the weather or another factor resulted in slower business on those days.

Excel indicates that a column has a filter applied by changing the appearance of the column's filter arrow to include an icon that looks like a funnel. After you finish examining your data by using a filter, you can clear the filter or turn off filtering entirely and hide the filter arrows.

To turn on filter arrows

1. Click any cell in the list of data you want to filter.

2. On the **Home** tab of the ribbon, in the **Editing** group, click **Sort & Filter**, and then click **Filter**.

To create a selection filter

1. Click **Sort & Filter**, and then click **Filter**.

2. Click the filter arrow for the column by which you want to filter your data.

3. Clear the check boxes next to the items you want to hide.

   Or

   Clear the **Select All** check box and select the check boxes next to the items you want to display.

4. Click **OK**.

To create a filter rule

1. Display the filter arrows for your list of data.

2. Click the filter arrow for the field by which you want to filter your data.

3. Point to the *Type* **Filters** item to display the available filters for the column's data type.

4. Click the filter you want to create.

5. Enter the arguments required to define the rule.

6. Click **OK**.

To create a Top 10 filter

1. Display the filter arrows for your list of data.

2. Click the filter arrow for a column that contains number values, point to **Number Filters**, and then click **Top 10**.

3. In the **Top 10 AutoFilter** dialog box, click the arrow for the first list box and select whether to display the top or bottom values.

4. Click the arrow for the last list box and select whether to base the rule on the number of items or the percentage of items.

5. Click in the middle box and enter the number or percentage of items to display.

6. Click **OK**.

To create a search filter

1. Display the filter arrows for your list of data.

2. Click the filter arrow for the field by which you want to filter your data.

3. Enter the character string that should appear in the values you want to display in the filter list.

4. Click **OK**.

To clear a filter

1. Click the filter arrow for the field that has the filter you want to clear.

2. Click **Clear Filter from** *Field*.

To turn off the filter arrows

1. Click any cell in the list of data.

2. Click **Sort & Filter**, and then click **Filter**.

Manipulate worksheet data

Excel includes a wide range of tools you can use to summarize worksheet data. This section describes how to select rows randomly by using the *RAND* and *RANDBETWEEN* functions, how to summarize worksheet data by using the *SUBTOTAL* and *AGGREGATE* functions, and how to display a list of unique values within a data set.

Select list rows at random

In addition to filtering the data stored in your Excel worksheets, you can choose rows at random from a list. Selecting rows randomly is useful for choosing which customers will receive a special offer, deciding which days of the month to audit, or picking prize winners at an employee party.

To choose rows randomly, you can use the *RAND* function—which generates a random decimal value between 0 and 1—and compare the value it returns with a test value included in a formula. If you recalculate the *RAND* function 10 times and check each time to find out whether the value is below 0.3, it's very unlikely that you would get exactly three instances where the value is below 0.3. Just as flipping a coin can result in the same result 10 times in a row by chance, so can the *RAND* function's results appear to be off if you only recalculate it a few times. However, if you were to recalculate the function 10,000 times, it is extremely likely that the number of values less than 0.3 would be very close to 30 percent.

> ✓ **TIP** Because the *RAND* function is a volatile function (that is, it recalculates its results every time you update the worksheet), you should copy the cells that contain the *RAND* function in a formula and paste the formulas' values back into their original cells. To do so, select the cells that contain the *RAND* formulas and paste them back into the same cells as values.

The *RANDBETWEEN* function generates a random whole number within a defined range. For example, the formula *=RANDBETWEEN(1,100)* would generate a random integer value from 1 to 100 (inclusive). The *RANDBETWEEN* function is very useful for creating sample data collections for presentations. Before the *RANDBETWEEN* function was introduced, you had to create formulas that added, subtracted, multiplied, and divided the results of the *RAND* function, which are always decimal values between 0 and 1, to create data.

To use *RAND* or *RANDBETWEEN* to select a row, create an *IF* formula that tests the random values. If you want to check 30 percent of the rows, a formula such as =IF(cell_address<0.3, "TRUE", "FALSE") would display *TRUE* in the formula cells for any value of 0.3 or less and *FALSE* otherwise.

Summarize data in worksheets that have hidden and filtered rows

The ability to analyze the data that's most vital to your current needs is important, but there are some limitations to how you can summarize your filtered data by using functions such as *SUM* and *AVERAGE*. One limitation is that any formulas you create that include the *SUM* and *AVERAGE* functions don't change their calculations if some of the rows used in the formula are hidden by the filter.

Excel provides two ways to summarize just the visible cells in a filtered data list. The first method is to use AutoCalculate. To use AutoCalculate, you select the cells you want to summarize. When you do, Excel displays the average of the values in the cells, the sum of the values in the cells, and the number of visible cells (the count) in the selection. You'll find the display on the status bar at the lower edge of the Excel window.

When you use AutoCalculate, you aren't limited to finding the sum, average, and count of the selected cells. You can add or remove calculations to suit your needs. A check mark appears next to a function's name if that function's result appears on the status bar.

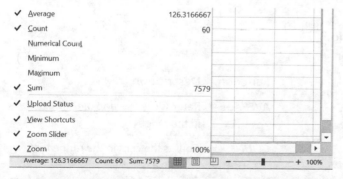

The status bar displays summary values when you select more than one cell that contains numeric data.

AutoCalculate is great for finding a quick total or average for filtered cells, but it doesn't make the result available in the worksheet. Formulas such as *=SUM(C3:C26)* always consider every cell in the range, regardless of whether you hide a cell's row manually, so you need to create a formula by using either the *SUBTOTAL* function or the *AGGREGATE* function to summarize just those values that are visible in your worksheet. The *SUBTOTAL* function lets you choose whether to summarize every value in a range or summarize only those values in rows you haven't manually hidden. The *SUBTOTAL* function has this syntax: *=SUBTOTAL(function_num, ref1, ref2, ...)*. The *function_num* argument holds the number of the operation you want to use to summarize your data. (The operation numbers are summarized in a table later in this section.) The *ref1*, *ref2*, and further arguments represent up to 29 ranges to include in the calculation.

As an example, suppose you have a worksheet in which you manually hid rows 20–26. In this case, the formula *=SUBTOTAL(9, C3:C26, E3:E26, G3:G26)* would find the sum of all values in the ranges C3:C26, E3:E26, and G3:G26, regardless of whether that range contained any hidden rows. The formula *=SUBTOTAL(109, C3:C26, E3:E26, G3:G26)* would find the sum of all values in cells C3:C19, E3:E19, and G3:G19, ignoring the values in the manually hidden rows.

> ⚠ **IMPORTANT** Be sure to place your *SUBTOTAL* formula in a row that is even with or above the headers in the range you're filtering. If you don't, your filter might hide the formula's result!

The following table lists the summary operations available for the *SUBTOTAL* formula. Excel displays the available summary operations as part of the Formula AutoComplete functionality, so you don't need to remember the operation numbers or look them up in the Help system.

Operation number (includes hidden values)	Operation number (ignores values in manually hidden rows)	Function	Description
1	101	*AVERAGE*	Returns the average of the values in the range
2	102	*COUNT*	Counts the cells in the range that contain a number

3	103	COUNTA	Counts the nonblank cells in the range
4	104	MAX	Returns the largest (maximum) value in the range
5	105	MIN	Returns the smallest (minimum) value in the range
6	106	PRODUCT	Returns the result of multiplying all numbers in the range
7	107	STDEV.S	Calculates the standard deviation of values in the range by examining a sample of the values
8	108	STDEV.P	Calculates the standard deviation of the values in the range by using all the values
9	109	SUM	Returns the result of adding all numbers in the range together
10	110	VAR.S	Calculates the variance of values in the range by examining a sample of the values
11	111	VAR.P	Calculates the variance of the values in the range by using all of the values

As the preceding table shows, the SUBTOTAL function has two sets of operations. The first set (operations 1–11) represents operations that include hidden values in their summary, and the second set (operations 101–111) represents operations that summarize only values visible in the worksheet. Operations 1–11 summarize all cells in a range, regardless of whether the range contains any manually hidden rows. By contrast, operations 101–111 ignore any values in manually hidden rows. What the SUBTOTAL function doesn't do, however, is change its result to reflect rows hidden by using a filter.

> ⚠️ **IMPORTANT** Excel treats the first cell in the data range as a header cell, so it doesn't consider the cell as it builds the list of unique values. Be sure to include the header cell in your data range!

The *AGGREGATE* function extends the capabilities of the *SUBTOTAL* function. With it, you can select from a broader range of functions and use another argument to determine which, if any, values to ignore in the calculation. *AGGREGATE* has two possible syntaxes, depending on the summary operation you select. The first syntax is =*AGGREGATE(function_num, options, ref1…)*, which is similar to the syntax of the *SUBTOTAL* function. The other possible syntax, =*AGGREGATE(function_num, options, array, [k])*, is used to create *AGGREGATE* functions that use the *LARGE*, *SMALL*, *PERCENTILE.INC*, *QUARTILE.INC*, *PERCENTILE.EXC*, and *QUARTILE.EXC* operations.

The following table describes the summary operations available for use in the *AGGREGATE* function.

Number	Function	Description
1	*AVERAGE*	Returns the average of the values in the range.
2	*COUNT*	Counts the cells in the range that contain a number.
3	*COUNTA*	Counts the nonblank cells in the range.
4	*MAX*	Returns the largest (maximum) value in the range.
5	*MIN*	Returns the smallest (minimum) value in the range.
6	*PRODUCT*	Returns the result of multiplying all numbers in the range.
7	*STDEV.S*	Calculates the standard deviation of values in the range by examining a sample of the values.
8	*STDEV.P*	Calculates the standard deviation of the values in the range by using all the values.
9	*SUM*	Returns the result of adding together all numbers in the range.
10	*VAR.S*	Calculates the variance of values in the range by examining a sample of the values.
11	*VAR.P*	Calculates the variance of the values in the range by using all of the values.
12	*MEDIAN*	Returns the value in the middle of a group of values.
13	*MODE.SNGL*	Returns the most frequently occurring number from a group of numbers.
14	*LARGE*	Returns the k-th largest value in a data set. k is specified by using the last function argument. If k is left blank, Excel returns the largest value.

15	SMALL	Returns the k-th smallest value in a data set. k is specified by using the last function argument. If k is left blank, Excel returns the smallest value.
16	PERCENTILE.INC	Returns the k-th percentile of values in a range, where k is a value from 0 to 1 (inclusive).
17	QUARTILE.INC	Returns the quartile value of a data set, based on a percentage from 0 to 1 (inclusive).
18	PERCENTILE.EXC	Returns the k-th percentile of values in a range, where k is a value from 0 to 1 (exclusive).
19	QUARTILE.EXC	Returns the quartile value of a data set, based on a percentage from 0 to 1 (exclusive).

5

You use the second argument, *options*, to select which items the *AGGREGATE* function should ignore. These items can include hidden rows, errors, and *SUBTOTAL* and *AGGREGATE* functions. The following table summarizes the values available for the *options* argument and the effect they have on the function's results.

Number	Description
0	Ignore nested *SUBTOTAL* and *AGGREGATE* functions.
1	Ignore hidden rows and nested *SUBTOTAL* and *AGGREGATE* functions.
2	Ignore error values and nested *SUBTOTAL* and *AGGREGATE* functions.
3	Ignore hidden rows, error values, and nested *SUBTOTAL* and *AGGREGATE* functions.
4	Ignore nothing.
5	Ignore hidden rows.
6	Ignore error values.
7	Ignore hidden rows and error values.

To summarize values by using AutoCalculate

1. Select the cells in your worksheet.

2. View the summaries on the status bar.

To change the AutoCalculate summaries displayed on the status bar

1. Right-click the status bar.

2. Click a summary operation without a check mark to display it.

   Or

   Click a summary operation with a check mark to hide it.

To create a SUBTOTAL formula

1. In a cell, enter a formula that uses the syntax *=SUBTOTAL(function_num, ref1, ref2, ...)*. The arguments in the syntax are as follows:

   • The *function_num* argument is the reference number of the function you want to use.

   • The *ref1*, *ref2*, and subsequent *ref* arguments refer to cell ranges.

To create an AGGREGATE formula

1. Do one of the following:

   • Create a formula of the syntax *=AGGREGATE(function_num, options, ref1...)*. The arguments in the syntax are as follows:

     • The *function_num* argument is the reference number of the function you want to use.

     • The *options* argument is the reference number for the options you want.

     • The *ref1*, *ref2*, and subsequent *ref* arguments refer to cell ranges.

   Or

   • Create a formula with the syntax *=AGGREGATE(function_num, options, array, [k])*. The arguments in the syntax are as follows:

     • The *function_num* argument is the reference number of the function you want to use.

     • The *options* argument is the reference number for the options you want to use.

     • The *array* argument represents the cell range (array) that provides data for the formula.

     • The optional *k* argument, used with *LARGE*, *SMALL*, *PERCENTILE.INC*, *QUARTILE.INC*, *PERCENTILE.EXC*, or *QUARTILE.EXC*, indicates which value, percentile, or quartile to return.

Find unique values within a data set

Summarizing numerical values can provide valuable information to help you run your business. It can also be helpful to know how many different values appear within a column. For example, you might want to display all the countries and regions in which your company has customers. If you want to display a list of the unique values in a column, you can do so by creating an advanced filter.

Use the Advanced Filter dialog box to find unique records in a list.

All you need to do is identify the rows that contain the values you want to filter and indicate that you want to display unique records so that you get only the information you want.

To find unique values within a data set

1. Click any cell in the range for which you want to find unique values.

2. On the **Data** tab of the ribbon, in the **Sort & Filter** group, click **Advanced**.

3. Click **Filter the list, in place**.

   Or

   Click **Copy to another location**.

4. Verify that the address of your data range appears in the **List range** box.

5. If necessary, click in the **Copy to** box and select the cells where you want the filtered list to appear.

6. Select the **Unique records only** check box.

7. Click **OK**.

Define valid sets of values for ranges of cells

Part of creating efficient and easy-to-use worksheets is to do what you can to ensure that the data entered into your worksheets is as accurate as possible. Although it isn't possible to catch every typographical or transcription error, you can set up a validation rule to make sure that the data entered into a cell meets certain standards. For example, you can specify the type of data you want, the range of acceptable values, and whether blank values are allowed. Setting accurate validation rules can, for example, help you and your colleagues avoid entering a customer's name in the cell designated to hold the phone number or setting a credit limit above a certain level.

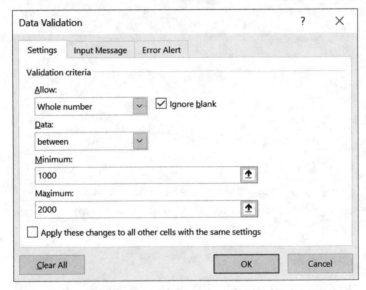

Create data-validation rules to ensure that appropriate data is entered into worksheet cells.

You can select the cells where you want to add a validation rule, even if those cells already contain data. Excel doesn't tell you whether existing data in any of those cells violates your rule at the moment you create the rule, but you can find out by having Excel circle any worksheet cells that contain data that violates the cell's validation rule. When you're done, you can have Excel clear the validation circles or have Excel turn off data validation for those cells entirely.

D	E	F	G	H	I	J
CustomerName	**Address**	**City**	**State**	**ZIP**	**Phone**	**Limit**
Contoso	11020 Microsoft Way	Redmond	WA	98073	(425) 555-0101	$ 26,000.00
Fabrikam	1480 Microsoft Way	Redmond	WA	98073	(425) 555-0173	$ 7,500.00
Northwind Traders	891A Microsoft Way	Redmond	WA	98073	(425) 555-0145	$ 15,000.00

Validation circles flag data previously entered into a worksheet that violates data-validation rules

To add a validation rule to a cell

1. On the **Data** tab, in the **Data Tools** group, click **Data Validation**.

2. In the **Data Validation** dialog box, on the **Settings** tab, click the **Allow** arrow, and then click the type of values to allow.

3. Use the controls to define the rule.

4. Select the **Ignore blank** check box to allow blank values.

   Or

   Clear the **Ignore blank** check box to require that a value be entered.

5. On the **Input Message** tab, enter an input message for the cell.

6. On the **Error Alert** tab, create an error alert message for values that violate the rule.

7. Click **OK**.

To edit a validation rule

1. Select one or more cells that contain the validation rule.

2. Click **Data Validation**.

3. On the **Settings** tab, select the **Apply these changes to all other cells with the same settings** check box to affect other cells with the same rule.

   Or

   Leave the **Apply these changes to all other cells with the same settings** check box cleared to affect only the selected cells.

4. Use the controls in the dialog box to edit the rule, input message, and error alert.

5. Click **OK**.

To circle invalid data in a worksheet

1. Click the **Data Validation** arrow.

2. Click **Circle Invalid Data**.

To remove validation circles

1. Click the **Data Validation** arrow.

2. Click **Clear Validation Circles**.

Skills review

In this chapter, you learned how to:

- Limit data that appears on your screen

- Manipulate worksheet data

- Define valid sets of values for ranges of cells

Practice tasks

The practice files for these tasks are located in the Excel2019SBS\Ch05 folder. You can save the results of the tasks in the same folder.

Limit data that appears on your screen

Open the LimitData workbook in Excel, and then perform the following tasks:

1. Create a filter that displays only those package exceptions that happened on **RT189**.

2. Clear the previous filter, and then create a filter that shows exceptions for the **Northeast** and **Northwest** centers.

3. With the previous filter still in place, create a filter that displays only those exceptions that occurred before April 1, 2019.

4. Clear the filter that shows values related to the **Northeast** and **Northwest** centers.

5. Turn off filtering for the list of data.

Manipulate worksheet data

Open the SummarizeValues workbook in Excel, and then perform the following tasks:

1. Combine the *IF* and *RAND* functions into formulas in cells **H3:H27** that display *TRUE* if the value is less than 0.3 and *FALSE* otherwise.

2. Use AutoCalculate to find the *SUM*, *AVERAGE*, and *COUNT* of cells **G12:G16**.

3. Remove the *COUNT* summary from the status bar and add the *MINIMUM* summary.

4. Create a *SUBTOTAL* formula that finds the average of the values in cells **G3:G27**.

5. Create an *AGGREGATE* formula that finds the maximum of values in cells **G3:G27**.

6. Create an advanced filter that finds the unique values in cells **F3:F27**.

Define valid sets of values for ranges of cells

Open the ValidateData workbook in Excel, and then perform the following tasks:

1. Create a data-validation rule in cells **J4:J7** that requires values entered into those cells be no greater than $25,000.

2. Attempt to type the value **30000** in cell **J7**, observe the message that appears, and then cancel data entry.

3. Edit the rule you created so it includes an input message and an error alert.

4. Display validation circles to highlight data that violates the rule you created, and then hide the circles.

Reorder and summarize data

6

One of the most important uses of business information is to record when something happens. Whether you ship a package to a client or pay a supplier, tracking when you took those actions, and in what order, helps you analyze your performance. Sorting your information based on the values in one or more columns helps you discover useful trends, such as whether your sales are generally increasing or decreasing, whether you do more business on specific days of the week, or whether you sell products to lots of customers from certain regions of the world.

Microsoft Excel has capabilities you might expect to find only in a database program—the ability to organize your data into levels of detail you can show or hide, and formulas that let you look up values in a list of data. Organizing your data by detail level lets you focus on the values you need to make a decision, and looking up values in a worksheet helps you find specific data. If a customer calls to ask about an order, you can use the order number or customer number to discover the information that customer needs.

This chapter guides you through procedures related to sorting your data by using one or more criteria, calculating subtotals, organizing your data into levels, and looking up information in a worksheet.

In this chapter

- Sort worksheet data
- Sort data by using custom lists
- Organize data into levels
- Look up information in a worksheet

Practice files

For this chapter, use the practice files from the Excel2019SBS\Ch06 folder. For practice file download instructions, see the introduction.

Sort worksheet data

Although Excel makes it easy to enter your business data and to manage it after you've saved it in a worksheet, unsorted data will rarely answer every question you want to ask it. For example, you might want to discover which of your services generates the most profits, or which service costs the most for you to provide. You can discover that information by sorting your data.

When you sort data in a worksheet, you rearrange the worksheet rows based on the contents of cells in a particular column or set of columns. For instance, you can sort a worksheet to find your highest-revenue services.

You can sort a group of rows in a worksheet in a number of ways, but the first step is to identify the column that will provide the values by which the rows should be sorted. In the revenue example, you could find the highest revenue totals by sorting on the cells in the *Revenue* column. You can do this by using the commands available from the Sort & Filter button on the Home tab of the ribbon.

> **TIP** The exact set of values that appears in the Sort & Filter list changes to reflect the data in your column. If your column contains numerical values, you'll get the options Sort Largest to Smallest, Sort Smallest to Largest, and Custom List. If your column contains text values, the options will be Sort A to Z (ascending order), Sort Z to A (descending order), and Custom List. And if your column contains dates, you'll get Sort Newest to Oldest, Sort Oldest to Newest, and Custom List.

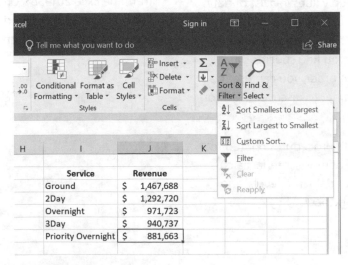

Revenue sorted in descending order.

The Sort Smallest to Largest and Sort Largest to Smallest options let you sort rows in a worksheet quickly, but you can use them only to sort the worksheet based on the contents of one column, even though you might want to sort by two columns. For example, you might want to order the worksheet rows by service category and then by total so that you can tell which service categories are used most frequently.

	A	B	C
1			
2	**Customer**	**Service**	**Revenue**
3	Contoso	2Day	$ 246,811
4	Fabrikam	2Day	$ 1,152,558
5	Tailspin Toys	2Day	$ 851,922
6	Contoso	3Day	$ 318,710
7	Fabrikam	3Day	$ 658,371
8	Tailspin Toys	3Day	$ 1,026,163
9	Contoso	Ground	$ 941,717
10	Fabrikam	Ground	$ 964,280
11	Tailspin Toys	Ground	$ 1,147,078
12	Contoso	Overnight	$ 675,122
13	Fabrikam	Overnight	$ 801,656
14	Tailspin Toys	Overnight	$ 35,456
15	Contoso	Priority Overnight	$ 955,755
16	Fabrikam	Priority Overnight	$ 175,699
17	Tailspin Toys	Priority Overnight	$ 161,061

Sort a list of data by more than one column.

You can sort rows in a worksheet by the contents of more than one column by using the Sort dialog box, in which you can pick any number of columns to use as sort criteria and choose whether to sort the rows in ascending or descending order. If you want to create two similar rules, perhaps changing just the field to which the rules are applied, you can create a rule for one field, copy it within the Sort dialog box, and change the field name.

If your data cells have fill colors applied to them, perhaps representing cells with values you want your colleagues to notice, you can sort your list of data by using those colors. In addition, you can create more detailed sorting rules, change the order in which rules are applied, and edit and delete rules by using the controls in the Sort dialog box.

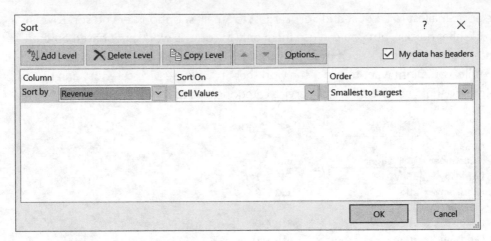

Use the Sort dialog box to create detailed sorting rules.

To sort worksheet data based on values in a single column

1. Click a cell in the column that contains the data by which you want to sort.

2. On the **Home** tab of the ribbon, in the **Editing** group, click the **Sort & Filter** button to display a menu of sorting and filtering choices.

3. Click **Sort A to Z** to sort the data in ascending order.

   Or

   Click **Sort Z to A** to sort the data in descending order.

To sort worksheet data based on values in multiple columns

1. Click a cell in the list of data you want to sort.

2. On the **Sort & Filter** menu, click **Custom Sort**.

3. If necessary, select the **My data has headers** check box.

4. In the **Sort by** list, select the first field.

5. In the **Sort On** list, select the option by which you want to sort the data (Cell Values, Cell Color, Font Color, or Conditional Formatting Icon).

6. In the **Order** list, select an order for the sort operation.

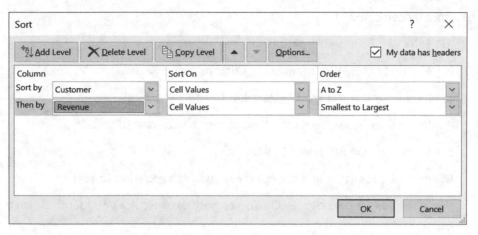

Create sorting rules in the Sort dialog box.

7. Click the **Add Level** button.

8. In the **Then by** list, create another rule by using the techniques described in steps 4 through 6.

9. When you are finished creating sort levels, click **OK** to sort the values.

	A	B	C	D	E
1					
2		**Customer**	**Season**	**Revenue**	
3		Contoso	Summer	$ 114,452.00	
4		Contoso	Fall	$ 118,299.00	
5		Contoso	Winter	$ 183,651.00	
6		Contoso	Spring	$ 201,438.00	
7		Fabrikam	Winter	$ 100,508.00	
8		Fabrikam	Spring	$ 139,170.00	
9		Fabrikam	Summer	$ 183,632.00	
10		Fabrikam	Fall	$ 255,599.00	
11		Northwind Traders	Spring	$ 120,666.00	
12		Northwind Traders	Summer	$ 129,732.00	
13		Northwind Traders	Winter	$ 174,336.00	
14		Northwind Traders	Fall	$ 188,851.00	

A list of data that has had sorting rules applied to it.

To sort by cell color

1. Select a cell in the list of data.

2. On the **Sort & Filter** menu, click **Custom Sort**.

3. If necessary, select the **My data has headers** check box.

4. In the **Sort by** list, select the field by which you want to sort.

5. In the **Sort On** list, select **Cell Color**.

6. In the **Order** list, select the cell color on which you want to sort.

7. In the last list box, choose **On Top** to position the color you identified on top.

   Or

   Choose **On Bottom** to position the color you identified on the bottom.

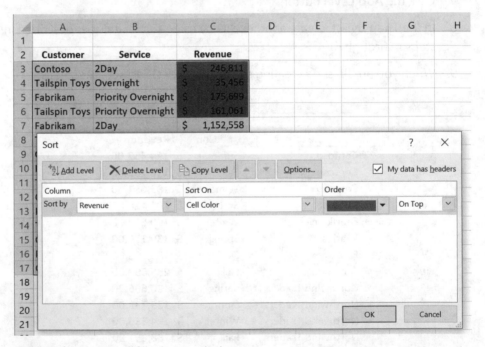

Sort lists of data using cell fill color as a criterion.

8. When you are done creating sorting rules, click **OK** to sort the values.

To copy a sorting level

1. Select a cell in the list of data.

2. On the **Sort & Filter** menu, click **Custom Sort**.

3. Select the sorting level you want to copy.

4. Click the **Copy Level** button, and edit the rule as needed.

5. Click **OK**.

To move a sorting rule up or down in priority

1. On the **Sort & Filter** menu, click **Custom Sort**.

2. Select the sorting rule you want to move.

3. Click the **Move Up** button to move the rule up in the order.

   Or

   Click the **Move Down** button to move the rule down in the order.

4. Click **OK**.

To delete a sorting rule

1. On the **Sort & Filter** menu, click **Custom Sort**.

2. Select the sorting level you want to delete.

3. Click the **Delete Level** button.

4. Click **OK**.

Sort data by using custom lists

The default setting for Excel is to sort numbers according to their values and to sort words in alphabetical order, but that pattern doesn't work for some sets of values. One example in which sorting a list of values in alphabetical order would yield incorrect results is the months of the year. In an "alphabetical" calendar, April is the first month and September is the last!

Fortunately, Excel recognizes a number of special lists, such as days of the week and months of the year. You can have Excel sort the contents of a worksheet based on values in a known list. And, if needed, you can create your own list of values. For example, the default lists of weekdays in Excel start with Sunday. If you keep your business records based on a Monday–Sunday week, you can create a new list with Monday as the first day and Sunday as the last.

You can create a new custom list by using the Custom Lists dialog box, which you access through the Excel Options dialog box. The Custom Lists dialog box gives you the choice of entering the values yourself or importing them from a cell range in your workbook.

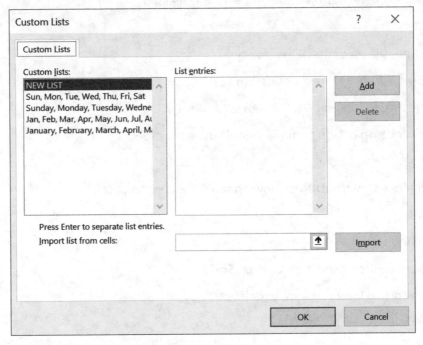

Manage your lists by using the Custom Lists dialog box.

> **TIP** Another benefit of creating a custom list is that dragging the fill handle of a list cell that contains a value causes Excel to extend the series for you. For example, if you create the list Spring, Summer, Fall, Winter, and then enter Summer in a cell and drag the cell's fill handle, Excel extends the series as Fall, Winter, Spring, Summer, Fall, and so on.

To define a custom list by entering its values

1. On the **File** tab, click **Options**.

2. In the **Excel Options** dialog box, click the **Advanced** category.

3. Scroll down to the **General** area, and then click the **Edit Custom Lists** button.

4. In the **Custom Lists** dialog box, enter a list of items in the **List entries** area. Press Enter after each item to move to the next line.

5. Click **Add**.

6. Click **OK**, and then click **OK** again to close the **Excel Options** dialog box.

To define a custom list by copying values from a worksheet

1. Select the cells that contain the values for your custom list.

2. Open the **Custom Lists** dialog box.

3. In the **Custom Lists** dialog box, click the **Import** button.

4. Click **OK**, and then click **OK** again to close the **Excel Options** dialog box.

To sort worksheet data by using a custom list

1. Click a cell in the list of data you want to sort.

2. On the **Home** tab, click the **Sort & Filter** button, and then click **Custom Sort**.

3. If necessary, select the **My data has headers** check box.

4. In the **Sort by** list, select the field that contains the data by which you want to sort.

5. If necessary, in the **Sort On** list, select **Values**.

6. In the **Order** list, select **Custom List**.

7. In the **Custom Lists** dialog box, select the list you want to use.

8. Click **OK**.

Organize data into levels

After you have sorted the rows in an Excel worksheet or entered the data so that it doesn't need to be sorted, you can have Excel calculate subtotals (totals for a portion of the data). In a worksheet with sales data for three different product categories, for example, you can sort the products by category, select all the cells that contain data, and then open the Subtotal dialog box.

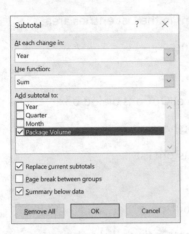

Apply subtotals to data by using the Subtotal dialog box.

In the Subtotal dialog box, you can choose the column on which to base your subtotals (such as every change of value in the *Week* column), the summary calculation you want to perform, and the column or columns with values to be summarized. After you define your subtotals, they appear in your worksheet.

	A	B	C	D
1	Year	Quarter	Month	Package Volume
2	2017	1	January	5,213,292
3	2017	1	February	2,038,516
4	2017	1	March	2,489,601
5	2017	2	April	9,051,231
6	2017	2	May	5,225,156
7	2017	2	June	3,266,644
8	2017	3	July	2,078,794
9	2017	3	August	1,591,434
10	2017	3	September	8,518,985
11	2017	4	October	1,973,050
12	2017	4	November	7,599,195
13	2017	4	December	9,757,876
14	**2017 Total**			58,803,774
15	2018	1	January	5,304,039
16	2018	1	February	5,465,096
17	2018	1	March	1,007,799

A list of data with Subtotal outlining applied.

When you add subtotals to a worksheet, Excel also defines groups based on the rows used to calculate a subtotal. The groupings form an outline of your worksheet based on the criteria you used to create the subtotals. For example, all the rows representing months in the year 2017 could be in one group, rows representing months in 2018 in another, and so on. The outline area at the left of your worksheet holds controls you can use to hide or display groups of rows in your worksheet.

	A	B	C	D
1	**Year**	**Quarter**	**Month**	**Package Volume**
14	**2017 Total**			58,803,774
15	2018	1	January	5,304,039
16	2018	1	February	5,465,096
17	2018	1	March	1,007,799
18	2018	2	April	4,010,287
19	2018	2	May	4,817,070
20	2018	2	June	8,155,717
21	2018	3	July	6,552,370
22	2018	3	August	2,295,635
23	2018	3	September	7,115,883
24	2018	4	October	1,362,767
25	2018	4	November	8,935,488
26	2018	4	December	9,537,077
27	**2018 Total**			64,559,228
28	**Grand Total**			123,363,002

A list of data with details for the year 2017 hidden.

When you hide a group of rows, the button displayed next to the group changes to a Show Detail button (the button with the plus sign) Clicking a group's Show Detail button restores the rows in the group to the worksheet.

The level buttons are the other buttons in the outline area of a worksheet with subtotals. Each button represents a level of organization in a worksheet. Clicking a level button hides all levels of detail below that of the button you clicked. The following table describes the data contained at each level of a worksheet with three levels of organization.

Level	Description
1	Grand total
2	Subtotals for each group
3	Individual rows in the worksheet

	A	B	C	D
1	**Year**	**Quarter**	**Month**	**Package Volume**
14	**2017 Total**			58,803,774
27	**2018 Total**			64,559,228
28	**Grand Total**			123,363,002
29				

A list of data with details hidden at level 2.

You can add levels of detail to the outline that Excel creates. For example, you might want to be able to hide revenues from January and February, which you know are traditionally strong months. You can also delete any groupings you no longer need or remove subtotals and outlining entirely.

 TIP If you want to remove all subtotals from a worksheet, open the Subtotal dialog box and click the Remove All button.

To organize data into levels

1. Click a cell in the group of data you want to organize.

2. On the **Data** tab of the ribbon, in the **Outline** group, click the **Subtotal** button.

3. In the **Subtotal** dialog box, in the **At each change in** list, select the field that controls when subtotals appear.

4. In the **Use function** list, select the summary function you want to use for each subtotal.

5. In the **Add subtotal to** group, select the check box next to any field you want to summarize.

6. Click **OK**.

To show or hide detail in a list with a subtotal summary

1. Do either of the following:

   - Click a **Hide Detail** control to hide a level of detail.

   - Click a **Show Detail** control to show a level of detail.

To create a custom group in a list that has a subtotal summary

1. Select the rows you want to include in the group.

	Year	Quarter	Month	Package Volume
1	Year	Quarter	Month	Package Volume
2	2017	1	January	5,213,292
3	2017	1	February	2,038,516
4	2017	1	March	2,489,601
5	2017	2	April	9,051,231

A data list with rows selected to create a custom group.

2. Click the **Group** button.

Look up information in a worksheet

To remove a custom group in a list that has a subtotal summary

1. Select the rows you want to remove from the group.

2. Click the **Ungroup** button.

To remove subtotals from a data list

1. Click any cell in the list.

2. Click the **Subtotal** button.

3. In the **Subtotal** dialog box, click **Remove All**.

Look up information in a worksheet

6

Whenever you create a worksheet that holds information about a list of distinct items, such as products offered for sale by a company, you should ensure that at least one column in the list contains a unique value that distinguishes that row (and the item the row represents) from every other row in the list. Assigning each row a column that contains a unique value means that you can associate data in one list with data in another list. For example, if you assign every customer a unique identification number, you can store a customer's contact information in one worksheet and all orders for that customer in another worksheet. You can then associate the customer's orders and contact information without writing the contact information in a worksheet every time the customer places an order.

In technical terms, the column that contains a unique value for each row is known as the primary key column. When you look up information in an Excel worksheet, it is very useful to position the primary key column as the first column in your list of data.

If you know an item's primary key value, it's no trouble to look through a list of 20 or 30 items to find it. If, however, you have a list of many thousands of items, looking through the list to find one would take quite a bit of time. Instead, you can use the *VLOOKUP* function to find the value you want.

	A	B	C	D	E	F
1						
2		**ShipmentID**	**Destination**			
3						
4						
5		**ShipmentID**	**CustomerID**	**Date**	**OriginationPostalCode**	**DestinationPostalCode**
6		SH210	CI384471	5/21/2015	59686	77408
7		SH211	CI495231	5/22/2015	24348	91936
8		SH212	CI429120	5/23/2015	70216	83501
9		SH213	CI418125	5/24/2015	84196	21660
10		SH214	CI782990	5/25/2015	13193	92518
11		SH215	CI102300	5/26/2015	27910	76842
12		SH216	CI560742	5/27/2015	73820	21393
13		SH217	CI483289	5/28/2015	34245	33975
14		SH218	CI762179	5/29/2015	87569	11471

An Excel table for use with VLOOKUP.

The *VLOOKUP* function finds a value in the leftmost column of a named range, such as a table, and then returns the value from the specified cell to the right of the cell with the found value. A properly formed *VLOOKUP* function has four arguments, as shown in the following definition: *=VLOOKUP(lookup_value, table_array, col_index_num, range_lookup)*.

The following table summarizes the values Excel expects for each of these arguments.

Argument	Expected value
lookup_value	The value to be found in the first column of the named range specified by the *table_array* argument. The *lookup_value* argument can be a value, a cell reference, or a text string.
table_array	The multicolumn range or name of the range or data table to be searched.
col_index_num	The number of the column in the named range that has the value to be returned.
range_lookup	A *TRUE* or *FALSE* value, indicating whether the function should find an approximate match (*TRUE*) or an exact match (*FALSE*) for the *lookup_value*. If this argument is left blank, the default value for it is *TRUE*.

⚠ **IMPORTANT** When *range_lookup* is left blank or set to *TRUE*, for *VLOOKUP* to work properly, the rows in the named range specified in the *table_array* argument must be sorted in ascending order based on the values in the leftmost column of the named range.

The *VLOOKUP* function works a bit differently depending on whether the *range_lookup* argument is set to *TRUE* or *FALSE*. The following list summarizes how the function works based on the value of *range_lookup*:

- If the *range_lookup* argument is left blank or set to *TRUE*, and *VLOOKUP* doesn't find an exact match for *lookup_value*, the function returns the largest value that is less than *lookup_value*.

- If the *range_lookup* argument is left blank or set to *TRUE*, and *lookup_value* is smaller than the smallest value in the named range, an #N/A error is returned.

- If the *range_lookup* argument is left blank or set to *TRUE*, and *lookup_value* is larger than all values in the named range, the largest value in the named range is returned.

- If the *range_lookup* argument is set to *FALSE*, and *VLOOKUP* doesn't find an exact match for *lookup_value*, the function returns an #N/A error.

As an example of a *VLOOKUP* function, consider the following data, which shows an Excel table with its headers in row 2 and the first column in column B of the worksheet.

CustomerID	Customer
CU01	Fabrikam
CU02	Northwind Traders
CU03	Tailspin Toys
CU04	Contoso

If the =*VLOOKUP (E3, B3:C6, 2, FALSE)* formula is used, when you enter CU02 in cell E3 and press Enter, the *VLOOKUP* function searches the first column of the table, finds an exact match, and returns the value *Northwind Traders* to cell F3.

F3		⋮	×	✓	*fx*	=VLOOKUP(E3,B3:C6,2,FALSE)	

◢	A	B	C	D	E	F
1						
2		CustomerID	Customer		LookupID	Customer
3		CU01	Fabrikam		CU02	Northwind Traders
4		CU02	Northwind Traders			
5		CU03	Tailspin Toys			
6		CU04	Contoso			

A VLOOKUP formula that looks up a customer name given a customer ID.

> ✓ **TIP** The related *HLOOKUP* function matches a value in a column of the first row of a table and returns the value in the specified row number of the same column. The letter *H* in the *HLOOKUP* function name refers to the horizontal layout of the data, just as the *V* in *VLOOKUP* refers to the data's vertical layout. For more information on using the *HLOOKUP* function, click the Excel Help button, enter HLOOKUP in the search terms box, and then click Search.

> ⚠ **IMPORTANT** Be sure to give the cell in which you type the *VLOOKUP* formula the same format as the data you want the formula to display. For example, if you create a *VLOOKUP* formula in cell G14 that finds a date, you must apply a date cell format to cell G14 for the result of the formula to display properly.

To look up worksheet values by using *VLOOKUP*

1. Ensure that the data list includes a unique value in each cell of the leftmost column and that the values are sorted in ascending order.

2. In the cell where you want to enter the *VLOOKUP* formula, enter a formula of the form =*VLOOKUP(lookup_value, table_array, col_index_num, range_lookup)*.

3. Enter **TRUE** for the *range_lookup* argument to allow an approximate match.

   Or

   Enter **FALSE** for the *range_lookup* argument to require an exact match.

4. Enter a lookup value in the cell named in the *VLOOKUP* formula's first argument, and press **Enter**.

Skills review

In this chapter, you learned how to:

- Sort worksheet data
- Sort data by using custom lists
- Organize data into levels
- Look up information in a worksheet

Practice tasks

The practice files for these tasks are located in the Excel2019SBS\Ch06 folder. You can save the results of the tasks in the same folder.

Sort worksheet data

Open the SortData workbook in Excel, and then perform the following tasks:

1. Sort the data in the list in ascending order based on the values in the *Revenue* column.

2. Sort the data in the list in descending order based on the values in the *Revenue* column.

3. Sort the data in the list in ascending order based on a two-level sort where the first sorting level is the *Customer* column and the second is the *Season* column.

4. Change the order of the fields in the previous sort so that the first criterion is the *Season* column and the second is the *Customer* column.

5. Sort the data so that the cells in the *Revenue* column that have a red fill color are at the top of the list.

Sort data by using custom lists

Open the SortCustomData workbook in Excel, and then perform the following tasks:

1. Create a custom list by using the values in cells **G4:G7**.

2. Sort the data in the cell range **B3:D14** by the values in the *Season* column based on the custom list you just created.

3. Create a two-level sort by using the values in the *Customer* column, in ascending order, as the first criterion, and the custom list–based sort for the *Season* column as the second criterion.

Organize data into levels

Open the OrganizeData workbook in Excel, and then perform the following tasks:

1. Outline the data list in cells **A1:D25** to find the subtotal for each year.

2. Hide the details of rows for the year 2018.

3. Create a new group consisting of the rows showing data for June and July 2017.

4. Hide the details of the group you just created.

5. Show the details of all months for the year 2018.

6. Remove the subtotal outline from the entire data list.

Look up information in a worksheet

Open the LookupData workbook in Excel, and then perform the following tasks:

1. Sort the values in the first table column in ascending order.

2. In cell C3, create a formula that finds the *CustomerID* value for a shipment ID entered into cell B3.

3. Edit the formula so that it finds the *DestinationPostalCode* value for the same package.

Combine data from multiple sources

Excel 2019 gives you a wide range of tools with which to format, summarize, and present your data. Once you've created a workbook to hold data, you can create as many worksheets as you need to make that data easier to find. If you want every workbook you create to have a similar appearance, you can create a workbook with the characteristics you want and save it as a template for similar workbooks you create in the future.

A consequence of organizing your data into different workbooks and worksheets is that you need ways to manage, combine, and summarize data from more than one Excel document. Of course, you can always copy data from one workbook or worksheet to another, but if a value in the original, or source, workbook or worksheet were to change, that change would not be reflected in the workbook or worksheet into which you copied the data. Rather than manually updating cells in the copy workbook or worksheet, you can create a link between the two. That way, whenever you open the copy workbook or worksheet, Excel will automatically update it to reflect the source workbook or worksheet. On a related note, if multiple worksheets hold related values, you can use links to summarize those values in a single worksheet.

This chapter guides you through procedures related to using a workbook as a template for other workbooks, linking to data in other workbooks, and consolidating multiple sets of data into a single workbook.

In this chapter

- Use workbooks as templates for other workbooks

- Link to data in other workbooks and worksheets

- Consolidate multiple sets of data into a single workbook

Practice files

For this chapter, use the practice files from the Excel2019SBS\Ch07 folder. For practice file download instructions, see the introduction.

Use workbooks as templates for other workbooks

Suppose you've established a design you like for your monthly sales-tracking workbook, and you want to create other workbooks with the same look and feel. With Excel 2019, you can save a workbook as a template for similar workbooks you will create in the future.

You can leave the workbook's labels to aid in data entry, but you should remove any existing data from a workbook that you save as a template, both to avoid data-entry errors and to remove any confusion as to whether the workbook is a template. You can also remove any worksheets you and your colleagues won't need by right-clicking the tab of an unneeded worksheet and, on the shortcut menu that appears, clicking Delete.

 TIP You can also save your Excel 2019 workbook either as an Excel 97–2003 template (.xlt) or as a macro-enabled Excel 2019 workbook template (.xltm). For information about using macros in Excel 2019 workbooks, see Chapter 12, "Automate repetitive tasks by using macros."

After you save a workbook as a template, you can use it as a model for new workbooks.

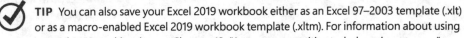 **IMPORTANT** Be sure to save your Excel template file in the Custom Office Templates folder so it's available for you to use later.

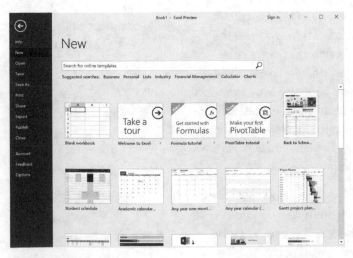

The Backstage view displays available Excel workbook templates.

When you create a new workbook by using the tools found in the Backstage view, the New page displays the blank workbook template, built-in templates, a search box you can use to locate helpful templates on Office.com, and a set of sample search terms.

From the list of available templates, you can click the template you want to use as the model for your workbook. Excel creates a new workbook (an .xlsx workbook file, not an .xltx template file) with the template's formatting and contents in place.

In addition to creating a workbook template, you can add a worksheet based on a worksheet template to your workbook by using the Insert dialog box.

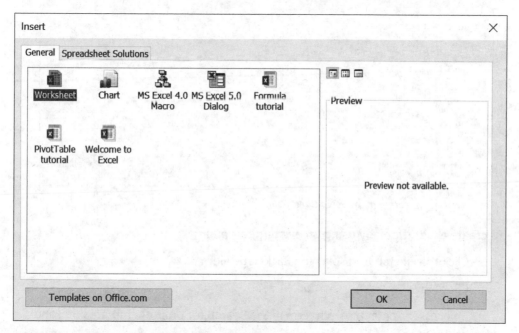

Add specific worksheet types using the Insert dialog box.

The Insert dialog box splits its contents into two tabs. The General tab contains icons you can click to insert a blank worksheet, a chart sheet, and any worksheet templates available to you.

> **TIP** The other two options on the General tab, MS Excel 4.0 Macro and MS Excel 5.0 Dialog, are there to help users include solutions built in earlier versions of Excel into Excel 2019.

The Spreadsheet Solutions tab contains a set of useful templates for a variety of financial and personal tasks. If you want to create a worksheet template, as opposed to a workbook template, you delete all but one worksheet from your file and save it as a template.

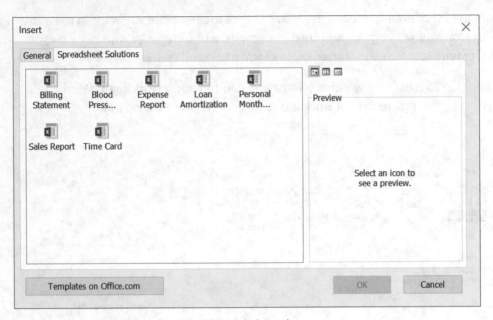

Create useful worksheets from the Spreadsheet Solutions tab.

To create a workbook by using an existing template

1. Click the **File** tab to display the Backstage view.

2. Click **New**.

3. If necessary, enter a search term in the **Search for online templates** box and press **Enter**.

4. Click the template you want to use.

5. Click **Create**.

To insert a worksheet template into a workbook

1. Right-click any sheet tab and, on the shortcut menu that appears, click **Insert**.

2. In the **Insert** dialog box, click the tab that contains the worksheet template you want to use.

3. Click the worksheet template.

4. Click **OK**.

To save a workbook as a template

1. Create the workbook you want to save as a template.

2. In the Backstage view, click **Save As**.

3. Click **Browse**.

4. Click the **Save as type** arrow, and then click **Excel Template**.

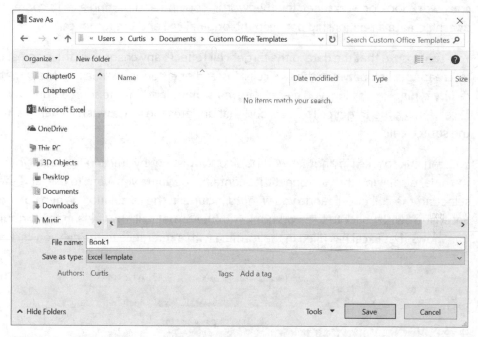

Click the Excel Template file type to use your file as a pattern for other workbooks.

5. In the **File name** box, enter a name for the template workbook.

6. Click **Save**.

To save a workbook as a macro-enabled template

1. Create the workbook you want to save as a macro-enabled template.

2. In the Backstage view, click **Save As**.

3. Click **Browse**.

4. Click the **Save as type** arrow, and then click **Excel Macro-Enabled Template**.

5. In the **File name** box, enter a name for the template workbook.

6. Click **Save**.

Link to data in other workbooks and worksheets

Copying and pasting data from one workbook or worksheet to another is a quick and easy way to gather related data in one place, but there is a substantial limitation: If data in the source workbook or worksheet changes, the change is not reflected in the copy workbook or worksheet. In other words, copying and pasting a cell's contents doesn't create a relationship between the original cell and the target cell.

You can ensure that the data in the target cell reflects any changes in the original cell by creating a link between the two cells. Instead of entering a value into the target cell by typing or pasting, you create a formula that identifies the source from which Excel derives the target cell's value, and that updates the value when it changes in the source cell.

You can link to a cell in another workbook or worksheet by starting to create your formula, displaying the worksheet that contains the value you want to use, and then selecting the cell or cell range you want to include in the calculation. When you press Enter and switch back to the workbook with the target cell, the value in the formula bar shows that Excel has filled in the formula with a reference to the cell you clicked.

I4		:	×	✓	fx	='[FleetOperatingCosts.xlsx]Truck Fuel'!$C$15		
	G		H			I	J	K
1								
2			**Transportation**					
3								
4			Truck Fuel		$	24,808,206		
5			Truck Maintenance					
6			Airplane Fuel					
7			Airplane Maintenance					

A cell reference to another workbook.

The reference *='[FleetOperatingCosts.xlsx]Truck Fuel'!$C$15* gives three pieces of information: the workbook, the worksheet, and the cell you linked to in the worksheet. The first element of the reference, the name of the workbook, is enclosed in brackets; the end of the second element (the worksheet) is marked with an exclamation point; and the third element, the cell reference, has a dollar sign before both the row and the column identifier. The single quotes around the workbook name and worksheet name are there to allow for the space in the Truck Fuel worksheet's name. This type of reference is known as a 3-D reference, reflecting the three dimensions (workbook, worksheet, and cell range) that you need to point to a group of cells in another workbook.

TIP For references to cells in the same workbook, the workbook information is omitted. Likewise, references to cells in the same worksheet don't use a worksheet identifier.

You can also link to cells in an Excel table. Such links include the workbook name, worksheet name, the name of the Excel table, and the row and column references of the cell to which you've linked. Creating a link to the *Cost* column's cell in a table's *Totals* row, for example, results in a reference such as =*'FleetOperatingCosts.xlsx'!Truck Maintenance[[#Totals],[Cost]]*.

7

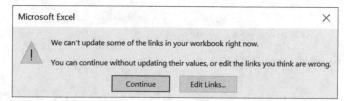

A2			*fx*	=FleetOperatingCosts.xlsx!Table1[[#Totals],[Cost]]					
	A		B	C	D	E	F	G
1	**Truck Maintenance Costs**							
2	$	4,189,600.00						
3								

Link to an Excel table value in another workbook.

IMPORTANT Hiding or displaying a table's *Totals* row affects any links to a cell in that row. Hiding the *Totals* row causes references to that row to display a *#REF!* error message.

Whenever you open a workbook containing a link to another document, Excel tries to update the information in linked cells. If the app can't find the source, as would happen if a workbook or worksheet were deleted or renamed, an alert box appears to indicate that there is a broken link. From within that alert box, you can access tools to fix the link reference.

Microsoft Excel	✕
⚠ We can't update some of the links in your workbook right now.	
You can continue without updating their values, or edit the links you think are wrong.	
[Continue] [Edit Links...]	

A dialog box that indicates the workbook you just opened contains one or more broken links.

If you enter a link into a cell and you make an error, a *#REF!* error message appears in the cell that contains the link.

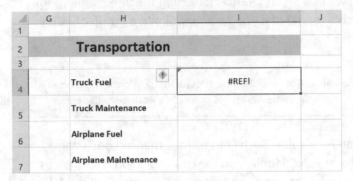

Cells that contain incorrect links display a #REF! error.

To fix the link, click the cell, delete its contents, and then either retype the link or create it with the point-and-click method described in the procedures for this topic. Excel might also display errors if the cell values in the worksheet cells you link to change in value and cause errors such as *DIV/0!* (divide by zero).

> ✓ **TIP** Excel tracks workbook changes, such as when you change a workbook's name, very well. Unless you delete a worksheet or workbook, or move a workbook to a new folder, odds are good that Excel can update your link references automatically to reflect the change.

To create a link to a cell or cell range on another worksheet

1. Start creating a formula that will include a value from a cell or cell range on another worksheet.

2. Click the sheet tab of the worksheet with the cell or cell range you want to include in the formula.

3. Select the cell or cells to include in the formula.

4. Press **Enter**.

To create a link to a cell or cell range in another workbook

1. Open the workbook where you want to create the formula that references an external cell or cell range.

2. Open the workbook that contains the cell or cell range you want to include in your formula.

3. Switch back to the first workbook and start creating a formula that will include a value from a cell or cell range in the other workbook.

4. Display the workbook that contains the cell or cell range you want to include in the formula.

5. Click the sheet tab of the worksheet with the cell or cell range you want to include in the formula.

6. Select the cell or cells to include in the formula.

7. Press **Enter**.

To create a link to cells in an Excel table

1. Start creating a formula that will include a value from cells in an Excel table.

2. Click the sheet tab of the worksheet with the Excel table that contains the cells you want to include in the formula.

3. Select the cell or cells to include in the formula.

4. Press **Enter**.

To open the source of a linked value

1. Open a workbook that contains a link to an external cell or cell range.

2. On the **Data** tab of the ribbon, in the **Queries & Connections** group, click the **Edit Links** button.

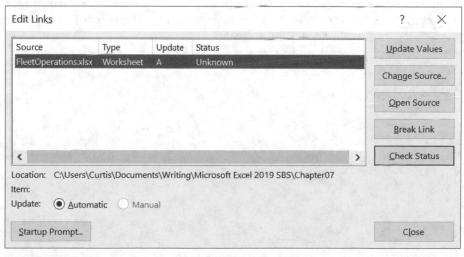

Manage workbook links by using the Edit Links dialog box.

3. In the **Edit Links** dialog box, click the link you want to work with.

4. Click the **Open Source** button.

To fix a link that returns an error because it references the wrong workbook

1. Click the **Edit Links** button.

2. In the **Edit Links** dialog box, click the link that returns an error.

3. Click **Change Source**.

4. Click the workbook that contains the correct source value.

5. If the **Select Sheet** dialog box appears, click the worksheet that contains the correct source value, and click **OK**.

6. Click **Close**.

To break a link

1. In a workbook that contains a link to a cell on another worksheet or in another workbook, click the **Edit Links** button.

2. In the **Edit Links** dialog box, click the link you want to edit.

3. Click the **Break Link** button.

4. When prompted, click **Break Links** to confirm that you want to break the link.

5. Click **Close**.

 TIP If you can't easily fix a link that returns an error, the best choice is often to delete the link from the formula and re-create it.

Consolidate multiple sets of data into a single workbook

When you create a series of worksheets that contain similar data, perhaps by using a template, you build a consistent set of workbooks in which data is stored in a predictable place. For example, consider a workbook template used to track the number of calls received from 9:00 A.M. to 10:00 P.M.

	A	B	C	D	E	F	G
1							
2							
3			**Hour**				
4		**Call Center**	9:00 AM	10:00 AM	11:00 AM	12:00 PM	1:00 PM
5		Northeast					
6		Atlantic					
7		Southeast					
8		North Central					
9		Midwest					
10		Southwest					
11		Mountain West					
12		Northwest					
13		Central					
14							

Consolidation targets should have labels but no data.

Using links to bring data from one worksheet to another gives you a great deal of power to combine data from several sources into a single resource. For example, you can create a worksheet that lists the number of calls you receive during specific hours of the day, use links to draw the values from the worksheets in which the call counts were recorded, and then create a formula to perform calculations on the data. However, for large worksheets with hundreds of cells filled with data, creating links from every cell is a time-consuming process. Also, to calculate a sum or an average for the data, you would need to include links to cells in every workbook.

Fortunately, there is an easier way to combine data from multiple worksheets in a single worksheet. By using this process, called data consolidation, you can define ranges of cells from multiple worksheets and have Excel summarize the data. You define these ranges in the Consolidate dialog box.

 IMPORTANT To consolidate data, every range included in the consolidation must be of the same shape and size.

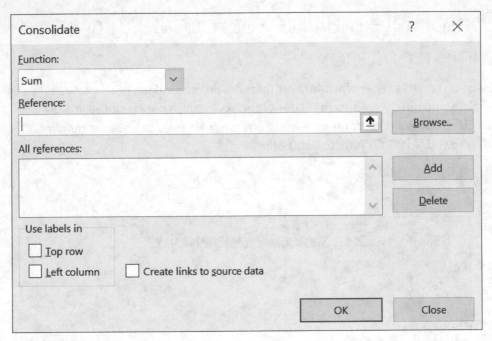

Summarize data sets of the same shape by using consolidation.

Cells in the same relative position in the ranges have their contents summarized together. When you consolidate the ranges, the cell in the upper-left corner of one range is added to the cell in the upper-left corner of every other range, even if those ranges are in different areas of the worksheet. After you choose the ranges to be used in your summary, you can choose the calculation to perform on the data. Excel sums the data by default, but you can select other functions to summarize the data.

 IMPORTANT You can define only one data consolidation summary per workbook.

To consolidate cell ranges from multiple worksheets or workbooks

1. Open the workbook into which you want to consolidate your data and the workbooks supplying the data for the consolidated range.

2. In the workbook into which you want to consolidate your data, on the **Data** tab, in the **Data Tools** group, click **Consolidate**.

3. In the **Consolidate** dialog box, click the **Collapse Dialog** button at the right edge of the **Reference** field to collapse the dialog box.

Clicking the Collapse Dialog button minimizes the Consolidate dialog box.

4. On the **View** tab, in the **Window** group, click **Switch Windows**.

5. In the list, click the first workbook that contains data you want to include.

6. Select the cell range, click the **Expand Dialog** button to restore the **Consolidate** dialog box to its full size, and click **Add** to add the selected range to the **All references** pane.

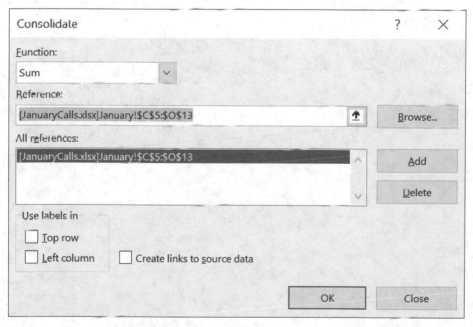

Add data ranges to create a consolidation range.

7. Repeat steps 3 through 6 to add additional ranges to the consolidation.

8. If you want to change the summary function, click the **Function** arrow in the **Consolidate** dialog box and select a new function from the list.

9. Click **OK**.

Skills review

In this chapter, you learned how to:

- Use workbooks as templates for other workbooks
- Link to data in other workbooks and worksheets
- Consolidate multiple sets of data into a single workbook

Practice tasks

The practice files for these tasks are located in the Excel2019SBS\Ch07 folder. You can save the results of the tasks in the same folder.

Use workbooks as templates for other workbooks

Open the CreateTemplate workbook in Excel, and then perform the following tasks:

1. Add a worksheet based on an existing template, such as the Sales Report template, to the workbook.

2. Save the new workbook as a template and close it.

3. In the Backstage view, click **New**.

4. Create a new workbook based on an existing template.

Link to data in other workbooks and worksheets

Open the CreateDataLinks and FleetOperatingCosts workbooks in Excel, and then perform the following tasks:

1. In the **CreateDataLinks** workbook, create links to the **FleetOperatingCosts** workbook that copy truck fuel, truck maintenance, airplane fuel, and airplane maintenance costs to the appropriate cells in column **I** on **Sheet1** of the **CreateDataLinks** workbook.

2. Close the **FleetOperatingCosts** workbook.

3. View the links in the **CreateDataLinks** workbook and show the source for one of the links.

4. Break the link to the airplane fuel source data cell.

Consolidate multiple sets of data into a single workbook

Open the ConsolidateData, JanuaryCalls, and FebruaryCalls workbooks in Excel, and then perform the following tasks:

1. In the **ConsolidateData** workbook, create a consolidation target by using cells **C5:O13**.

2. Add call data from the **JanuaryCalls** workbook's cell range **C5:O13** as a consolidation range.

3. Add call data from the **FebruaryCalls** workbook's cell range **C5:O13** as a consolidation range.

4. Click **OK**.

	A	B	C	D	E	F	G
				Hour			
3							
4		Call Center	9:00 AM	10:00 AM	11:00 AM	12:00 PM	1:00 PM
5		Northeast	15931	15958	13140	25367	19558
6		Atlantic	28432	22326	15436	20884	30000
7		Southeast	13132	12568	19732	14762	18885
8		North Central	17588	26324	24121	24453	20048
9		Midwest	24875	19965	19386	11374	26007
10		Southwest	15353	27755	19718	17889	22116
11		Mountain West	21516	28321	9754	26384	15926
12		Northwest	19806	24154	12389	10151	24078
13		Central	21018	24884	18655	31525	13407
14							

A completed consolidation summary.

Analyze alternative data sets

When you store data in an Excel 2019 workbook, you can use that data, either by itself or as part of a calculation, to discover important information about your organization. You can summarize your data quickly by using the Quick Analysis Lens to create charts, calculate totals, or apply conditional formatting.

The data in your worksheets is great for answering "what-if" questions, such as, "How much money would we save if we reduced our labor to 20 percent of our total costs?" You can always save an alternative version of a workbook and create formulas that calculate the effects of your changes, but you can do the same thing in your existing workbooks by defining one or more alternative data sets. You can also create a data table that calculates the effects of changing one or two variables in a formula, find the input values required to generate the result you want, and describe your data statistically.

This chapter guides you through procedures related to examining data by using the Quick Analysis Lens, defining an alternative data set, defining multiple alternative data sets, analyzing data by using data tables, varying data to get a specific result by using Goal Seek, finding optimal solutions by using Solver, and analyzing data by using descriptive statistics.

In this chapter

- Examine data by using the Quick Analysis Lens
- Define an alternative data set
- Define multiple alternative data sets
- Analyze data by using data tables
- Vary your data to get a specific result by using Goal Seek
- Find optimal solutions by using Solver
- Analyze data by using descriptive statistics

Practice files

For this chapter, use the practice files from the Excel2019SBS\Ch08 folder. For practice file download instructions, see the introduction.

Examine data by using the Quick Analysis Lens

One useful tool in Excel 2019 is the Quick Analysis Lens, which brings the most commonly used formatting, charting, and summary tools into one convenient location. After you select the data you want to summarize, clicking the Quick Analysis button displays the tools you can use to analyze your data.

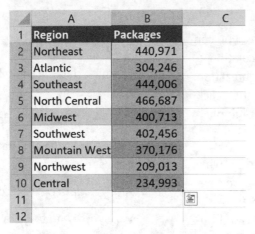

	A	B	C
1	Region	Packages	
2	Northeast	440,971	
3	Atlantic	304,246	
4	Southeast	444,006	
5	North Central	466,687	
6	Midwest	400,713	
7	Southwest	402,456	
8	Mountain West	370,176	
9	Northwest	209,013	
10	Central	234,993	
11			
12			

Click the Quick Analysis button, shown here in the bottom-right corner of the selected cells, to display analysis tools.

TIP To display the Quick Analysis toolbar by using a keyboard shortcut, press Ctrl+Q.

The Quick Analysis toolbar makes a wide range of tools available, including the ability to create an Excel table or PivotTable, insert a chart, or add conditional formatting. You can also add total columns and rows to your data range.

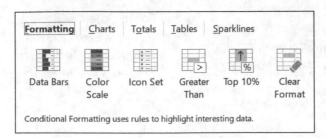

Select from several categories of analysis tools.

As an example, you can use the tools on the Totals tab of the Quick Analysis toolbar to add summary operations to your data. You can add one summary column and one summary row to each data range. If you select a new summary column or row when one exists, Excel displays a confirmation dialog box to verify that you want to replace the existing summary.

To add formatting by using the Quick Analysis Lens

1. Select the cells you want to analyze.

2. Click the **Quick Analysis** button.

3. If necessary, click the **Formatting** tab in the Quick Analysis toolbar.

4. Click the button that represents the formatting you want to apply.

To add totals by using the Quick Analysis Lens

1. Select the cells you want to analyze.

2. Click the **Quick Analysis** button.

3. If necessary, click the **Totals** tab.

4. Click the button that represents the total you want to apply.

To add tables by using the Quick Analysis Lens

1. Select the cells you want to analyze.

2. Click the **Quick Analysis** button.

3. If necessary, click the **Tables** tab.

4. Click the button that represents the type of table you want to create.

Define an alternative data set

When you save data in an Excel worksheet, you create a record that reflects the characteristics of an event or object. For example, that data could represent the number of deliveries in an hour on a particular day, the price of a new delivery option, the percentage of total revenue accounted for by a delivery option—the possibilities are endless. After the data is in place, you can create formulas to generate totals, find averages, and sort the rows in a worksheet based on the contents of one or more columns. However, if you want to perform a what-if analysis or explore the impact that changes in your data would have on any of the calculations in your workbooks, you need to change your data.

The problem with manipulating data that reflects an event or item is that when you change any data to affect a calculation, you run the risk of destroying the original data if you accidentally save your changes. You can avoid ruining your original data by creating a duplicate workbook and making your changes to it, but you can also create an alternative data set, or scenario, within an existing workbook.

When you create a scenario, you give Excel alternative values for a list of cells in a worksheet. You use the Scenario Manager dialog box to add, delete, and edit scenarios.

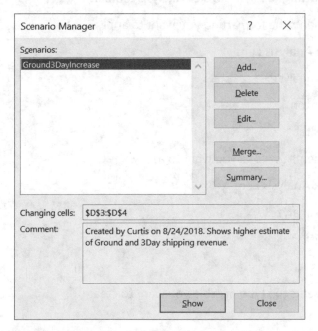

Track and change scenarios by using the Scenario Manager dialog box.

When you're ready to add a scenario, you start by providing its name and, if you want, a comment describing the scenario.

> **TIP** Adding a comment gives you and your colleagues valuable information about the scenario and your purpose for creating it. Many Excel users create scenarios without comments, but comments are extremely useful when you work on a team or revisit a workbook after several months.

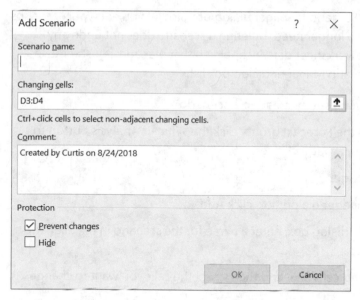

Define a scenario in the Add Scenario dialog box.

After you name your scenario, you can define its values.

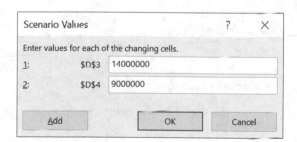

Enter alternative data in the Scenario Values dialog box.

After you have created your scenario, clicking the Show button in the Scenario Manager dialog box replaces the values in the original worksheet with the alternative values you just defined in the scenario. Any formulas that reference cells with changed values will recalculate their results.

You can remove the scenario by clicking the Undo button on the Quick Access Toolbar.

> ⚠ **IMPORTANT** If you save and close a workbook while a scenario is in effect, those values become the default values for the cells changed by the scenario! You should seriously consider creating a scenario that contains the original values of the cells you change or creating a scenario summary worksheet (a subject covered in the next section).

8

The tools available in the Scenario Manager dialog box also let you edit your scenarios and delete the ones you no longer need. Deleting a scenario does not undo any changes you made to the worksheet data by applying that scenario; it just removes the scenario from the Scenario Manager dialog box list.

To define an alternative data set by creating a scenario

1. On the **Data** tab, in the **Forecast** group, click the **What-If Analysis** button to display a menu of the what-if choices.

2. Click **Scenario Manager**.

3. In the **Scenario Manager** dialog box, click **Add**.

4. In the **Add Scenario** dialog box, enter a name for the scenario in the **Scenario name** box.

5. Click in the **Changing cells** box, and then select the cells you want to change.

6. Click **OK**.

7. In the **Scenario Values** dialog box, enter new values for each of the changing cells.

8. Click **OK**.

9. Click **Close** to close the **Scenario Manager** dialog box.

To display an alternative data set

1. On the **What-if Analysis** menu, click **Scenario Manager**.

2. In the **Scenario Manager** dialog box, click the scenario you want to display.

3. Click **Show**.

4. If you want to close the **Scenario Manager** dialog box, click **Close**.

To edit an alternative data set

1. On the **What-If Analysis** menu, click **Scenario Manager**.

2. In the **Scenario Manager** dialog box, click the scenario you want to edit.

3. Click **Edit**.

4. In the **Edit Scenario** dialog box, change the values in the **Scenario name**, **Changing cells**, or **Comment** box.

5. Click **OK**.

6. In the **Scenario Values** dialog box, enter new values for each of the changing cells.

7. Click **OK**.

8. Click **Close** to close the **Scenario Manager** dialog box.

To delete an alternative data set

1. On the **What-if Analysis** menu, click **Scenario Manager**.

2. In the **Scenario Manager** dialog box, click the scenario you want to delete.

3. Click **Delete**.

4. Click **Close** to close the **Scenario Manager** dialog box.

Define multiple alternative data sets

One great feature of Excel scenarios is that you're not limited to creating one alternative data set. You can create as many scenarios as you want and apply them by using the Scenario Manager dialog box.

> ✓ **TIP** If you apply a scenario to a worksheet and then apply another scenario to the same worksheet, both sets of changes appear. If multiple scenarios change the same cell, the cell will contain the value in the most recently applied scenario.

Applying multiple scenarios alters the values in your worksheets. You can see how those changes affect your formulas, but Excel also lets you create a record of your different scenarios by using the Scenario Summary dialog box. From within the dialog box, you can choose the type of summary worksheet you want to create and the cells you want to display in the summary worksheet.

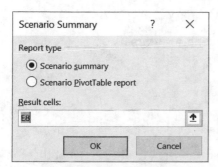

*Summarize scenarios by using the
Scenario Summary dialog box.*

8

> ⚠ **IMPORTANT** Make sure you don't have any scenarios applied to your workbook when you create the summary worksheet. If you do have an active scenario, Excel will record the scenario's changed values as the originals, and your summary will be inaccurate.

It's a good idea to create an "undo" scenario named *Normal* that holds the original values of the cells you're going to change before you change them in other scenarios. For example, if you create a scenario that changes the values in three cells, your *Normal* scenario will restore those cells to their original values. That way, even if you accidentally modify your worksheet, you can apply the *Normal* scenario and not have to reconstruct the worksheet from scratch.

> ⚠ **IMPORTANT** Each scenario can change a maximum of 32 cells, so you might need to create more than one scenario to ensure that you can restore a worksheet.

To apply multiple alternative data sets

1. On the **Data** tab, in the **Forecast** group, click the **What-If Analysis** button to display a menu of the what-if choices, and then click **Scenario Manager**.

2. In the **Scenario Manager** dialog box, click the scenario you want to display.

3. Click **Show**.

4. Repeat steps 2 and 3 for any additional scenarios you want to display.

5. Click **Close**.

To create a scenario summary worksheet

1. On the **What-if Analysis** menu, click **Scenario Manager**.

2. In the **Scenario Manager** dialog box, click **Summary**.

3. In the **Scenario Summary** dialog box, click **Scenario summary**.

4. Click **OK**.

Analyze data by using data tables

When you examine business data in Excel, you will often want to discover what the result of a formula would be with different input values. In Excel 2019, you can calculate the results of those changes by using a data table. To create a data table with one variable, you create a worksheet that contains the data required to calculate the variations in the table.

	A	B	C	D	E
1	**Revenue Increases**			**Revenue**	
2	Year	2016		$ 2,102,600.70	
3	Increase	0%	2%		
4	Package Count	237,582	5%		
5	Rate	$ 8.85	8%		
6					

Perform data analysis by changing one variable.

 IMPORTANT You must lay out the data and formulas in a rectangle so the data table you create will appear in the lower-right corner of the cell range you select.

For example, you can put the formula used to summarize the base data in cell D2, the cells with the changing values in the range C3:C5, and the cells to contain the calculations based on those values in D3:D5. Given the layout of this specific worksheet, you would select cells C2:D5, which contain the summary formula, the changing values, and the cells where the new calculations should appear.

After you select the data and the formula, you can use the Data Table dialog box to perform your analysis.

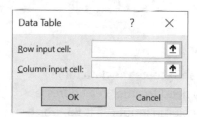

Identify input cells for your data table.

To change a single variable, you identify the cell that contains the summary formula's value that will change in the data table's cells. In this example, that cell is B3. Because the target cells D3:D5 are laid out as a column, you would identify that range as the column input cell.

TIP If your target cells were laid out as a row, you would enter the address of the cell containing the value to be changed in the Row Input Cell box.

When you click OK, Excel fills in the results of the data table, using the replacement values in cells C3:C5 to provide the values for cells D3:D5.

	A	B	C	D	E
1	**Revenue Increases**			**Revenue**	
2	Year	2016		$ 2,102,600.70	
3	Increase	0%	2%	$ 2,107,352.34	
4	Package Count	237,582	5%	$ 2,114,479.80	
5	Rate	$ 8.85	8%	$ 2,121,607.26	
6					

A completed one-variable data table.

To create a two-variable data table, you lay out your data with one set of replacement values as row headers and the other set as column headers.

	A	B	C	D	E
1	**Revenue Increases**		**Revenue**		
2	Year	2016	$ 2,102,600.70	260,000	300,000
3	Increase	0%	2%		
4	Package Count	237,582	5%		
5	Rate	$ 8.85	8%		
6			10%		
7					

Two-variable data tables replace both row and column values.

In this example, you would select the cell range C2:E6 and create the data table. Because you're creating a two-variable data table, you need to enter cell addresses for both the column input cell and row input cell. The column input cell is B3, which represents the rate increase, and the row input cell is B4, which contains the package count. When you're done, Excel creates your data table.

	A	B	C	D	E
1	**Revenue Increases**		**Revenue**		
2	Year	2016	$ 2,102,600.70	260,000	300,000
3	Increase	0%	2%	$ 2,306,200.00	$ 2,661,000.00
4	Package Count	237,582	5%	$ 2,314,000.00	$ 2,670,000.00
5	Rate	$ 8.85	8%	$ 2,321,800.00	$ 2,679,000.00
6			10%	$ 2,327,000.00	$ 2,685,000.00
7					

Replacing both row and column values generates multiple outcomes.

 TIP For a two-value data table, the summary formula should be the top-left cell in the range you select before creating the data table.

To create a one-variable data table

1. Create a worksheet containing the following:

   - A summary formula

   - The input values that the summary formula uses to calculate its value

   - A series of adjacent cells that contain alternative values for one of the summary formula's input values

2. Select the cells representing the summary formula and the changing values, and the cells where the alternative summary formula results should appear.

3. On the **Data** tab, in the **Forecast** group, click the **What-If Analysis** button to display a menu of the what-if choices, and then click **Data Table**.

4. In the **Data Table** dialog box, do either of the following:

   - If the changing values appear in a row, in the **Row input cell** box, enter the cell address of the changing value.

   - If the changing values appear in a column, in the **Column input cell** box, enter the cell address of the changing value.

5. Click **OK**.

8

To create a two-variable data table

1. Create a worksheet containing the following:

   - A summary formula

   - The input values that the summary formula uses to calculate its value

   - Two series of adjacent cells (one in a row, one in a column) that contain alternative values for two of the summary formula's input values

2. Select the cells representing the summary formula and the changing values, and the cells where the alternative summary formula results should appear.

3. On the **What-If Analysis** menu, click **Data Table**.

4. In the **Data Table** dialog box, in the **Row input cell** box, enter the cell address of the cell that has alternative values that appear in a worksheet row.

5. In the **Column input cell** box, enter the cell address of the cell that has alternative values that appear in a worksheet column.

6. Click **OK**.

Vary your data to get a specific result by using Goal Seek

When you run an organization, you must track how every element performs, both in absolute terms and in relation to other parts of the organization. There are many ways to measure your operations, but one useful technique is to limit the percentage of total costs contributed by a specific item.

As an example, consider a worksheet that contains the actual costs and percentage of total costs for several production input values.

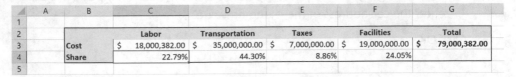

	A	B	C	D	E	F	G
1							
2			Labor	Transportation	Taxes	Facilities	Total
3		Cost	$ 18,000,382.00	$ 35,000,000.00	$ 7,000,000.00	$ 19,000,000.00	$ 79,000,382.00
4		Share	22.79%	44.30%	8.86%	24.05%	
5							

A worksheet that calculates the percentage of total costs for each of four categories.

Under the current pricing structure, labor represents 22.79 percent of the total costs for the product. If you'd prefer that labor represent no more than 20 percent of total costs, you can change the cost of labor manually until you find the number you want. Rather than doing so manually, though, you can use Goal Seek to have Excel find the solution for you.

When you use Goal Seek, you identify the cell that contains the formula you use to evaluate your data, the target value, and the cell you want to change to generate that target value.

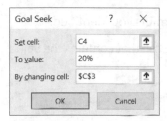

Identify the cell that contains the formula
you want to use to generate a target value.

Clicking OK tells Excel to find a solution for the goal you set. When Excel finishes its work, the new values appear in the designated cells, and the Goal Seek Status dialog box opens.

 IMPORTANT If you save a workbook with the results of a Goal Seek calculation in place, you will overwrite the values in your workbook.

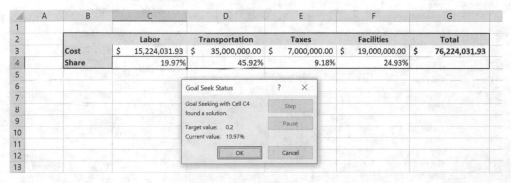

	A	B	C	D	E	F	G
1							
2			Labor	Transportation	Taxes	Facilities	Total
3		Cost	$ 15,224,031.93	$ 35,000,000.00	$ 7,000,000.00	$ 19,000,000.00	$ 76,224,031.93
4		Share	19.97%	45.92%	9.18%	24.93%	

A worksheet where Goal Seek found a solution to a problem.

TIP Goal Seek finds the closest solution it can without exceeding the target value.

To find a target value by using Goal Seek

1. On the **Data** tab, in the **Forecast** group, click the **What-If Analysis** button, and then click **Goal Seek**.

2. In the **Goal Seek** dialog box, in the **Set cell** box, enter the address of the cell that contains the formula you want to use to produce a specific value.

3. In the **To value** box, enter the target value for the formula you identified.

4. In the **By changing cell** box, enter the address of the cell that contains the value you want to vary to produce the result you want.

5. Click **OK**.

Find optimal solutions by using Solver

Goal Seek is a great tool for finding out how much you need to change a single input value to generate a specific result from a formula, but it's of no help if you want to find the best mix of several input values. For more complex problems that seek to maximize or minimize results based on several input values and constraints, you need to use Solver.

	A	B	C	D	E	F	G	H	I	J
1		**Boxes**						**Constraints**		
2			**Maple**	**Elm**	**Ash**	**Total Boxes**		**Product**	**Available**	
3		Apples	1	1	1	3		Apples	50	
4		Pears	1	1	1	3		Pears	45	
5		Strawberries	1	1	1	3		Strawberries	80	
6		Blueberries	1	1	1	3		Blueberries	100	
7		Blackberries	1	1	1	3		Blackberries	100	
8		**Total Boxes**	5	5	5					
9								**Market**	**Maximum**	
10		**Sale Price**						Maple	40	
11			**Maple**	**Elm**	**Ash**					
12		Apples	$ 14.95	$ 12.95	$ 12.95					
13		Pears	$ 9.95	$ 10.95	$ 10.95					
14		Strawberries	$ 8.95	$ 8.95	$ 8.95					
15		Blueberries	$ 8.95	$ 8.95	$ 10.95					
16		Blackberries	$ 8.95	$ 10.95	$ 9.95					
17										
18						**Total Revenue**				
19						$ 158.25				
20										

Use Solver to select a product distribution to maximize revenue.

TIP It helps to spell out every aspect of your problem so that you can identify the cells you want Solver to use in its calculations.

If you performed a complete installation when you installed Excel on your computer, the Solver button will appear on the Data tab in the Analyze group. If not, you can install the Solver add-in from the Add-Ins page of the Excel Options dialog box. After the installation is complete, Solver appears on the Data tab in the Analyze group, and you can create your model.

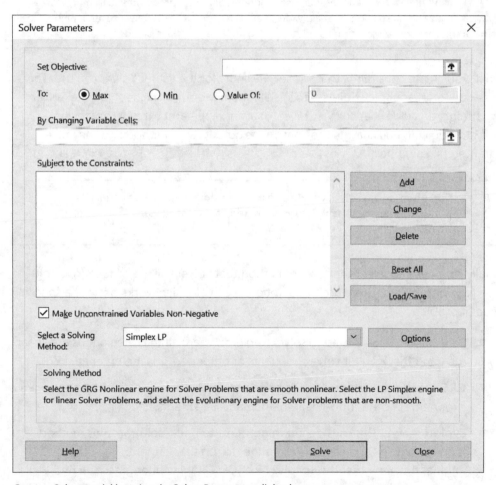

Create a Solver model by using the Solver Parameters dialog box.

The first step in setting up your Solver problem is to identify the cell that contains the summary formula you want to establish as your objective. After that, you indicate whether you want to minimize the cell's value, maximize the cell's value, or make the cell take on a specific value. Next, you select the cells Solver should vary to change the value in the objective cell. You can, if you want, require Solver to find solutions that use only integer values (that is, values that are whole numbers and have no decimal component).

> ⚠️ **IMPORTANT** Finding integer-only solutions, or *integer programming*, is much harder than finding solutions that allow decimal values. It might take Solver several minutes to find a solution or to discover that a solution using just integer values isn't possible.

Next, you create constraints that will set the limits for the values Solver can use. The best way to set your constraints is to specify them in your worksheet. Basing Solver constraints on worksheet cell values lets you add labels and explanatory text in neighboring cells and change the constraints quickly, without opening the Solver Parameters dialog box.

> ✅ **TIP** After you run Solver, you can use the commands in the Solver Results dialog box to save the results as changes to your worksheet or create a scenario based on the changed data.

Finally, you need to select the solving method that Solver will use to look for a solution to your problem. There are three options, each of which works best for a specific type of problem:

- **Simplex LP**   This is used to solve problems where all the calculations are linear, meaning they don't involve exponents or other non-linear elements.

- **GRG Nonlinear**   This is used to solve problems where the calculations involve exponents or other non-linear mathematical elements.

- **Evolutionary**   This uses genetic algorithms to find a solution. This method is quite complex and can take far longer to run than either of the other two engines, but if neither the Simplex LP or GRG Nonlinear engines can find a solution, the Evolutionary engine might be able to.

> ✅ **TIP** If you're using the Simplex LP engine and Solver returns an error immediately, indicating that it can't find a solution, try using the GRG Nonlinear engine.

To add Solver to the ribbon

1. Click the **File** tab, and then in the Backstage view, click **Options**.

2. In the **Excel Options** dialog box, click the **Add-Ins** category.

3. If necessary, in the **Manage** list at the bottom of the dialog box, click **Excel Add-ins**.

4. When **Excel Add-ins** appears in the **Manage** box, click **Go**.

5. In the **Add-Ins** dialog box, select the **Solver Add-in** check box.

6. Click **OK**.

To open the Solver Parameters dialog box

1. On the **Data** tab, in the **Analyze** group, click **Solver**.

To identify the objective cell of a model

1. Click **Solver**.

2. In the **Solver Parameters** dialog box, click in the **Set Objective** box.

3. Click the cell that includes the formula you want to optimize.

To specify the type of result your Solver model should return

1. In the **Solver Parameters** dialog box, do any of the following:

   - Select **Max** to maximize the objective cell's value.

   - Select **Min** to minimize the objective cell's value.

   - Select **Value Of** and enter the target value in the box to the right to generate a specific result.

To identify the cells with values that can be changed

1. In the **Solver Parameters** dialog box, click in the **By Changing Variable Cells** box.

2. Select the cells you will allow Solver to change to generate a solution.

8

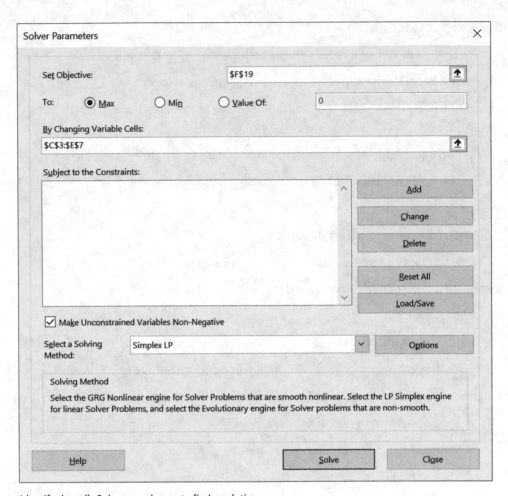

Identify the cells Solver can change to find a solution.

To add a constraint to your Solver model

1. In the **Solver Parameters** dialog box, click **Add**.

2. In the **Add Constraint** dialog box, in the **Cell Reference** box, identify the cells to which you want to apply the constraint.

3. In the middle list box, click the arrow, and then click the type of constraint you want to apply.

4. Click in the **Constraint** box and do either of the following:

- Enter the address of the cell that contains the constraint's comparison value.

- Select the cell that contains the constraint's comparison value.

Add constraints to reflect the specified circumstances of your business.

5. Click **Add** to create a new constraint.

Or

Click **OK** to close the **Add Constraint** dialog box.

To require a value to be a binary number (0 or 1)

1. In the **Add Constraint** dialog box, in the **Cell Reference** box, identify the cells to which you want to apply the constraint.

2. In the middle list box, click the arrow, and then click **bin**.

3. Click **OK**.

To require a value to be an integer

1. In the **Add Constraint** dialog box, in the **Cell Reference** box, identify the cells to which you want to apply the constraint.

2. In the middle list box, click the arrow, and then click **int**.

3. Click **OK**.

To edit a constraint

1. In the **Solver Parameters** dialog box, click the constraint you want to edit.

2. Click **Change**.

3. In the **Change Constraint** dialog box, in the **Cell Reference** box, identify the cells to which you want to apply the constraint.

4. In the middle list box, click the arrow, and then click the type of constraint you want to apply.

5. Click in the **Constraint** box and do either of the following:

   - Enter the address of the cell that contains the constraint's comparison value.

   - Select the cell that contains the constraint's comparison value.

6. Click **OK**.

To delete a constraint

1. In the **Solver Parameters** dialog box, click the constraint you want to delete.

2. Click **Delete**.

To require changing cells to contain non-negative values

1. In the **Solver Parameters** dialog box, select the **Make Unconstrained Variables Non-Negative** check box.

To select a solving method

1. In the **Solver Parameters** dialog box, click the **Select a Solving Method** arrow.

2. Click the method you want to use.

To reset the Solver model

1. In the **Solver Parameters** dialog box, click **Reset All**.

2. Click **OK**.

3. Click **Close**.

Analyze data by using descriptive statistics

Experienced business people can tell a lot about numbers just by looking at them to determine if they "look right"—that is, the sales figures are approximately where they're supposed to be for a particular hour, day, or month; the average seems about right; and whether sales have increased from year to year. When you need more than an informal assessment, however, you can use the tools in the Analysis ToolPak.

If the Data Analysis button, which displays a set of analysis tools when clicked, doesn't appear in the Analyze group on the Data tab, you can install it by using tools available on the Excel Options dialog box Add-Ins page. After you complete its installation, the Data Analysis button appears in the Analyze group on the Data tab.

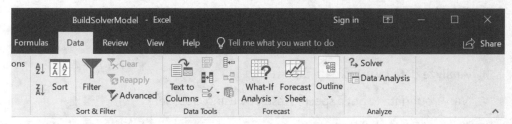

Adding Data Analysis, Solver, or both adds the Analyze group to the Data tab.

To add the Data Analysis button to the ribbon

1. In the Backstage view, click **Options**.

2. In the **Excel Options** dialog box, click the **Add-Ins** category.

3. If necessary, click the **Manage** arrow and then click **Excel Add-ins**.

4. When **Excel Add-ins** appears in the **Manage** box, click **Go**.

5. In the **Add-Ins** dialog box, select the **Analysis ToolPak** check box.

6. Click **OK**.

To analyze your data by using descriptive statistics

1. On the **Data** tab, in the **Analyze** group, click **Data Analysis**.

2. In the **Data Analysis** dialog box, click **Descriptive Statistics**.

3. Click **OK** to display the **Descriptive Statistics** dialog box.

4. Click in the **Input Range** box, and then select the cells that contain the data you want to summarize.

5. Select the **Summary statistics** check box.

6. Click **OK**.

Skills review

In this chapter, you learned how to:

- Examine data by using the Quick Analysis Lens
- Define an alternative data set
- Define multiple alternative data sets
- Analyze data by using data tables
- Vary your data to get a specific result by using Goal Seek
- Find optimal solutions by using Solver
- Analyze data by using descriptive statistics

Practice tasks

The practice files for these tasks are located in the Excel2019SBS\Ch08 folder. You can save the results of the tasks in the same folder.

Examine data by using the Quick Analysis Lens

Open the PerformQuickAnalysis workbook in Excel, and then perform the following tasks:

1. Select cells **B2:B10**.

2. Use the **Quick Analysis** button to add a total row to the bottom of the selected range.

3. Use the **Quick Analysis** button to add a running total column to the right of the selected range.

Define an alternative data set

Open the CreateScenarios workbook in Excel, and then perform the following tasks:

1. Create a scenario called **Overnight** that changes the **Base Rate** value for **Overnight** and **Priority Overnight** packages (in cells **C6** and **C7**) to $18.75 and $25.50.

2. Apply the scenario.

3. Undo the scenario application by pressing **Ctrl+Z**.

4. Close the **Scenario Manager** dialog box.

Define multiple alternative data sets

Open the ManageMultipleScenarios workbook in Excel, and then perform the following tasks:

1. Create a scenario called **HighVolume** that increases **Ground** packages to 17,000,000 and **3Day** to 14,000,000.

2. Create a second scenario called **NewRates** that increases the **Ground** rate to $9.45 and the **3Day** rate to $12.

3. Open the **Scenario Manager** dialog box and create a summary worksheet.

4. Apply the **HighVolume** scenario, and then apply the **NewRates** scenario.

5. Close the **Scenario Manager** dialog box.

Analyze data by using data tables

Open the DefineDataTables workbook in Excel, and then perform the following tasks:

1. On the **RateIncreases** worksheet, select cells **C2:D5**.

2. Use the **What-If Analysis** button to start creating a data table.

3. In the **Column input cell** box, enter B3.

4. Click **OK**.

5. On the **RateAndVolume** worksheet, select cells **C2:E6**.

6. On the **What-If Analysis** menu, click **Data Table**.

7. In the **Row input cell** box, enter B4.

8. In the **Column input cell** box, enter B3.

9. Click **OK**.

Vary your data to get a specific result by using Goal Seek

Open the PerformGoalSeekAnalysis workbook in Excel, and then perform the following tasks:

1. Click cell **C4**.

2. Open the **Goal Seek** dialog box.

3. Verify that **C4** appears in the **Set cell** box.

4. In the **To value** box, enter 20%.

5. In the **By changing cell** box, enter C3.

6. Click **OK**.

Find optimal solutions by using Solver

Open the BuildSolverModel workbook in Excel, and then perform the following tasks:

1. Click cell **F19**, and then open the **Solver Parameters** dialog box.

2. Verify that cell **F19** appears in the **Set Objective** box, and then select **Max**.

3. In the **By Changing Variable Cells** box, select cells **C3:E7**.

4. Add a constraint to require cell **C8** to be less than or equal to the value in cell **I10**.

5. Add a constraint that requires the values in cells **F3:F7** to be less than or equal to the values in cells **I3:I7**.

6. Make the unconstrained variables non-negative.

7. Solve the model by using the **GRG Nonlinear** engine.

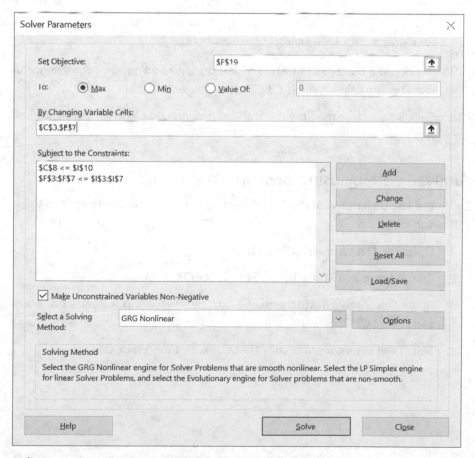

Define your solution by using the Solver Parameters dialog box.

8. Click **OK** to close the **Solver Results** dialog box and examine the result.

	A	B	C	D	E	F	G	H	I	J
1		**Boxes**						**Constraints**		
2			**Maple**	**Elm**	**Ash**	**Total Boxes**		**Product**	**Available**	
3		Apples	40	10	0	50		Apples	50	
4		Pears	0	45	0	45		Pears	45	
5		Strawberries	0	80	0	80		Strawberries	80	
6		Blueberries	0	0	100	100		Blueberries	100	
7		Blackberries	0	100	0	100		Blackberries	100	
8		**Total Boxes**	40	235	100					
9								**Market**	**Maximum**	
10		**Sale Price**						Maple	40	
11			**Maple**	**Elm**	**Ash**					
12		Apples	$ 14.95	$ 12.95	$ 12.95					
13		Pears	$ 9.95	$ 10.95	$ 10.95					
14		Strawberries	$ 8.95	$ 8.95	$ 8.95					
15		Blueberries	$ 8.95	$ 8.95	$ 10.95					
16		Blackberries	$ 8.95	$ 10.95	$ 9.95					
17										
18						Total Revenue				
19						$ 4,126.25				
20										

Solver generates a solution without integer constraints.

9. Reopen the **Solver Parameters** dialog box and add another constraint that requires the values in cells **C3:E7** to be integers.

10. Click **Solve**, close the **Solver Parameters** dialog box, and note how the solution has changed.

Analyze data by using descriptive statistics

Open the UseDescriptiveStatistics workbook in Excel, and then perform the following tasks:

1. Open the **Data Analysis** dialog box.

2. Click **Descriptive Statistics**, and then click **OK**.

3. In the **Descriptive Statistics** dialog box, click in the **Input Range** box and select cells **C3:C17**.

4. Select the **Summary statistics** check box, and then click **OK**.

Create charts and graphics

When you enter data into an Excel 2019 worksheet, you create a record of important events, whether they are individual sales, sales for an hour of a day, the price of a product, or something else entirely. What a list of values in cells can't communicate easily, however, are the overall trends in the data. The best way to communicate trends in a large collection of data is by creating a chart, which summarizes data visually. In addition to standard charts, with Excel 2019 you can create compact charts called sparklines, which summarize a data series by using a graph contained within a single cell.

You have a great deal of control over the appearance of your charts. You can change the color of any chart element, choose a different chart type to better summarize the underlying data, and change the display properties of text and numbers in a chart. If the data in the worksheet used to create a chart represents a progression through time, such as sales over several months, you can have Excel extrapolate future sales and add a trendline to the graph representing that prediction.

This chapter guides you through procedures related to creating charts (including six new chart types in Excel 2019), customizing chart elements, finding trends in your data, summarizing data by using sparklines, creating and formatting diagrams, and creating shapes and mathematical equations.

In this chapter

- Create charts
- Perform business intelligence analysis using charts
- Customize chart appearance
- Find trends in your data
- Create combo charts
- Summarize your data by using sparklines
- Create diagrams by using SmartArt
- Create and manage shapes
- Create and manage mathematical equations

Practice files

For this chapter, use the practice files from the Excel2019SBS\Ch09 folder. For practice file download instructions, see the introduction.

Create charts

Excel 2019 lets you create charts quickly by using the Quick Analysis Lens, which displays recommended charts to summarize your data. When you select the entire data range you want to chart, clicking the Quick Analysis button that appears in the bottom-right corner of the selection lets you display the types of charts Excel recommends.

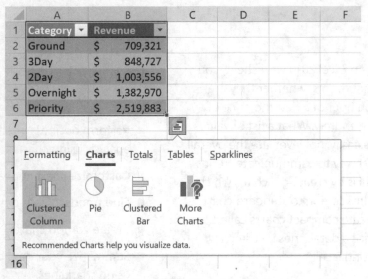

Use the Quick Analysis Lens to add a chart to your worksheet.

You can display a preview of each recommended chart by pointing to the icon representing that chart. Clicking the icon adds the chart to your worksheet.

> ✓ **TIP** Press the F11 key to create a chart of the default type on a new chart sheet, which is a distinct type of sheet that only contains a chart and not worksheet cells. Unless you or another user changed the default, Excel creates a column chart.

If the chart you want to create doesn't appear in the list of charts recommended by the Quick Analysis Lens, you can select the chart type you want from a gallery on the Insert tab of the ribbon. When you point to a subtype in the gallery, Excel displays a preview of the chart you will create by clicking that subtype. When you click a chart subtype, Excel creates the chart by using the default layout and color scheme defined in your workbook's theme.

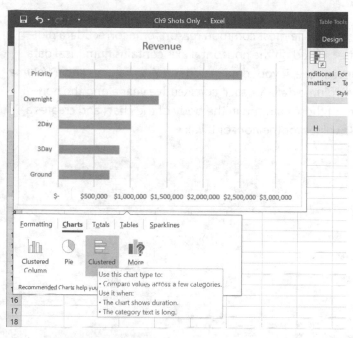

Display a live preview of a chart.

9

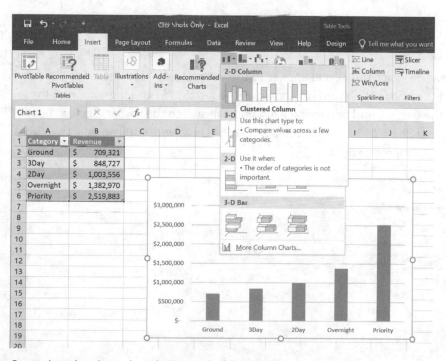

Create charts by using tools on the Insert tab of the ribbon.

If Excel doesn't plot your data the way you want it to, you can change the axis on which Excel plots a data column. The most common reason for incorrect data plotting is that the column to be plotted on the horizontal axis contains numerical data instead of textual data. For example, if your data includes a *Year* column and a *Volume* column, instead of plotting volume data for each consecutive year along the horizontal axis, Excel plots both of those columns in the body of the chart and creates a sequential series to provide values for the horizontal axis.

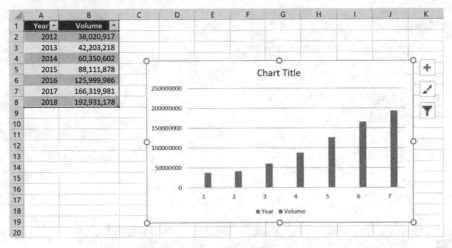

A chart with horizontal axis labels plotted as data.

You can change which data Excel applies to the vertical axis (also known as the *y-axis*) and the horizontal axis (also known as the *x-axis*). If Excel has swapped the values for the vertical and horizontal axes, you can switch the row and column data to update your chart. If the problem is a little more involved, you can edit how Excel interprets your source data.

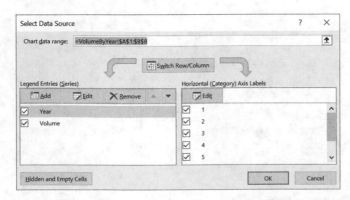

Change how Excel plots your data by using the Select Data Source dialog box.

The *Year* column should appear on the horizontal axis as a data category, which Excel refers to as the axis labels.

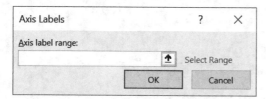

Identify horizontal (category) labels by using the Axis Labels dialog box.

After you identify the cell range that provides the values for your axis labels, Excel will revise your chart.

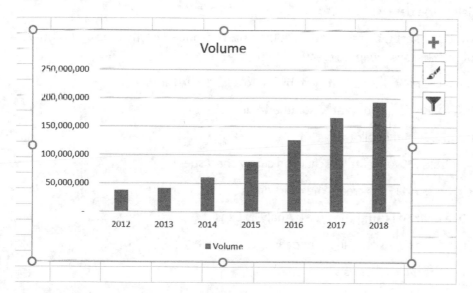

A chart with horizontal and vertical axis values plotted correctly.

After you create your chart, you can change its size to reflect whether the chart should dominate its worksheet or take on a role as another informative element on the worksheet.

Just as you can control a chart's size, you can also control its location. You can drag a chart to a new location on its current worksheet, move the chart to another worksheet, or move the chart to its own chart sheet.

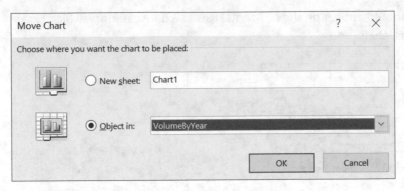

Pick a destination for a chart by using the Move Chart dialog box.

To create a chart

1. Select the data you want to appear in your chart.

2. On the **Insert** tab of the ribbon, in the **Charts** group, click the type and subtype of the chart you want to create.

To create a chart of the default type by using a keyboard shortcut

1. Select the data you want to summarize in a chart.

2. Do either of the following:

   • Press **F11** to create the chart on a new chart sheet.

   • Press **Alt+F1** to create the chart on the active worksheet.

To create a chart by using the Quick Analysis Lens

1. Select the data you want to appear in your chart.

2. Click the **Quick Analysis** button.

3. In the gallery that appears, click the **Charts** tab.

4. Click the type of chart you want to create.

To create a recommended chart

1. Select the data you want to visualize.

2. On the **Insert** tab, in the **Charts** group, click the **Recommended Charts** button.

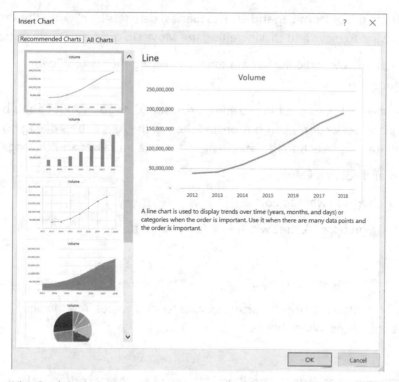

View Excel chart recommendations.

3. In the **Insert Chart** dialog box, click the chart you want to create.

4. Click **OK**.

To change how Excel plots your data in a chart

1. Click the chart you want to change.

2. On the **Design** tool tab of the ribbon, in the **Data** group, click **Select Data**.

3. In the **Select Data Source** dialog box, do any of the following:

   • Delete a **Legend Entries (Series)** data set by clicking the series and clicking the **Remove** button.

   • Add a **Legend Entries (Series)** data set by clicking the **Add** button and, in the **Edit Series** dialog box that appears, selecting the cells that contain the data you want to add, and then clicking **OK**.

   • Edit a **Legend Entries (Series)** data set by clicking the series you want to edit, clicking the **Edit** button, and, in the **Edit Series** dialog box, selecting the cells that provide values for the series, and then clicking **OK**.

- Change the order of **Legend Entries (Series)** data sets by clicking the series you want to move and clicking either the **Move Up** or **Move Down** button.

- Switch the row and column data series by clicking the **Switch Row/Column** button.

- Change the values used to provide **Horizontal (Category) Axis Labels** by clicking that section's **Edit** button and then, in the **Axis Labels** dialog box that appears, selecting the cells to provide the label values and clicking **OK**.

To switch row and column values

1. Click the chart you want to edit.

2. In the **Data** group, click the **Switch Row/Column** button.

To resize a chart

1. Click the chart you want to edit.

2. On the **Format** tool tab, in the **Size** group, enter new values into the **Shape Height** and **Shape Width** boxes.

   Or

   Drag a handle to change the position of the chart's edge or corner. You can do any of the following:

   - Drag the handle in the middle of the top or bottom chart border to change the chart's height.

   - Drag a handle in the middle of the left or right chart border to change the chart's width.

   - Drag a handle at a corner of the chart border to change both the chart's height and its width.

To reposition a chart within a worksheet

1. Click the chart.

2. Drag it to its new position.

To move a chart to another worksheet

1. Click the chart.

2. On the **Design** tool tab, in the **Location** group, click the **Move Chart** button.

3. In the **Move Chart** dialog box, click the **Object in** arrow.

4. In the **Object in** list, click the sheet to which you want to move the chart.

5. Click **OK**.

To move a chart to its own chart sheet

1. Click the chart.

2. In the **Location** group, click the **Move Chart** button.

3. In the **Move Chart** dialog box, click in the **New sheet** box.

4. Enter a name for the new sheet.

5. Click **OK**.

Perform business intelligence analysis using charts

Excel 2019 introduces one new type of chart, the funnel chart, and the ability to create 2D maps of your data. A funnel chart shows how many items in a process continue to the next step. For example, a business might track sales leads, successful contacts, and customers who place an order. The top level of the funnel would depict the leads, the second the successful contacts, and the third customers who placed orders.

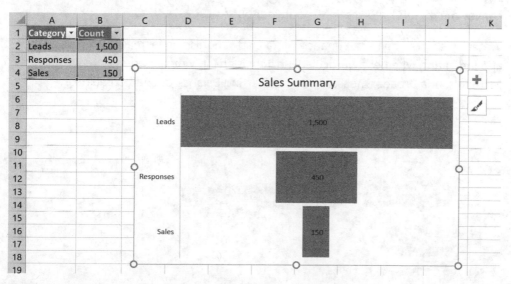

Use a funnel chart to summarize processes where each stage of the process has fewer participants.

If you collect geographical data, such as your customers' state of residence, you can summarize that data using a two-dimensional (2D) map. You can mark states from which a customer placed an order or use color or marker size to show the relative number or value of orders from those states.

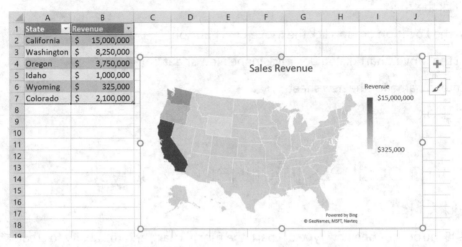

View geographic data by using a 2D map.

Excel also includes six types of charts that enhance your ability to analyze and display business data: waterfall, histogram, Pareto, box-and-whisker, treemap, and sunburst. Each of these new chart types enhances your ability to summarize your data and convey meaningful information about your business.

Waterfall charts summarize financial data by distinguishing increases from decreases and indicating whether a particular line item is an individual account, such as Direct Materials, or a broader measure, such as Starting Balance or Ending Balance.

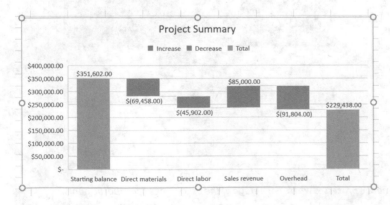

Use waterfall charts to summarize financial data.

Excel doesn't automatically recognize which entries should be treated as totals, but you can double-click any columns that represent totals (or subtotals) and identify them so Excel knows how to handle them.

Histograms count the number of occurrences of values within a set of ranges, where each range is called a *bin*. For example, a summary of daily package volumes for a delivery area could fall into several ranges.

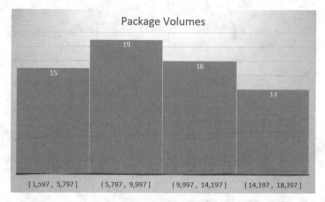

Histograms summarize values by using groups called bins.

A Pareto chart combines a histogram and a line chart to show both the contributions of categories of values, such as package delivery options (for example, overnight, priority overnight, and ground), and the cumulative contributions after each category is counted.

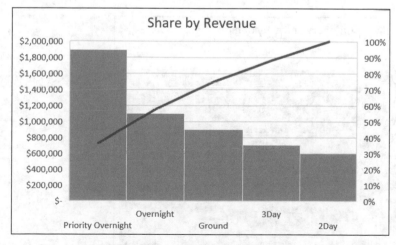

Pareto charts show category revenue and share of the total.

A box-and-whisker chart combines several statistical measures, including the average (or mean), median, minimum, and maximum values for a data series, into a single chart. These charts provide a compact yet informative view of your data from a statistical standpoint.

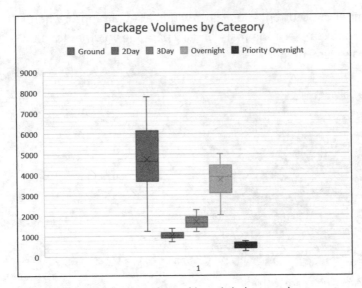

Box-and-whisker charts provide graphic statistical summaries.

The treemap chart divides data into categories, which are represented by colors, and shows the hierarchy of values within each category by using the size of the rectangles within the category. For example, you could represent regional frequencies for each package delivery option available to customers.

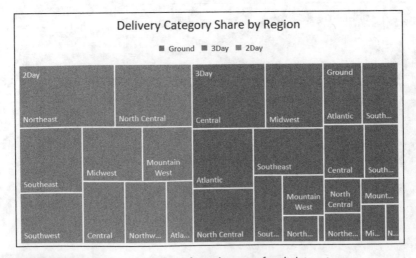

Treemap charts display contributions from elements of each data category.

A sunburst chart breaks down a data set's hierarchy to an even deeper level, showing the details of how much each subcategory of data contributes to the whole.

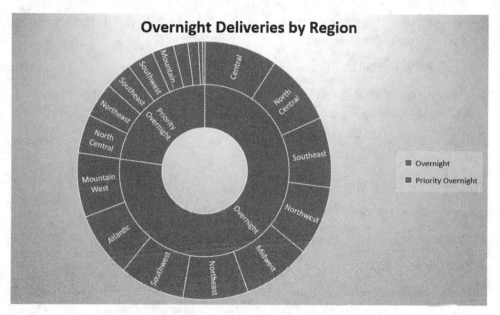

Sunburst charts show category contributions in detail.

To create a funnel chart

1. Select the data you want to visualize.

2. On the **Insert** tab, in the **Charts** group, click the **Insert Waterfall, Funnel, Stock, Surface, or Radar Chart** button.

3. In the **Funnel** group, click the **Funnel** chart type.

To create a 2D map chart

1. Select the data you want to visualize.

2. On the **Insert** tab, in the **Charts** group, click the **Maps** button, and then click the **Filled Map** chart type.

3. If necessary, give Excel permission to upload your data to Bing Maps to create the chart.

> ⚠ **IMPORTANT** If you attempt to map data that does not include an identifiable geographic element, Excel displays an error message. If that error occurs, verify the data range you selected.

To create a waterfall chart

1. Select the data you want to visualize.

2. On the **Insert** tab, in the **Charts** group, click the **Insert Waterfall, Funnel, Stock, Surface, or Radar Chart** button.

3. Click the **Waterfall** chart type.

4. If necessary, identify a column as a total by clicking the column once to select the series, clicking the column again to select it individually, right-clicking the column, and then clicking **Set as Total**.

To create a histogram chart

1. Select the data you want to visualize.

2. In the **Charts** group, click the **Insert Statistic Chart** button.

3. In the **Histogram** group, click the **Histogram** subtype.

To create a Pareto chart

1. Select the data you want to visualize.

2. Click the **Insert Statistic Chart** button.

3. In the **Histogram** group, click the **Pareto** subtype.

To create a box-and-whisker chart

1. Select the data you want to visualize.

2. Click the **Insert Statistic Chart** button.

3. In the **Histogram** group, click the **Box and Whisker** subtype.

To create a treemap chart

1. Select the data you want to visualize.

2. In the **Charts** group, click the **Insert Hierarchy Chart** button.

3. In the **Treemap** group, click the **Treemap** subtype.

To create a sunburst chart

1. Select the data you want to visualize.

2. Click the **Insert Hierarchy Chart** button.

3. In the **Sunburst** group, click the **Sunburst** subtype.

Customize chart appearance

If you want to change a chart's appearance, you can do so by using the Chart Styles button, which appears in a group of three buttons next to a selected chart. These buttons put chart formatting and data controls within easy reach.

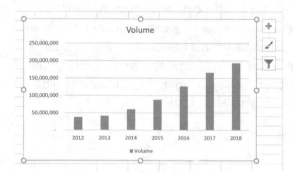

Customize your chart by using the buttons that appear beside the chart.

Clicking the Chart Styles button opens a gallery that has two tabs: Style and Color. The Style tab contains 14 styles from which to choose, and the Color tab displays a series of color schemes you can select to change your chart's appearance.

> **TIP** If you prefer to work with the ribbon, these same styles appear in the Chart Styles gallery on the Design tab.

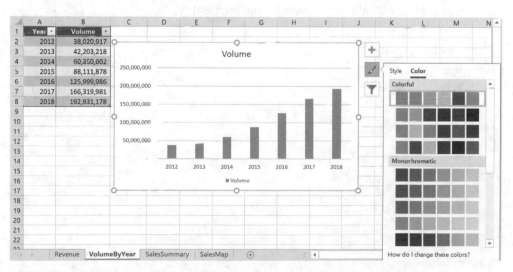

Select a color palette for your chart.

TIP The colors and styles in the Chart Styles gallery are tied to your workbook's theme. If you change your workbook's theme, Excel changes the colors available in the Chart Styles gallery, as well as your chart's appearance, to reflect the new theme's colors.

When you create a chart, Excel creates a visualization that focuses on the data. In most cases, the chart has a title, a legend (a list of the data series displayed in the chart), horizontal lines in the body of the chart to make it easier to discern individual values, and axis labels. If you want to create a chart that has more or different elements, such as additional data labels for each data point plotted on your chart, you can do so by selecting a new layout. If it's still not quite right, you can show or hide individual elements by using the Chart Elements button.

Click the Chart Elements button to display or hide elements in the active chart.

After you select a chart element, you can change its size and appearance by using controls specifically created to work with that element type.

Format a chart element by using a task pane designed for that element.

230

You can use the third button, Chart Filters, to focus on specific data in your chart. Clicking the Chart Filters button displays a filter interface that is very similar to that used to limit the data displayed in an Excel table.

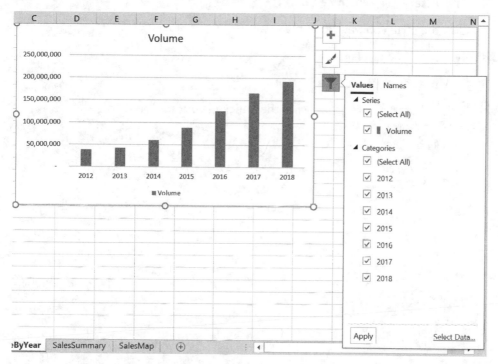

Focus on the data you want by using a chart filter.

Selecting or clearing a check box displays or hides data related to a specific value within a series. You can also use the check boxes in the Series section of the panel to display or hide entire data series.

If you think you want to apply the same set of changes to charts you'll create in the future, you can save your chart as a chart template. When you select the data you want to summarize visually and apply the chart template, you'll create consistently formatted charts in a minimum of steps.

To apply a built-in chart style

1. Click the chart you want to format.

2. On the **Design** tool tab, in the **Chart Styles** gallery, click the style you want to apply.

Or

1. Click the chart you want to format.

2. Click the **Chart Styles** button.

3. If necessary, click the **Style** tab.

4. Click the style you want to apply.

To apply a built-in chart layout

1. Click the chart you want to format.

2. In the **Chart Layouts** group, click the **Quick Layout** button.

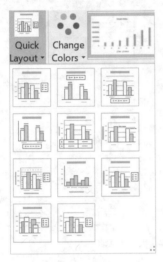

Select a new layout from the Quick Layout gallery.

3. Click the layout you want to apply.

To change a chart's color scheme

1. Click the chart you want to format.

2. In the **Chart Styles** group, click the **Change Colors** button.

3. Click the color scheme you want to apply.

Or

1. Click the chart you want to format.

2. Click the **Chart Styles** button.

3. If necessary, click the **Color** tab.

4. Click the color scheme you want to apply.

To select a chart element

1. Click the chart element.

Or

1. Click the chart.

2. On the **Format** tool tab, in the **Current Selection** group, click the **Chart Elements** arrow.

3. Click the chart element you want to select.

To format a chart element

1. Select the chart element.

2. Use the tools on the **Format** tool tab to change the element's formatting.

   Or

   In the **Current Selection** group, click the **Format Selection** button to display the **Format** *Chart Element* task pane.

3. Change the element's formatting.

To display or hide a chart element

1. Click the chart and do either of the following:

   - On the **Design** tool tab, in the **Chart Layouts** group, click the **Add Chart Element** button, point to the element on the list, and click **None** to hide the element, or click one of the other options to show the element.

   - Click the **Chart Elements** button and select or clear the check box next to the element you want to show or hide.

To create a chart filter

1. Click the chart you want to filter.

2. Click the **Chart Filters** button.

3. Use the tools on the **Values** and **Names** tabs to create your filter.

9

To save a chart as a chart template

1. Right-click the chart.

2. Click **Save as Template**.

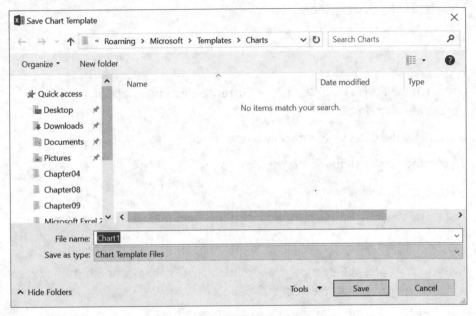

Save a chart as a template so that you can apply consistent formatting quickly.

3. In the **File name** box, enter a name for the template.

4. Click **Save**.

To apply a chart template

1. Click the chart to which you want to apply a template.

2. On the **Design** tool tab, in the **Type** group, click **Change Chart Type**.

3. If necessary, click the **All Charts** tab.

4. Click the **Templates** category.

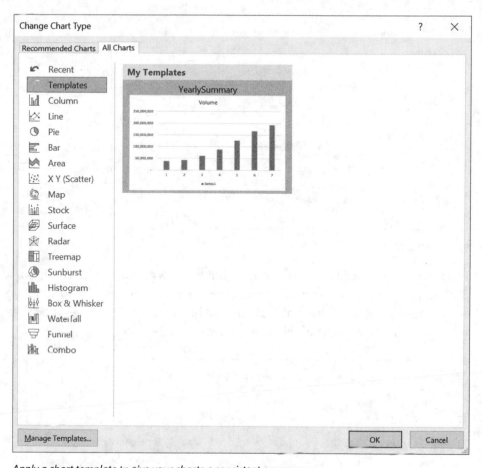

Apply a chart template to give your charts a consistent appearance.

5. Click the template you want to apply.

6. Click **OK**.

Find trends in your data

You can use the data in Excel workbooks to discover how your business has performed in the past, but you can also have Excel 2019 make its best guess, for example, as to future shipping revenues if the current trend continues. As an example, consider a line chart that shows package volume data for the years 2012 through 2018.

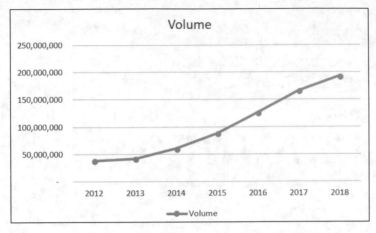

A line chart that shows data over time.

The total has increased from 2012 to 2018, but the growth hasn't been uniform, so guessing how much package volume would increase if the overall trend continued would require detailed mathematical computations. Fortunately, Excel knows that math and can use it to add a trendline to your data.

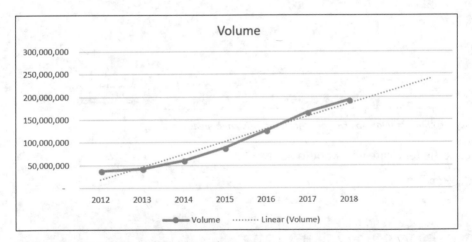

Create a trendline to forecast future data values.

You can choose the data distribution that Excel should expect when it makes its projection. The right choice for most business data is Linear; other distributions (such as Exponential, Logarithmic, and Polynomial) are used for scientific and operations research applications. You can also tell how far ahead Excel should look. Looking ahead by zero periods shows the best-fit line for the current data set, whereas looking ahead two periods would project two periods into the future, assuming current trends continue.

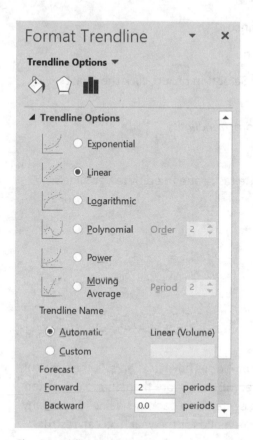

Change trendline characteristics by using the Format Trendline task pane.

> **TIP** When you select a chart, click the Chart Elements button, and click the right-pointing triangle beside Trendline, one of the options Excel displays is Linear Forecast, which adds a trendline with a two-period forecast.

As with other chart elements, you can double-click the trendline to open a formatting dialog box and change the line's appearance.

To add a trendline to a chart

1. Click the chart to which you want to add a trendline.

2. On the **Design** tool tab, in the **Chart Layouts** group, click the **Add Chart Element** button.

3. Point to **Trendline** and click the type of trendline you want to add.

To edit a trendline's properties and appearance

1. Click the chart that contains the trendline.

2. On the **Format** tool tab, in the **Current Selection** group, click the **Chart Elements** arrow.

3. Click the element that ends with the word *Trendline*.

4. Click **Format Selection**.

5. Use the controls in the **Format Trendline** task pane to edit the trendline's properties and appearance.

To delete a trendline

1. Click the trendline.

2. Press the **Delete** key.

Create combo charts

The Excel 2019 charting engine is powerful, but it does have its quirks. Some data collections you might want to summarize in Excel will have more than one value related to each category. For example, each regional center for a package-delivery company could have both overall package volume and revenue for the year. You can restructure the data in your Excel table to create a combo chart, which uses two vertical axes to show both value sets in the same chart.

 TIP A Pareto chart, discussed earlier in this chapter, is a type of dual-axis chart.

To create a dual-axis chart

1. Select the data you want to visualize.

2. On the **Insert** tab, in the **Charts** group, click the **Insert Combo Chart** button.

3. Click the type of combo chart you want to create.

   Or

   Click **Create Custom Combo Chart** and use the settings in the **Combo** category of the **All Charts** tab to define your combo chart.

Summarize your data by using sparklines

You can create charts in Excel to summarize your data visually by using legends, labels, and colors to highlight aspects of your data. It is possible to create very small charts to summarize your data in an overview worksheet, but you can also use a sparkline to create a compact, informative chart that provides valuable context for your data.

Edward Tufte introduced sparklines in his book *Beautiful Evidence* (Graphics Press, 2006), with the goal of creating charts that imparted their information in approximately the same space as a word of printed text. In Excel, a sparkline occupies a single cell, which makes it ideal for use in summary worksheets.

	A	B	C	D	E	F
1						
2		Month	Revenue	Target	Difference	
3		January	$ 1,538,468	$ 1,600,000	$ (61,532)	
4		February	$ 1,474,289	$ 1,600,000	$ (125,711)	
5		March	$ 1,416,242	$ 1,600,000	$ (183,758)	
6		April	$ 1,685,377	$ 1,600,000	$ 85,377	
7		May	$ 1,573,046	$ 1,600,000	$ (26,954)	
8		June	$ 1,979,077	$ 1,600,000	$ 379,077	
9		July	$ 1,600,000	$ 1,600,000	$ -	
10		August	$ 2,417,226	$ 1,600,000	$ 817,226	
11		September	$ 1,872,026	$ 1,600,000	$ 272,026	
12		October	$ 2,097,478	$ 1,600,000	$ 497,478	
13		November	$ 2,876,025	$ 2,750,000	$ 126,025	
14		December	$ 3,825,430	$ 4,000,000	$ (174,570)	
15						

Data that Excel can summarize by using sparklines.

You can create three types of sparklines: line, column, and win/loss. The line and column sparklines are compact versions of the standard line and column charts. The win/loss sparkline indicates whether a cell value is positive (a win), negative (a loss), or zero (a tie).

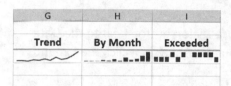

G	H	I
Trend	By Month	Exceeded

Examples of line, column, and win/loss sparklines.

After you create a sparkline, you can change its appearance. Because a sparkline takes up the entire interior of a single cell, resizing that cell's row or column resizes the sparkline. You can also change a sparkline's formatting, modify its labels, or delete it entirely.

9

Format sparklines by using tools on the Sparkline Tools Design tool tab of the ribbon.

> ✓ **TIP** Sparklines work best when displayed in compact form. If you find yourself adding markers and labels to a sparkline, you might consider using a regular chart to take advantage of its wider range of formatting and customization options.

To create a sparkline

1. Select the data you want to visualize.

2. On the **Insert** tab, in the **Sparklines** group, do one of the following:

   - Click the **Line** button.

   - Click the **Column** button.

   - Click the **Win/Loss** button.

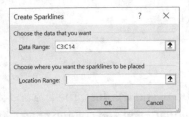

Insert a sparkline by using the Create Sparklines dialog box.

3. In the **Create Sparklines** dialog box, verify that the data you selected appears in the **Data Range** box.

   If the wrong data appears, click the **Collapse Dialog** button next to the **Data Range** box, select the cells that contain your data, and then click the **Expand Dialog** button.

4. Click the **Collapse Dialog** button next to the **Location Range** box, click the cell where you want the sparkline to appear, and then click the **Expand Dialog** button.

5. Click **OK**.

To format a sparkline

1. Click the cell that contains the sparkline.

2. Use the tools on the **Design** tool tab to format the sparkline.

To delete a sparkline

1. Click the cell that contains the sparkline.

2. On the **Design** tool tab, in the **Group** group, click the **Clear** button.

Create diagrams by using SmartArt

Businesses define processes to manage product development, sales, and other essential functions. Excel 2019 comes with a selection of built-in diagram types, referred to as SmartArt, that you can use to illustrate processes, lists, and hierarchies within your organization.

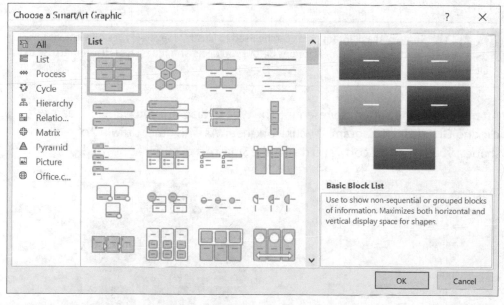

Create SmartArt graphics by using the Choose a SmartArt Graphic dialog box.

Clicking one of the buttons in the dialog box selects the type of diagram the button represents and causes a description of the diagram type to appear in the rightmost pane of the dialog box. The following table lists the nine categories of diagrams from which you can choose.

Diagram	Description
List	Shows a series of items that typically require a large amount of text to explain
Process	Shows a progression of sequential steps through a task, process, or workflow
Cycle	Shows a process with a continuous cycle or relationships of core elements
Hierarchy	Shows hierarchical relationships, such as those within a company
Relationship	Shows the relationship between two or more items
Matrix	Shows the relationship of components to a whole by using quadrants
Pyramid	Shows proportional, foundation-based, or hierarchical relationships such as a series of skills
Picture	Shows one or more images with captions
Office.com	Shows diagrams available from Office.com

> **TIP** Some of the diagram types can be used to illustrate several types of relationships. Be sure to examine all your options before you decide on the type of diagram to use to illustrate your point.

After you click the button representing the type of diagram you want to create, clicking OK adds the diagram to your worksheet. As with other drawing objects and shapes, you can move, copy, and delete the SmartArt diagram as needed.

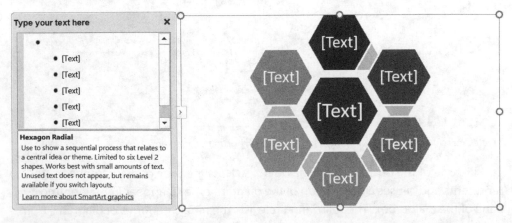

Show how your ideas relate by using SmartArt.

While the diagram is selected, you can add and edit text; add, edit, or reposition shapes; and use the buttons on the ribbon to change the shapes' formatting. To add text, you can either type directly into the shape or use the Text Pane, which appears beside the SmartArt diagram. When you're done, click outside the shape to stop editing.

 TIP Pressing the Enter key after you edit the text in a SmartArt shape adds a new shape to the diagram.

To create a SmartArt graphic

1. Display the worksheet where you want the SmartArt graphic to appear.

2. On the **Insert** tab, in the **Illustrations** group, click the **SmartArt** button.

3. In the **Choose a SmartArt Graphic** dialog box, click the category from which you want to choose your graphic style.

4. Click the style of graphic you want to create.

5. Click **OK**.

To edit text in a SmartArt graphic shape

1. Click the shape, and then do either of the following:

   - Edit the text directly in the shape.

   - Click the corresponding line in the **Type Your Text Here** pane and edit the text there.

To format shape text

1. Click the shape that contains the text you want to format.

2. Use the tools on the mini toolbar or the **Home** tab of the ribbon to format the text.

To add a shape

1. Click the shape next to where you want the new shape to appear.

2. On the **Design** tool tab, in the **Create Graphic** group, click the **Add Shape** arrow (not the button) and select where you want the new shape to appear.

 TIP If you click the Add Shape button (not the arrow), Excel adds a shape below or to the left of the current shape.

9

To delete a shape

1. Click the shape.

2. Press **Delete**.

To change a shape's position

1. Click the shape you want to move.

2. In the **Create Graphic** group, do either of the following:

   - Click **Move Up**.

   - Click **Move Down**.

To change a shape's level

1. Click the shape you want to move.

2. In the **Create Graphic** group, do either of the following:

   - Click **Promote**.

   - Click **Demote**.

To change a SmartArt graphic's layout

1. Click the SmartArt graphic.

2. On the **Design** tool tab, in the **Layouts** group, click the **More** button in the lower-right corner of the **Layouts** gallery.

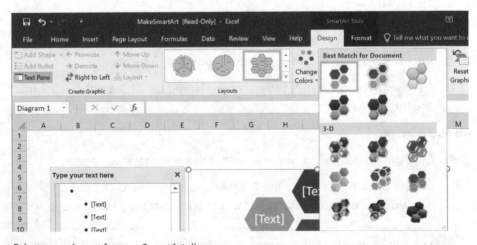

Select a new layout for your SmartArt diagram.

3. Click the new layout.

To change a SmartArt graphic's color scheme

1. Click the SmartArt graphic.

2. On the **Design** tool tab, in the **SmartArt Styles** group, click the **Change Colors** button and click a new color scheme.

To apply a SmartArt Style

1. Click the SmartArt graphic.

2. In the **SmartArt Styles** group, click the **More** button in the lower-right corner of the **SmartArt Styles** gallery, and click the style you want to apply.

To format a shape

1. Click the shape you want to format.

2. Use the tools on the **Format** tool tab to change the shape's formatting.

To delete a SmartArt diagram

1. Right-click the diagram, and then click **Cut**.

Create and manage shapes

With Excel, you can analyze your worksheet data in many ways, including summarizing your data and business processes visually by using charts and SmartArt. You can also augment your worksheets by adding objects such as geometric shapes, lines, flowchart symbols, and banners.

 TIP A SmartArt diagram is a collection of shapes that Excel treats as a collective unit. The shapes described in this topic are individual objects that Excel manages independently.

After you draw a shape on a worksheet, or select it after you've drawn it, you can use the controls on the Format tool tab of the ribbon to change its appearance.

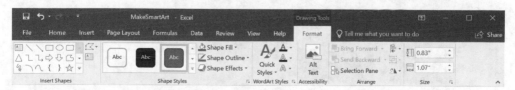

Change shape formatting by using tools on the Drawing Tools Format tool tab.

> ✓ **TIP** Holding down the Shift key while you draw a shape keeps the shape's height, width, and other characteristics equal. For example, clicking the Rectangle tool and then holding down the Shift key while you draw the shape causes you to draw a square.

You can resize a shape by clicking the shape and then dragging one of the resizing handles that appears around the edge of the shape. You can drag a handle on a side of the shape to drag that side to a new position; if you drag a handle on the corner of the shape, you affect height and width simultaneously. If you hold down the Shift key while you drag a shape's corner, Excel keeps the shape's height and width in proportion as you drag the corner. You can also rotate a shape until it is in the orientation you want.

> ✓ **TIP** You can assign your shape a specific height and width by clicking the shape and then, on the Format tool tab, in the Size group, entering the values you want in the Shape Height and Shape Width boxes.

After you create a shape, you can use the controls on the Format tool tab to change its formatting. You can apply predefined styles or use the options accessible from the Shape Fill, Shape Outline, and Shape Effects buttons to change those aspects of the shape's appearance.

> ✓ **TIP** When you point to a formatting option, such as a style or option displayed in the Shape Fill, Shape Outline, or Shape Effects lists, Excel displays a live preview of how your shape would appear if you applied that formatting option. You can preview as many options as you want before committing to a change.

If you want to use a shape as a label or header in a worksheet, you can add text to the shape's interior by clicking the shape and typing. If you want to edit a shape's text, point to the text. When the mouse pointer is in position, it will change from a white pointer with a four-pointed arrow to a black I-bar. You can then click the text to start editing it or change its formatting.

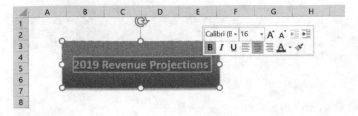

Add text to shapes to make your labels stand out.

You can move a shape within your worksheet by dragging it to a new position. If your worksheet contains multiple shapes, you can align and distribute them within the worksheet. Aligning shapes horizontally means arranging them so they are lined up by their top edge, bottom edge, or horizontal center. Aligning them vertically means lining them up so that they have the same right edge, left edge, or vertical center. Distributing shapes moves the shapes so they have a consistent horizontal or vertical distance between them.

If you have multiple shapes on a worksheet, you will find that Excel arranges them from front to back, placing newer shapes in front of older shapes.

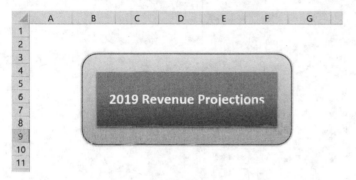

Align shapes to make more attractive worksheets.

You can change the order of the shapes to create exactly the arrangement you want, whether by moving a shape one step forward or backward, or by moving it all the way to the front or back of the stack.

Create and manage mathematical equations

One other way to enhance your Excel files is to add mathematical equations to a worksheet. You can create a wide range of formulas by using built-in structures and symbols.

Build an equation by using the tools on the Equation Tools Design tool tab of the ribbon.

> **TIP** Clicking the arrow at the bottom of the Equation button at the left end of the Equation Tools tab displays a list of common equations, such as the Pythagorean Theorem, that you can add with a single click.

Excel 2019 also provides the new capability of interpreting a handwritten equation that you draw directly into your worksheet.

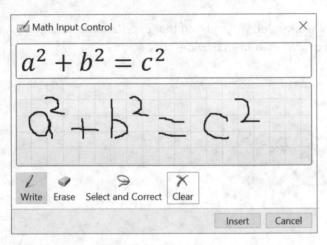

Create an equation by writing it in the Ink Equation dialog box.

To add a shape to a worksheet

1. On the **Insert** tab, in the **Illustrations** group, click the **Shapes** button to display the **Shapes** list.

2. Click the shape you want to add.

3. Click and drag in the body of the worksheet to define the shape.

To move a shape

1. Click the shape and drag it to its new location.

To resize a shape

1. Do either of the following:

   • Grab a handle on an edge or corner of the shape and drag inward or outward to move one or more edges.

   • On the **Format** tool tab, in the **Size** group, enter new values in the **Shape Height** and **Shape Width** boxes.

To rotate a shape

1. Click the shape and do one of the following:

   - Drag the rotate handle (it looks like a clockwise-pointing circular arrow) above the shape to a new position.

   - On the **Format** tool tab, in the **Arrange** group, click the **Rotate** button, and then select the rotate option you want.

   - Click the **Rotate** button, and then click **More Rotation Options** to use the tools in the **Format Shape** task pane.

To change shape formatting

1. Click the shape you want to format.

2. Use the tools on the **Format** tool tab to change the shape's appearance.

To add text to a shape

1. Click the shape.

2. Enter the text you want to appear in the shape.

3. Click outside the shape to stop editing its text

To edit shape text

1. Point to the text in the shape. When the mouse pointer changes to a thin I-bar, click once.

2. Edit the shape's text.

3. Click outside the shape to stop editing its text.

To format shape text

1. Point to the text in the shape. When the mouse pointer changes to a thin I-bar, click once.

2. Select the text you want to edit.

3. Use the tools on the mini toolbar and the **Home** tab of the ribbon to format the text.

4. Click outside the shape to stop editing its text.

9

To align shapes

1. Select the shapes you want to align.

2. On the **Format** tool tab, in the **Arrange** group, click the **Align** button.

3. Click the alignment option you want to apply to your shapes.

To distribute shapes

1. Select three or more shapes.

2. Click the **Align** button, and do either of the following:

    *   Click **Distribute Horizontally** to place the shapes on the worksheet with evenly spaced horizontal gaps between them.

    *   Click **Distribute Vertically** to place the shapes on the worksheet with evenly spaced vertical gaps between them.

To reorder shapes

1. Click the shape you want to move.

2. In the **Arrange** group, do either of the following:

    *   Click the **Bring Forward** arrow, and then click **Bring Forward** or **Bring to Front**.

    *   Click the **Send Backward** arrow, and then click **Send Backward** or **Send to Back**.

To delete a shape

1. Click the shape.

2. Press **Delete**.

To add a preset equation to a worksheet

1. On the **Insert** tab, in the **Symbols** group, click the **Equation** arrow (not the button).

2. Click the equation you want to add.

To add an equation to a worksheet

1. In the **Symbols** group, click the **Equation** button.

2. Use the tools on the **Design** tool tab of the ribbon to create the equation.

To add a handwritten equation to a worksheet

1. Click the **Equation** arrow.

2. Click **Ink Equation**.

3. In the **Write Math Here** area, write the equation you want to enter.

4. Click **Insert**.

To edit an equation

1. Click the part of the equation you want to edit.

2. Enter new values for the equation.

To delete an equation

1. Click the edge of the equation's shape to select it.

2. Press **Delete**.

Skills review

In this chapter, you learned how to:

- Create charts
- Perform business intelligence analysis using charts
- Customize chart appearance
- Find trends in your data
- Create combo charts
- Summarize your data by using sparklines
- Create diagrams by using SmartArt
- Create and manage shapes
- Create and manage mathematical equations

9

Practice tasks

The practice files for these tasks are located in the Excel2019SBS\Ch09 folder. You can save the results of the tasks in the same folder.

Create charts

Open the CreateCharts workbook in Excel, and then perform the following tasks:

1. Using the values on the **Data** worksheet, create a column chart.

2. Change the column chart so it uses the **Year** values in cells **A3:A9** as the horizontal (category) axis values, and the **Volume** values in cells **B3:B9** as the vertical axis values.

3. Using the same set of values, create a line chart.

4. Using the Quick Analysis Lens, create a pie chart from the same data.

Perform business intelligence analysis using charts

Open the CreateNewCharts workbook in Excel, and then perform the following tasks:

1. Use the data on the **Funnel** worksheet to create a funnel chart.

2. Use the data on the **Mapping** worksheet to create a 2D map by state.

3. Use the data on the **Waterfall** worksheet to create a waterfall chart. Identify the **Starting Balance** and **Total** values as totals.

4. Use the data on the **Histogram** worksheet to create a histogram.

5. Use the data on the **Pareto** worksheet to create a Pareto chart.

6. Use the data on the **BoxAndWhisker** worksheet to create a box-and-whisker chart.

7. Use the data on the **Treemap** worksheet to create a treemap chart.

8. Use the data on the **Sunburst** worksheet to create a sunburst chart.

Customize chart appearance

Open the CustomizeCharts workbook in Excel, and then perform the following tasks:

1. Using the chart on the **Presentation** worksheet, change the chart's color scheme.

2. Change the same chart's layout.

3. Using the chart on the **Yearly Summary** worksheet, change the chart's type to a line chart.

4. Move the chart on the **Yearly Summary** worksheet to a new chart sheet.

Find trends in your data

Open the IdentifyTrends workbook in Excel, and then perform the following tasks:

1. Using the chart on the **Data** worksheet, add a linear trendline that draws the best-fit line through the existing data.

2. Edit the trendline so it shows a forecast two periods into the future.

3. Delete the trendline.

Create combo charts

Open the MakeComboCharts workbook in Excel, and then perform the following tasks:

1. Using the data on the **Summary** worksheet, create a dual-axis chart that displays the **Volume** series as a column chart and the **Exceptions** series as a line chart.

2. Ensure that the **Exceptions** values are plotted on the minor vertical axis at the right edge of the chart.

Summarize your data by using sparklines

Open the CreateSparklines workbook in Excel, and then perform the following tasks:

1. Using the data in cells **C3:C14**, create a line sparkline in cell **G3**.

2. Using the data in cells **C3:C14**, create a column sparkline in cell **H3**.

3. Using the data in cells **E3:E14**, create a win/loss sparkline in cell **I3**.

4. Change the color scheme of the win/loss sparkline.

5. Delete the sparkline in cell **H3**.

Create diagrams by using SmartArt

Open the MakeSmartArt workbook in Excel, and then perform the following tasks:

1. Create a process SmartArt diagram.

2. Fill in the shapes with the steps for a process with which you're familiar.

3. Add a shape to the process.

4. Change the place where one of the shapes appears in the diagram.

5. Change the diagram's color scheme.

6. Delete a shape from the diagram.

Create and manage shapes and mathematical equations

Open the CreateShapes workbook in Excel, and then perform the following tasks:

1. Create three shapes and add text to each of them.

2. Edit and format the text in one of the shapes.

3. Move the shapes so you can determine which is in front, which is in the middle, and which is in back.

4. Change the shapes' order and observe how it changes the appearance of the worksheet.

5. Align the shapes so their middles are on the same line.

6. Distribute the shapes evenly in the horizontal direction.

7. Delete one of the shapes.

Create and manage mathematical equations

Open the CreateEquations workbook in Excel, and then perform the following tasks:

1. Add a built-in equation such as the quadratic formula.

2. Enter an equation manually.

Use PivotTables and PivotCharts

10

In this chapter

When you create Excel 2019 worksheets, you must consider how you want the data to appear when you show it to your colleagues. You can change the formatting of your data to emphasize the contents of specific cells, sort and filter your worksheets based on the contents of specific columns, or hide rows containing data that isn't relevant to the point you're trying to make.

One limitation of the standard Excel worksheet is that you can't easily change how the data is organized on the page. Fortunately, there is an Excel tool with which you can create worksheets that can be sorted, filtered, and rearranged dynamically to emphasize different aspects of your data. That tool is the PivotTable.

This chapter guides you through procedures related to creating and editing PivotTables from an existing worksheet, focusing your PivotTable data by using filters and slicers, formatting PivotTables, creating a PivotTable with data imported from a text file, and summarizing your data visually by using a PivotChart.

- Analyze data dynamically by using PivotTables

- Filter, show, and hide PivotTable data

- Edit PivotTables

- Format PivotTables

- Create PivotTables from external data

- Create dynamic charts by using PivotCharts

Practice files

For this chapter, use the practice files from the Excel2019SBS\Ch10 folder. For practice file download instructions, see the introduction.

Analyze data dynamically by using PivotTables

In Excel worksheets, you can gather and present important data, but the standard worksheet can't be easily changed from its original configuration. As an example, consider a worksheet that records monthly package volumes for each of nine distribution centers in the United States. The data in the worksheet is organized so that each row represents a distribution center, and each column represents a month of the year.

	A	B	C	D	E	F	G	H
1								
2		January	February	March	April	May	June	July
3	Atlantic	6042842	3098663	3210406	3002529	3368888	3208696	3115294
4	Central	6006191	2932222	3167785	2989245	3576763	2973980	3364482
5	Midwest	5720977	3456904	3046753	3125231	3280768	3035619	2945492
6	Mountain West	5872046	2935951	3265252	3071049	3159233	3063572	3456576
7	North Central	6236863	3785068	2929397	2677853	3079267	3040653	3521947
8	Northeast	6370982	3281469	3725669	3148289	3165070	2990986	3329821
9	Northwest	6108382	4216668	3640750	2997048	3236144	2849014	3403395
10	Southeast	6396724	4877758	4387252	3583479	3513158	3009637	3175859
11	Southwest	5949454	4413610	3226583	3006170	3019281	2801259	3087404
12	Grand Total	54704461	32998313	30599847	27600893	29398572	26973416	29400270

Static worksheets summarize data one way.

Such a neutral presentation of your data is useful, but it has limitations. First, although you can use sorting and filtering to restrict the rows or columns shown, it's difficult to change the worksheet's organization. For example, in this worksheet, you can't easily reorganize its contents so that the months are assigned to the rows and the distribution centers are assigned to the columns.

To reorganize and redisplay your data dynamically, you can use the PivotTable. In Excel 2019, you can quickly create a PivotTable from the Recommended PivotTables dialog box.

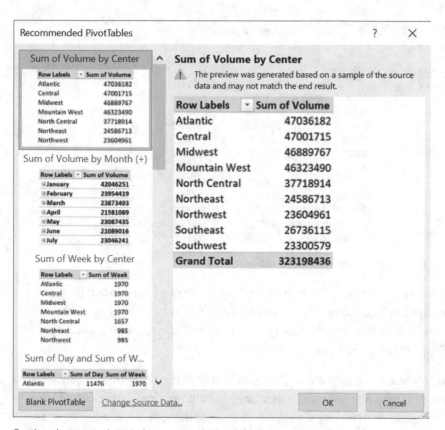

Excel analyzes your data and recommends PivotTable layouts.

Pointing to a recommended PivotTable shows a preview of what that PivotTable would look like if you clicked that option, so you can view several possibilities before deciding which one to create.

 TIP If Excel 2019 has no recommended PivotTables for your data, it gives you the option to create a blank PivotTable.

If none of the recommended PivotTables meet your needs, you can create a PivotTable by adding individual fields. For instance, you can create a PivotTable with the same layout as the worksheet described previously, which emphasizes totals by month, and then change the PivotTable layout to have the rows represent the months of the year and the columns represent the distribution centers. The new layout emphasizes the totals by regional distribution center.

	A	B	C	D	E
1					
2					
3	Sum of Volume	Column Labels ▾			
4	Row Labels ▾	Atlantic	Central	Midwest	Mountain West
5	January	6042842	6006191	5720977	5872046
6	February	3098663	2932222	3456904	2935951
7	March	3210406	3167785	3046753	3265252
8	April	3002529	2989245	3125231	3071049
9	May	3368888	3576763	3280768	3159233
10	June	3208696	2973980	3035619	3063572
11	July	3115294	3364482	2945492	3456576
12	August	3237645	3191591	3441757	3371850
13	September	3072723	2807222	3166599	2942925
14	October	3261585	3362250	3333751	3182437
15	November	6137174	6083306	6236356	6121929

Reorganize your PivotTable by changing the order of fields.

To create a PivotTable quickly, you must have your data collected in a list. Excel tables mesh perfectly with PivotTable dynamic views. Excel tables have a well-defined column and row structure, and the ability to refer to an Excel table by its name greatly simplifies PivotTable creation and management.

In an Excel table used to create a PivotTable, each row of the table should contain a value representing the attribute described by each column. Columns could include data on distribution centers, years, months, days, weekdays, and package volumes, for example. Excel needs that data when it creates the PivotTable so that it can maintain relationships among the data.

> ⚠️ **IMPORTANT** It's OK if some cells in the source data list or Excel table are blank, but the source must not contain any blank rows. If Excel encounters a blank row while creating a PivotTable, it stops looking for additional data.

	A	B	C	D	E	F	G	H	I
1									
2		Center ▾	Date ▾	Year ▾	Month ▾	Week ▾	Day ▾	Weekday ▾	Volume ▾
3		Atlantic	1/1/2017	2017	January	1	1	Wednesday	120933
4		Atlantic	1/2/2017	2017	January	1	2	Thursday	52979
5		Atlantic	1/3/2017	2017	January	1	3	Friday	45683
6		Atlantic	1/4/2017	2017	January	1	4	Saturday	53152
7		Atlantic	1/5/2017	2017	January	1	5	Sunday	149776
8		Atlantic	1/6/2017	2017	January	1	6	Monday	108772
9		Atlantic	1/7/2017	2017	January	1	7	Tuesday	99919
10		Atlantic	1/8/2017	2017	January	2	8	Wednesday	138271
11		Atlantic	1/9/2017	2017	January	2	9	Thursday	77451
12		Atlantic	1/10/2017	2017	January	2	10	Friday	130536
13		Atlantic	1/11/2017	2017	January	2	11	Saturday	119809

Use an Excel table or list of data to create a PivotTable.

After you identify the data you want to summarize, you can start creating your PivotTable.

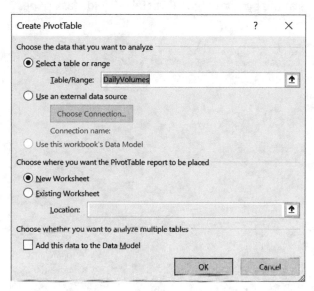

Verify the data source and target location of your PivotTable.

In most cases, the best choice is to place your new PivotTable on its own worksheet to avoid cluttering the display. If you do want to put it on an existing worksheet, perhaps as part of a summary worksheet with multiple visualizations, you can do so.

10

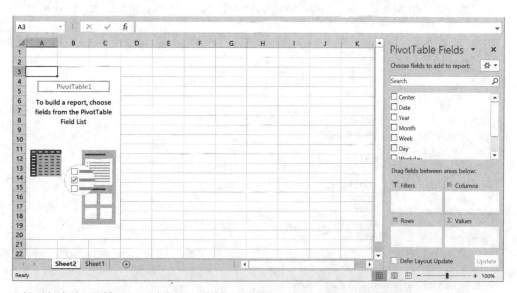

Add a blank PivotTable to a worksheet, and then add data and organization information.

PivotTables have four areas where you can place fields: Rows, Columns, Values, and Filters. To define your PivotTable's data structure, drag field names from the PivotTable field list to the four areas at the bottom of the PivotTable Fields task pane.

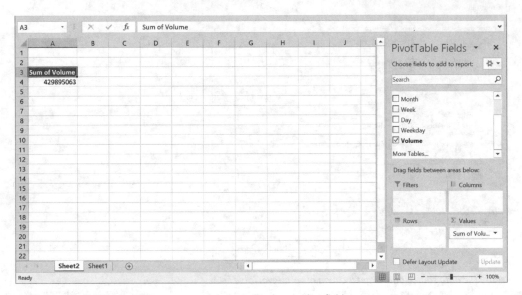

Adding a data field to the Values area summarizes all values in that field.

It's important to note that the order in which you enter the fields in the Rows and Columns areas affects how Excel organizes the data in your PivotTable. As an example, consider a PivotTable that groups the PivotTable rows by distribution center and then by month.

	A	B
3	Row Labels	Sum of Volume
4	Atlantic	47036182
5	January	6042842
6	February	3098663
7	March	3210406
8	April	3002529
9	May	3368888
10	June	3208696
11	July	3115294
12	August	3237645
13	September	3072723
14	October	3261585
15	November	6137174
16	December	6279737
17	Central	47001715
18	January	6006191
19	February	2932222

A PivotTable with package volume data arranged by distribution center and then by month.

The same PivotTable data could also be organized by month and then by distribution center.

Row Labels	Sum of Volume
⊟ January	54704461
Atlantic	6042842
Central	6006191
Midwest	5720977
Mountain West	5872046
North Central	6236863
Northeast	6370982
Northwest	6108382
Southeast	6396724
Southwest	5949454
⊟ February	32998313
Atlantic	3098663
Central	2932222

A PivotTable with package volume data arranged by month and then by distribution center.

In the preceding examples, all the field headers are in the Rows area. If you drag the Distribution Center header from the Rows area to the Columns area in the PivotTable Fields pane, the PivotTable reorganizes (pivots) its data to form a different configuration.

Sum of Volume	Column Labels				
Row Labels	Atlantic	Central	Midwest	Mountain West	North Central
January	6042842	6006191	5720977	5872046	6236863
February	3098663	2932222	3456904	2935951	3785068
March	3210406	3167785	3046753	3265252	2929397
April	3002529	2989245	3125231	3071049	2677853
May	3368888	3576763	3280768	3159233	3079267
June	3208696	2973980	3035619	3063572	3040653
July	3115294	3364482	2945492	3456576	3521947
August	3237645	3191591	3441757	3371850	3166710
September	3072723	2807222	3166599	2942925	2996901
October	3261585	3362250	3333751	3182437	3125591
November	6137174	6083306	6236356	6121929	6026826
December	6279737	6546678	6099560	5880670	6093514
Grand Total	47036182	47001715	46889767	46323490	46680590

A PivotTable arranged in cross-tabular format.

10

If your data set is large or if you based your PivotTable on a data collection on another computer, it might take some time for Excel to reorganize the PivotTable after a pivot. You can have Excel delay redrawing the PivotTable until you're ready for Excel to display the reorganized contents.

If you expect your PivotTable source data to change, such as when you link to an external database, you should ensure that your PivotTable summarizes all the available data. To do that, you can refresh the PivotTable connection to its data source. If Excel detects new data in the source table, it updates the PivotTable contents accordingly.

To organize your data for use in a PivotTable

1. Do either of the following:

   - Create an Excel table.

   - Create a data list that contains no blank rows or columns and has no extraneous data surrounding the list.

To create a recommended PivotTable

1. Click a cell in the Excel table or data list you want to summarize.

2. On the **Insert** tab of the ribbon, in the **Tables** group, click **Recommended PivotTables**.

3. In the **Recommended PivotTables** dialog box, click the recommended PivotTable you want to create.

4. Click **OK** to create the recommended PivotTable on a new worksheet.

To create a PivotTable

1. Click a cell in the Excel table or data list you want to summarize.

2. In the **Tables** group, click **PivotTable**.

3. In the **Create PivotTable** dialog box, verify that Excel has correctly identified the data source you want to use.

4. Click **New Worksheet**.

   Or

   Click **Existing Worksheet**, click in the **Location** box, and click the cell where you want the PivotTable to start.

5. Click **OK**.

To add fields to a PivotTable

1. Click a cell in the PivotTable.

2. On the **Analyze** tool tab of the ribbon, in the **Show** group, click **Field List** to display the **PivotTable Fields** pane.

3. In the **PivotTable Fields** pane, drag a field header from the field list to the **Data**, **Columns**, **Rows**, or **Filters** area.

To remove a field from a PivotTable

1. In the **PivotTable Fields** pane, drag a field header from the **Data**, **Columns**, **Rows**, or **Filters** area to the field list.

To pivot a PivotTable

1. In the **PivotTable Fields** pane, drag a field header from the **Data**, **Columns**, **Rows**, or **Filters** area to another area.

To defer PivotTable updates

1. In the **PivotTable Fields** pane, select the **Defer Layout Update** check box.

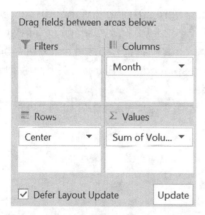

Defer PivotTable updates that might take a while to execute.

2. When you want to update your PivotTable, click **Update**.

3. To turn updating back on, clear the **Defer Layout Update** check box.

Filter, show, and hide PivotTable data

PivotTables often summarize huge data sets in a relatively small worksheet. The more details you can capture and write to a table, the more flexibility you have in analyzing the data. As an example, consider a table in which each row contains a value representing the distribution center, date, month, week, weekday, day, and volume for every day of the year. You could filter this data to only display values for Mondays.

	Center	Date	Year	Month	Week	Day	Weekday	Volume
4	Atlantic	1/2/2017	2017	January	1	2	Monday	52979
11	Atlantic	1/9/2017	2017	January	2	9	Monday	77451
18	Atlantic	1/16/2017	2017	January	3	16	Monday	119081
25	Atlantic	1/23/2017	2017	January	4	23	Monday	49040
32	Atlantic	1/30/2017	2017	January	5	30	Monday	108356
39	Atlantic	2/6/2017	2017	February	1	6	Monday	18459
46	Atlantic	2/13/2017	2017	February	2	13	Monday	28649
53	Atlantic	2/20/2017	2017	February	3	20	Monday	74467
60	Atlantic	2/27/2017	2017	February	4	27	Monday	46684
67	Atlantic	3/6/2017	2017	March	1	6	Monday	27525
74	Atlantic	3/13/2017	2017	March	2	13	Monday	29137

Filter Excel tables to focus on relevant data.

Each column, in turn, contains numerous values: There are nine distribution centers, data from two years, 12 months in a year, seven weekdays, and as many as five weeks and 31 days in a month. Just as you can filter the data that appears in an Excel table or other data collection, you can filter the data displayed in a PivotTable by selecting which values you want the PivotTable to include.

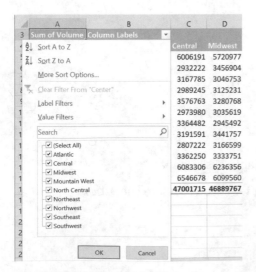

Filter a PivotTable by clicking a filter arrow.

SEE ALSO For more information about filtering an Excel table, see "Limit data that appears on your screen" in Chapter 5, "Manage worksheet data."

Clicking the column header in the PivotTable displays several sorting options, commands for different categories of filters, and a list of items that appear in the field you want to filter. Every list item has a check box next to it. Items whose check boxes are selected are currently displayed in the PivotTable, and items whose check boxes are cleared are hidden.

The first entry at the top of the item list is the Select All check box. The Select All check box can have one of three states:

- **Displaying a check mark** If the Select All check box displays a check mark, the PivotTable displays every item in the list.

- **Displaying a black square** If the Select All check box contains a black square, it means that some, but not all, of the items in the list are displayed.

- **Cleared** If the Select All check box is cleared, no filter items are selected.

Selecting only the Northwest check box, for example, leads to a PivotTable configuration in which only the data for the Northwest center is displayed.

	A	B	C
3	Sum of Volume	Column Labels	
4	Row Labels	Northwest	Grand Total
5	2017	23604961	23604961
6	January	3023030	3023030
7	February	1662538	1662538
8	March	1708446	1708446
9	April	1648903	1648903
10	May	1607655	1607655
11	June	1373976	1373976
12	July	1570950	1570950
13	August	1767367	1767367
14	September	1582032	1582032
15	October	1744048	1744048
16	November	2982666	2982666
17	December	2933350	2933350
18	2018	25028389	25028389
19	January	3085352	3085352

Sheet2 Sheet1 +

Limit data by using selection filters.

If you'd rather display PivotTable data on the entire worksheet, you can hide the PivotTable Fields pane and filter the PivotTable by using the filter arrows on the Row Labels and Column Labels headers within the body of the PivotTable. Excel indicates that a PivotTable has filters applied by placing a filter indicator next to the Column Labels or Row Labels header, as appropriate, and next to the filtered field name in the PivotTable Fields task pane.

So far, all the fields by which we've talked about filtering the PivotTable will change the organization of the data in the PivotTable. Adding some fields to a PivotTable, however, might create unwanted complexity. For example, you might want to filter a PivotTable by month, but adding the Month field to the body of the PivotTable expands the table unnecessarily.

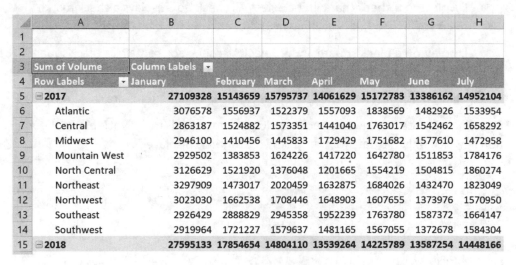

	A	B	C	D	E	F	G	H
1								
2								
3	Sum of Volume	Column Labels						
4	Row Labels	January	February	March	April	May	June	July
5	2017	27109328	15143659	15795737	14061629	15172783	13386162	14952104
6	Atlantic	3076578	1556937	1522379	1557093	1838569	1482926	1533954
7	Central	2863187	1524882	1573351	1441040	1763017	1542462	1658292
8	Midwest	2946100	1410456	1445833	1729429	1751682	1577610	1472958
9	Mountain West	2929502	1383853	1624226	1417220	1642780	1511853	1784176
10	North Central	3126629	1521920	1376048	1201665	1554219	1504815	1860274
11	Northeast	3297909	1473017	2020459	1632875	1684026	1432470	1823049
12	Northwest	3023030	1662538	1708446	1648903	1607655	1373976	1570950
13	Southeast	2926429	2888829	2945358	1952239	1763780	1587372	1664147
14	Southwest	2919964	1721227	1579637	1481165	1567055	1372678	1584304
15	2018	27595133	17854654	14804110	13539264	14225789	13587254	14448166

Adding multiple fields to an area substantially expands PivotTables.

Instead of adding the Month field to the Rows or Columns area, adding the field to the Filters area leaves the body of the PivotTable unchanged, but adds a new filter control above the PivotTable in its worksheet. When you click the filter arrow of a field in the Filters area, Excel displays a list of the values in the field. You can choose to filter based on one or more values.

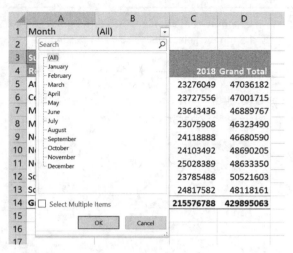

Add a field to the Filter area to filter a PivotTable without changing its organization.

 TIP In Excel 2003 and earlier versions, the Filter area was called the Page Field area.

If your PivotTable has more than one field in the Rows area of the PivotTable Fields pane, you can filter values in a PivotTable by hiding and collapsing levels of detail within the report. To do that, you click the Hide Detail control (which looks like a box with a minus sign in it) or the Show Detail control (which looks like a box with a plus sign in it) next to a header.

Summarize levels of data by using the Show Detail and Hide Detail controls.

10

Excel 2019 provides two other ways for you to filter PivotTables: search filters and slicers. By using a search filter, you can enter a series of characters for Excel to use to filter that field's values.

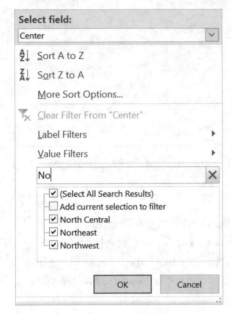

Filter a PivotTable field by using a search filter.

In versions of Excel prior to Excel 2013, the only visual indication that you had applied a filter to a field was the indicator added to a field's filter arrow. The indicator told users that there was an active filter applied to that field but provided no information on which values were displayed and which were hidden. In Excel 2019, slicers provide a visual indication of which items are currently displayed or hidden in a PivotTable.

When you're ready to create a slicer, you display the Insert Slicers dialog box and select the data you want to filter.

Select fields for which you want to display a slicer.

After you make your selections, Excel displays a slicer for each field you identified.

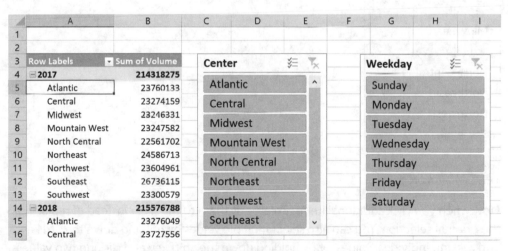

Slicers provide visually summarized values affected by filters.

TIP If you have already applied a filter to the field for which you display a slicer, the slicer reflects the filter's result.

A slicer displays the values within the PivotTable field you identified. Any value displayed in color (or gray if you have a gray-and-white color scheme) appears within the PivotTable. Values displayed in light gray or white do not appear in the PivotTable.

Clicking an item in a slicer changes that item's state. If a value is currently displayed in a PivotTable, clicking it hides it. If it's hidden, clicking its value in the slicer displays it in the PivotTable. As with other objects in an Excel 2019 workbook, you can use the Shift and Ctrl keys to help define your selections.

Clicking a value creates a filter that limits the data displayed to only that value, and clicking a selected value removes it from the filter. If you want to display values related to multiple items in the slicer, click the Multi-Select button on the slicer's title bar. The Multi-Select button looks like a list of items preceded by check marks.

Select multiple items in a slicer by using Multi-Select.

Now when you click additional items, Excel adds them to the slicer instead of replacing the original selection. You can also select multiple values by holding down the Ctrl key and clicking individual values, or by holding down the Shift key and clicking two values in sequence, which selects the two values you clicked and all values between them.

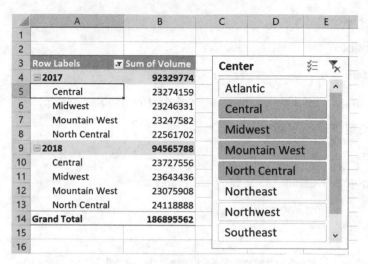

Slicers provide a visual reference for filtered fields.

As with other drawing objects in Excel, you can move and resize the slicer as needed. When you're done filtering values, you can clear the slicer filter and get rid of the slicer entirely.

 TIP You can change a slicer's formatting by clicking the slicer and then, on the Slicer Tools Options tool tab on the ribbon, clicking a style in the Slicer Styles gallery.

10

To filter a PivotTable by using the values in a field

1. In the body of a PivotTable, click the filter arrow at the right edge of a field header.

2. Use the controls in the filter list to create your filter.

3. Click **OK**.

To hide the PivotTable Fields pane

1. Click the **Close** button in the upper-right corner of the **PivotTable Fields** pane.

Or

1. Click a cell in the body of the PivotTable.

2. On the **Analyze** tool tab of the ribbon, in the **Show** group, click the **Field List** button.

To show the PivotTable Fields task pane

1. Click a cell in the body of the PivotTable.

2. Click the **Field List** button.

To filter a PivotTable by using a field in the Filters area of the PivotTable Fields pane

1. Display the **PivotTable Fields** pane.

2. Drag a field to the **Filters** area.

3. In the **Filter** area of the PivotTable, click the field's filter arrow.

4. Click the value by which you want to filter.

   Or

   Select the **Select Multiple Items** check box and select the check boxes next to the items you want to appear in the PivotTable.

To hide a level of detail in a PivotTable

1. Click the **Hide Detail** control next to a PivotTable field's row header.

To show a level of detail in a PivotTable

1. Click the **Show Detail** control next to a PivotTable field's row header.

To add a slicer to your workbook

1. Click a cell in the body of the PivotTable.

2. On the **Analyze** tool tab, in the **Filter** group, click the **Insert Slicer** button.

3. In the **Insert Slicers** dialog box, select the check box next to the field for which you want to create a slicer.

4. Click **OK**.

To select multiple values in a slicer filter

1. On the **Slicer** title bar, click the **Multi-Select** button.

2. Click the values you want to appear in the PivotTable.

To filter a field by using a slicer

1. In the body of the **slicer**, do any of the following:

   • Click the single value you want to display.

- Hold down the **Ctrl** key and click the values you want to display.

- Hold down the **Shift** key and click two values to display those values and all values between them.

To clear the filter in a slicer

1. On the **slicer** title bar, click the **Clear Filter** button.

To change the appearance of a slicer

1. Right-click the slicer's title bar and then click **Size and Properties**.

2. Use the settings in the **Format Slicer** pane to change the slicer's appearance.

3. Click the pane's **Close** button to close it and apply the changes.

To remove a slicer

1. Right-click the slicer and then click **Remove** *field*.

Edit PivotTables

After you create a PivotTable, you can rename it, edit it to control how it summarizes your data, and use the PivotTable cell data in a formula. As an example, consider a PivotTable named *PivotTable1* that summarizes package volume data.

10

| Sum of Volume | Column Labels ▾ | | |
Row Labels ▾	2017	2018	Grand Total
⊟ **January**	**27109328**	**27595133**	**54704461**
Atlantic	3076578	2966264	6042842
Central	2863187	3143004	6006191
Midwest	2946100	2774877	5720977
Mountain West	2929502	2942544	5872046
North Central	3126629	3110234	6236863
Northeast	3297909	3073073	6370982
Northwest	3023030	3085352	6108382
Southeast	2926429	3470295	6396724
Southwest	2919964	3029490	5949454
⊟ **February**	**15143659**	**17854654**	**32998313**
Atlantic	1556937	1541726	3098663
Central	1524882	1407340	2932222
Midwest	1410456	2046448	3456904
Mountain West	1383853	1552098	2935951
North Central	1521920	2263148	3785068

PivotTables summarize large data sets in a compact format.

Excel assigns the PivotTable a name, such as *PivotTable1*, when you create it. Of course, the name *PivotTable1* doesn't help you or your colleagues understand the data the PivotTable contains, particularly if you use the PivotTable data in a formula on another worksheet. You can provide more information about your PivotTable and the data it contains by changing its name to something more descriptive.

When you create a PivotTable with at least one field in the Rows area and one field in the Columns area of the PivotTable Fields pane, Excel adds a grand total row and column to summarize your data. You can control which totals and subtotals appear, and where they appear, to best suit your data and analysis goals.

After you create a PivotTable, Excel determines the best way to summarize the data in the column you assign to the Values area. For numeric data, for example, Excel uses the *SUM* function, but you can change the function used to summarize your data.

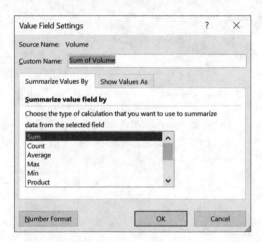

Control how your PivotTable summarizes your values.

You can also change how the PivotTable displays the data in the Values area. Some of these methods include displaying each value as a percentage of the grand total, row total, or column total, or as a running total.

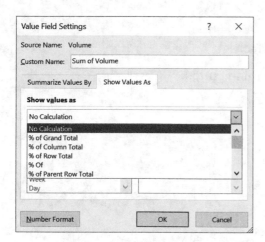

You can change how Excel summarizes values in the body of a PivotTable.

If you want, you can create a formula that incorporates a value from a PivotTable cell. When you get to a point in your formula where you want to use PivotTable data, click the cell that contains the value you want to include in the formula. When you do, a *GETPIVOTDATA* formula appears in the formula bar of the worksheet that contains the PivotTable. When you press the Enter key, Excel creates the *GETPIVOTDATA* formula and displays the contents of the PivotTable cell in the target cell.

To rename a PivotTable

1. Click any cell in the body of the PivotTable.

2. On the **Analyze** tool tab, in the **PivotTable** group, click in the **PivotTable Name** box.

3. Enter a new name for the PivotTable and press the **Enter** key.

To show or hide PivotTable subtotals

1. Click any cell in the body of the PivotTable.

2. On the **Design** tool tab of the ribbon, in the **Layout** group, click the **Subtotals** button.

3. In the list, click any of the following items:

   - **Do Not Show Subtotals**

   - **Show all Subtotals at Bottom of Group**

   - **Show all Subtotals at Top of Group**

To show or hide PivotTable grand totals

1. Click any cell in the body of the PivotTable.

2. In the **Layout** group, click the **Grand Totals** button.

3. In the list, click any of the following items:

   - **Off for Rows and Columns**

   - **On for Rows and Columns**

   - **On for Rows Only**

   - **On for Columns Only**

To change the summary operation for the Values area

1. Click any cell in the body of the PivotTable that contains data.

2. On the **Analyze** tool tab, in the **Active Field** group, click **Field Settings**.

3. In the **Value Field Settings** dialog box, on the **Summarize Values By** tab, click the operation you want to use to summarize your PivotTable data.

4. Click **OK**.

To change how Excel displays data in the Values area

1. Click any cell in the body of the PivotTable that contains data.

2. In the **Value Field Settings** dialog box, on the **Show Values As** tab, click the **Shows values as** arrow.

3. Click the calculation you want to use.

4. If necessary, in the **Base item** list, click the value on which you want to base your calculation.

5. Click **OK**.

To use PivotTable data in a formula

1. Start entering a formula in a cell.

2. When you want to use data from a PivotTable cell in your formula, click the PivotTable cell that contains the data you want to use.

3. Complete the formula and press **Enter**.

Format PivotTables

PivotTables are the ideal tools for summarizing and examining large data tables, even those containing more than 10,000 or even 100,000 rows. Although PivotTables often end up as compact summaries, you should do everything you can to make your data more comprehensible. One way to improve your data's readability is to apply a number format to the PivotTable Values field.

 SEE ALSO For more information about selecting and defining cell formats by using the Format Cells dialog box, see "Format cells" in Chapter 4, "Change workbook appearance."

Analysts often use PivotTables to summarize and examine organizational data for the purpose of making important decisions about the company. Excel extends the capabilities of your PivotTables by enabling you to apply a conditional format to the PivotTable cells. Additionally, you can select whether to apply the conditional format to every cell in the Values area, to every cell at the same level as the selected cell (that is, a regular data cell, a subtotal cell, or a grand total cell), or to every cell that contains or draws its values from the selected cell's field.

	A	B	C
1			
2			
3	Sum of Volume	Column Labels	
4	Row Labels	2017	2018
5	⊟ January		
6	Atlantic	3076578	2966264
7	Central	2863187	3143004
8	Midwest	2946100	2774877
9	Mountain West	2929502	2942544
10	North Central	3126629	3110234
11	Northeast	3297909	3073073
12	Northwest	3023030	3085352
13	Southeast	2926429	3470295
14	Southwest	2919964	3029490
15	⊟ February		
16	Atlantic	1556937	1541726
17	Central	1524882	1407340
18	Midwest	1410456	2046448

Summarize values visually by adding a conditional format.

10

When you apply a conditional format to a PivotTable, Excel displays a Formatting Options button, which offers three options for applying the conditional format:

- **Selected Cells** Applies the conditional format to the selected cells only

- **All Cells Showing Sum of *field* Values** Applies the conditional format to every cell in the body of the PivotTable that contains data, regardless of whether the cell is in the data area, a subtotal row or column, or a grand total row or column

- **All Cells Showing Sum of *field* Values for Fields** Applies the conditional format to every cell at the same level (for example, data cell, subtotal, or grand total) as the selected cells

 SEE ALSO For more information about creating conditional formats, see "Change the appearance of data based on its value" in Chapter 4, "Change workbook appearance."

In Excel, you can take full advantage of the Microsoft Office system enhanced formatting capabilities to apply existing formats to your PivotTables. Just as you can create Excel table formats, you can also create your own PivotTable formats to match your organization's preferred color scheme. After you give the new style a name, you can format each element of PivotTables to which you apply the style.

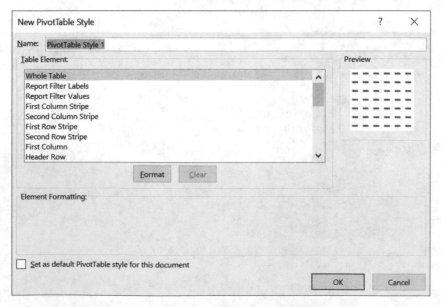

Define custom styles by using the New PivotTable Style dialog box.

The Design tool tab contains many other tools you can use to format your PivotTable, but one of the most useful is the Banded Columns check box. If you select a PivotTable style that offers banded rows as an option, selecting the Banded Rows check box turns banding on. If you prefer not to have Excel band the rows in your PivotTable, clearing the check box turns banding off.

To apply a number format to PivotTable data

1. Click any data cell in the body of the PivotTable.

2. On the **Analyze** tool tab, in the **Active Field** group, click **Field Settings**.

3. In the **Value Field Settings** dialog box, click the **Number Format** button.

4. Use the tools on the **Number** tab of the **Format Cells** dialog box to define a number format for your PivotTable data field.

5. Click **OK** to close the **Format Cells** dialog box, and again to close the **Value Field Settings** dialog box.

To apply a conditional format to a PivotTable

1. Click any data cell in the body of the PivotTable.

2. On the **Home** tab of the ribbon, in the **Styles** group, click the **Conditional Formatting** button, and define the conditional format you want to apply.

3. Next to the cell you selected, click the **Formatting Options** button.

4. Do any of the following:

    • Click **Selected Cells** to apply the conditional format only to the cell you clicked before creating the format.

    • Click **All cells showing "Sum of *field*" values** to format all data cells, including subtotals and grand totals.

    • Click **All cells showing "Sum of *field*" values for "*Field1*" and "*Field2*"** to format all data cells that are not subtotals or grand totals.

To apply an existing PivotTable style

1. Click any cell in the PivotTable.

2. On the **Design** tool tab, in the **PivotTable Styles** group, click the style you want to apply.

10

To create a new PivotTable style

1. Click any cell in the PivotTable.

2. In the **PivotTable Styles** group, click the **More** button (which looks like a downward-pointing black triangle) in the lower-right corner of the **PivotTable Styles** gallery.

3. Click **New PivotTable Style**.

4. In the **New PivotTable Style** dialog box, click in the **Name** box and enter a name for the new **PivotTable style**.

5. In the **Table Element** list, click the element for which you want to define a format.

6. Click the **Format** button.

7. Define a format for the selected element by using the settings in the **Format Cells** dialog box.

8. Click **OK**.

9. Repeat steps 5 through 8 to define formats for other PivotTable elements.

10. Click **OK** to close the **New PivotTable Style** dialog box and apply the style.

To apply banded rows to a PivotTable

1. Click any cell in the body of a PivotTable.

2. If necessary, apply a **PivotTable Style** that includes banded rows.

3. On the **Design** tool tab, in the **PivotTable Style Options** group, select the **Banded Rows** check box.

Create PivotTables from external data

Although most often you will create PivotTables from data stored in Excel worksheets, you can also bring data from outside sources into Excel. For example, you might need to work with data created in another spreadsheet program with a file format that Excel can't read directly. Fortunately, you can export the data from the original program into a text file, which Excel can then translate into a worksheet.

 TIP The data import technique shown here isn't exclusive to PivotTables. You can use this procedure to bring data into your worksheets for any purpose.

Spreadsheet programs store data in cells, so the goal of representing spreadsheet data in a text file is to indicate where the contents of one cell end and those of the next cell begin. The character that marks the end of a cell is a delimiter, in that it marks the end (or "limit") of a cell. The most common cell delimiter is the comma, so the delimited sequence *15, 18, 24, 28* represents data in four cells. The problem with using commas to delimit financial data is that larger values—such as *52,802*—often use a comma as a thousands marker. To avoid confusion when importing a text file, some financial data programs export their data with the tab character as a delimiter.

 TIP You can open files in which the values are separated by commas, called *comma-separated value files*, directly into Excel. These files often have *.csv* extensions.

To start importing data from a text file, you identify the file that contains the data you want to work with.

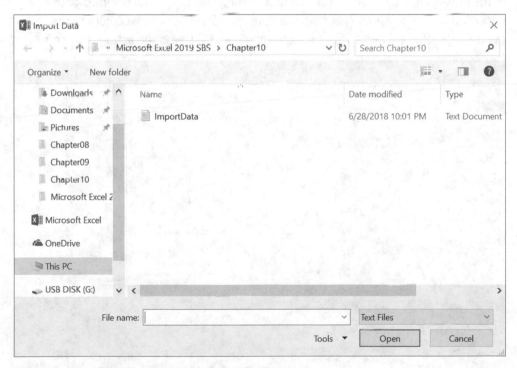

Identify the file you want to import in the Import Data dialog box.

After you identify the file that holds the data you want to import, Excel displays the Get Data dialog box.

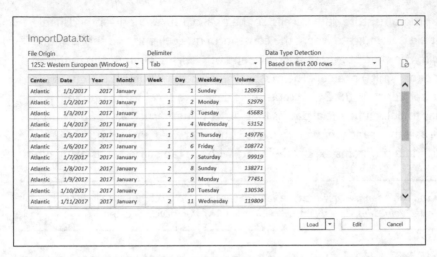

Identify the file origin and delimiter for the data to import.

In the Power Query Editor, you can change settings for individual columns of the imported data, such as by changing the data type assigned to that column or by combining columns. Right-clicking a column header displays the actions you can take to affect that column.

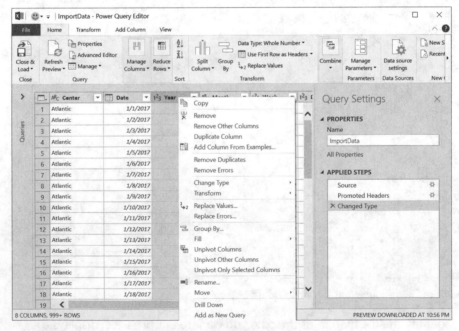

Right-click a column header in the Power Query Editor to control how Excel handles data in the file you want to import.

After you make the necessary changes, you can close the Power Query Editor and load the data into the workbook as an Excel table linked to the original data source, such as a text file. After the data is in Excel, you can work with it normally—including using it to create a PivotTable.

	A	B	C	D	E	F	G	H
1	Center	Date	Year	Month	Week	Day	Weekday	Volume
2	Atlantic	1/1/2017	2017	January	1	1	Sunday	120933
3	Atlantic	1/2/2017	2017	January	1	2	Monday	52979
4	Atlantic	1/3/2017	2017	January	1	3	Tuesday	45683
5	Atlantic	1/4/2017	2017	January	1	4	Wednesday	53152
6	Atlantic	1/5/2017	2017	January	1	5	Thursday	149776
7	Atlantic	1/6/2017	2017	January	1	6	Friday	108772
8	Atlantic	1/7/2017	2017	January	1	7	Saturday	99919
9	Atlantic	1/8/2017	2017	January	2	8	Sunday	138271
10	Atlantic	1/9/2017	2017	January	2	9	Monday	77451
11	Atlantic	1/10/2017	2017	January	2	10	Tuesday	130536
12	Atlantic	1/11/2017	2017	January	2	11	Wednesday	119809
13	Atlantic	1/12/2017	2017	January	2	12	Thursday	64125
14	Atlantic	1/13/2017	2017	January	2	13	Friday	146927
15	Atlantic	1/14/2017	2017	January	2	14	Saturday	62505

Excel stores your imported data as an Excel table.

To import data from a text file

1. Display the worksheet where you want the imported data to appear.

2. On the **Data** tab, in the **Get External Data** group, click **From Text/CSV**.

3. In the **Get Data** dialog box that appears, navigate to the folder that contains the file you want to import, click the file, and then click **Import**.

4. On the first page of the **Get Data** dialog box, verify that the **File Origin** and **Delimiter** values are correct.

5. Click **Load** to import the data into Excel as an Excel table.

   Or

   Click **Edit**, use the controls in the **Power Query Editor** to change the settings of the imported data, and click **Close & Load**.

To create a PivotTable from imported data

1. Click a cell in the imported data list.

2. On the **Insert** tab, in the **Tables** group, click **PivotTable**.

10

3. In the **Create PivotTable** dialog box, verify that Excel has correctly identified the data source you want to use.

4. Select the **New Worksheet** option button.

   Or

   Select the **Existing Worksheet** option button, click in the **Location** box, and click the cell where you want to the PivotTable to start.

5. Click **OK**.

Create dynamic charts by using PivotCharts

Just as you can create a PivotTable that you can reorganize whenever you want to emphasize different aspects of the data in a list, you can also create a dynamic chart, or PivotChart, to reflect the contents and organization of a PivotTable.

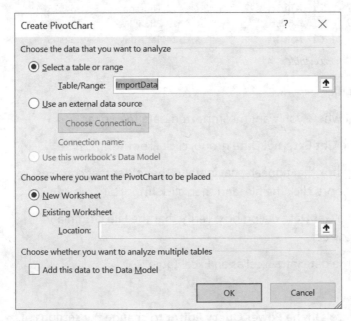

Define a PivotChart in the Create PivotChart dialog box

You can create a PivotTable and its associated PivotChart at the same time, or you can create a PivotChart from an existing PivotTable. If you create the PivotTable and PivotChart at the same time, blank outlines for each appear in your worksheet.

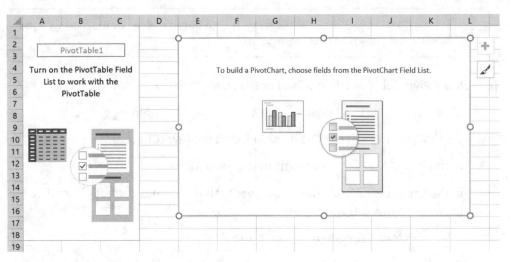

Creating a PivotChart also creates a PivotTable.

Any changes to the PivotTable on which the PivotChart is based are reflected in the PivotChart. For example, applying a PivotTable filter that limits the data displayed to values for the year 2014 focuses the chart on that data.

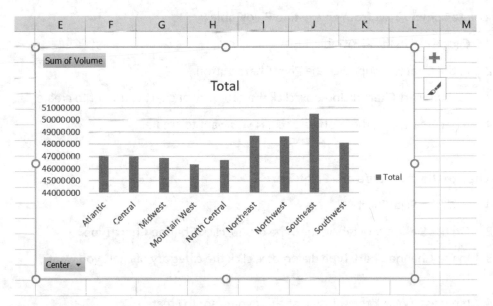

Summarize your data visually by using a PivotChart.

You can also filter a PivotChart by using tools available in the body of the PivotChart or change the PivotChart's chart type to represent your data differently.

IMPORTANT If your data is of the wrong type to be represented by the chart type you select, Excel displays an error message.

To create a PivotTable and PivotChart at the same time

1. Click a cell in the Excel table or data list you want to summarize.

2. On the **Insert** tab, in the **Charts** group, click the **PivotChart** arrow.

3. In the **PivotChart** list, click **PivotChart & PivotTable**.

4. In the **Create PivotTable** dialog box, verify that Excel has correctly identified the data source you want to use.

5. Select the **New Worksheet** option button.

   Or

   Select the **Existing Worksheet** option button, click in the **Location** box, and click the cell where you want to the PivotTable to start.

6. Click **OK**.

To create a PivotChart from an existing PivotTable

1. Click a cell in the PivotTable.

2. In the **Charts** group, click the **PivotChart** button.

3. In the **Insert Chart** dialog box, click the category of chart you want to create.

4. If necessary, click the subtype of chart you want to create.

5. Click **OK**.

To change the chart type of a PivotChart

1. Click the PivotChart.

2. On the **Design** tool tab, in the **Type** group, click **Change Chart Type**.

3. In the **Change Chart Type** dialog box, click the category of chart you want to create.

4. If necessary, click the subtype of chart you want to create.

5. Click **OK**.

Skills review

In this chapter, you learned how to:

- Analyze data dynamically by using PivotTables
- Filter, show, and hide PivotTable data
- Edit PivotTables
- Format PivotTables
- Create PivotTables from external data
- Create dynamic charts by using PivotCharts

10

Practice tasks

The practice files for these tasks are located in the Excel2019SBS\Ch10 folder. You can save the results of the tasks in the same folder.

Analyze data dynamically by using PivotTables

Open the CreatePivotTables workbook in Excel, and then perform the following tasks:

1. Click a cell in the Excel table on **Sheet1** and create a PivotTable based on that data.

2. In the **PivotTable Fields** pane, add the **Year** field to the **Columns** area, the **Center** field to the **Rows** area, and the **Volume** field to the **Values** area.

3. Pivot the PivotTable so the **Year** field is above the **Center** field in the **Rows** area.

Filter, show, and hide PivotTable data

Open the FilterPivotTables workbook in Excel, and then perform the following tasks:

1. Using the **Month** field, create a selection filter that displays data for **January**, **April**, and **July**.

2. Remove the filter.

3. Add the **Weekday** field to the **Filters** area and limit the data shown to **Tuesday**.

4. Change the **Weekday** field's filter to include multiple values, and then set it to display values for **Tuesday** and **Wednesday**.

5. Create a slicer for the **Month** field, and then display values for the month of **December**.

6. Change the slicer filter to allow multiple selections, and then display values for **January** and **December**.

7. Clear the slicer filter, and then delete the slicer.

Edit PivotTables

Open the EditPivotTables workbook in Excel, and then perform the following tasks:

1. Change the name of the PivotTable on **Sheet2** to PackageVolume.

2. Change the PivotTable's subtotals so they appear at the bottom of each group.

3. Change the summary function for the body of the PivotTable from **Sum** to **Average**.

4. In cell **E3**, create a formula that displays the data from cell B5 (the **Sum of Volume** value for the Atlantic center).

Format PivotTables

Open the FormatPivotTables workbook in Excel, and then perform the following tasks:

1. Change the format of the **Volume** field, currently providing data for the **Values** area, so that the numbers are displayed in the **Comma** number format with no digits after the decimal point.

2. Click any cell in the data area of the PivotTable, and then create a conditional format that changes the fill color of cells that contain a value that is above average for the field.

3. Apply a different PivotTable style to the PivotTable.

4. Create a new PivotTable style and apply it.

Create PivotTables from external data

Open the ImportPivotData workbook in Excel, and then perform the following tasks:

1. On the **Data** tab, use the tools in the **Get External Data** group to start importing data from the text file **ImportData.txt**.

2. In the **Get Data** dialog box, identify the tab character as the data file's delimiter, and finish importing the data.

3. Create a PivotTable from the data list consisting of the data you just imported.

Create dynamic charts by using PivotCharts

Open the CreatePivotCharts workbook in Excel, and then perform the following tasks:

1. Click any cell in the Excel table on **Sheet1** and create a clustered column PivotChart with the **Center** field in the **Legend (Series)** area and **Volume** (which will be displayed as *Sum of Volume*) in the **Values** area.

2. Remove the **Center** field from the body of the PivotTable, and then drag the **Year** field to the **Axis (Category)** area.

3. Change the chart type of the PivotChart to a line chart.

4. Add the **Center** field to the **Legend (Series)** area.

Part 3

Collaborate and share in Excel

Print worksheets and charts

11

Microsoft Excel 2019 gives you a wide range of tools with which to create and manipulate your data. By using filters, by sorting, and by creating PivotTables and charts, you can change your worksheets so that they convey the greatest possible amount of information. After you configure your worksheet so that it shows your data to best advantage, you can print your Excel documents to use in a presentation or include in a report. You can choose to print all or part of any of your worksheets, change how your data and charts appear on the printed page, and even suppress any error messages that might appear in your worksheets.

This chapter guides you through procedures related to adding headers and footers to your worksheets, preparing your worksheets for printing, printing all or part of a worksheet, and printing charts.

In this chapter

- Add headers and footers to printed pages
- Prepare worksheets for printing
- Print worksheets
- Print parts of worksheets
- Print charts

Practice files

For this chapter, use the practice files from the Excel2019SBS\Ch11 folder. For practice file download instructions, see the introduction.

Add headers and footers to printed pages

If you want to ensure that the same information appears at the top or bottom of every printed page, you can do so by using headers or footers. A header is a section that appears at the top of every printed page; a footer is a section that appears at the bottom of every printed page.

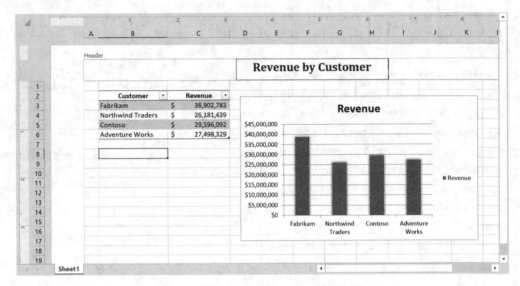

Headers and footers provide space to add information about your workbook.

To view your workbook's headers and footers, you display the workbook in Page Layout view. Page Layout view shows you exactly how your workbook will look when printed, while still enabling you to edit your file—a capability not provided by Print Preview.

Excel divides its headers and footers into left, middle, and right sections. When you point to an editable header or footer section, Excel highlights the section to indicate that clicking will open that header or footer section for editing.

> **TIP** If you have a chart selected when you click the Header & Footer button on the Insert tab, Excel displays the Header/Footer page of the Page Setup dialog box instead of opening a header or footer section for editing.

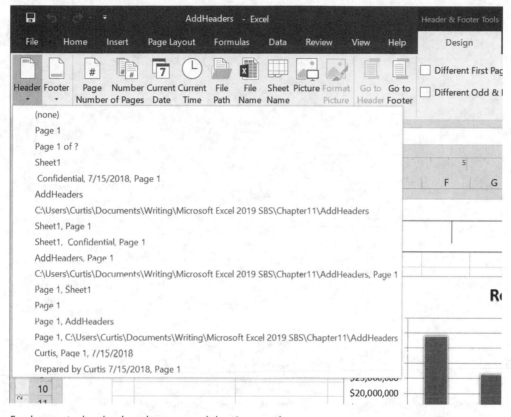

Excel generates headers based on your worksheet's properties.

When you activate a header or footer section, you can add one of several standard headers and footers, such as page numbers by themselves or followed by the name of the workbook. The list of headers that appears will vary depending on the properties and contents of your worksheet and workbook.

You can also create custom headers by entering your own or adding a graphic, such as a company logo, to a worksheet. By adding graphics, you can identify the worksheet as referring to your company and help reinforce your company's brand if you include the worksheet in a printed report distributed outside your company. After you insert a graphic into a header or footer, you can make it larger or smaller, change its appearance, and add borders.

When you print or display a worksheet, you might want to have different headers for odd and even pages, or perhaps just for the first page. After you indicate that you want separate headers, Excel indicates whether a header or footer applies to the first page or, if appropriate, an odd or even page.

Your worksheet's header and footer will always be the same width as the printed worksheet, but you can adjust their vertical size.

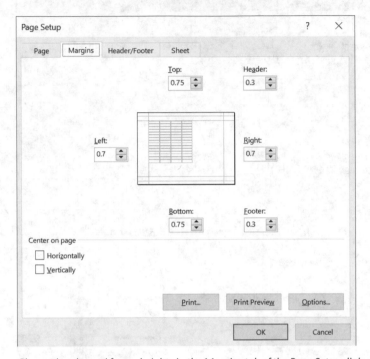

Change header and footer heights in the Margins tab of the Page Setup dialog box.

To edit headers and footers

1. On the **Insert** tab of the ribbon, in the **Text** group, click **Header & Footer**.

2. Click in the header or footer section you want to edit.

To switch between the header and the footer

1. Click **Header & Footer**.

2. Click the **Go to Footer** button to move to the footer.

   Or

   Click the **Go to Header** button to move to the header.

To add text to a header or footer

1. Open a header or footer section for editing.

2. On the **Design** tab of the ribbon, in the **Header & Footer Elements** group, click a button representing the text you want to add to your header or footer.

3. Enter any additional text you want to appear in the header or footer.

4. Use the controls on the **Home** tab to format the text.

To add an automatically generated header or footer

1. Open a header or footer section for editing.

2. In the **Header & Footer** group, click the **Header** button and click the automatically generated header you want to add.

   Or

   Click the **Footer** button and click the automatically generated footer you want to add.

To add a graphic from your computer to a header or footer

1. Open a header or footer section for editing.

2. In the **Header & Footer Elements** group, click **Picture**.

Add a graphic to a header or footer from the Insert Pictures dialog box.

3. In the **Insert Pictures** dialog box, click **From a file**.

4. Navigate to the folder that contains the picture you want to add.

5. Double-click the file.

To edit a graphic in a header or footer

1. Activate the header or footer section that contains the *&[Picture]* code.

2. In the **Header & Footer Elements** group, click **Format Picture**.

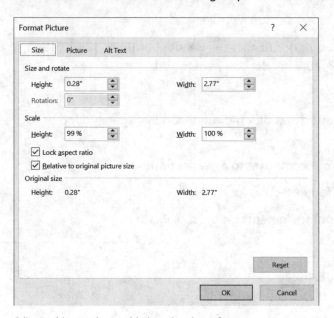

Edit graphics you have added to a header or footer.

3. Make the changes you want in the **Format Picture** dialog box.

4. Click **OK**.

To put a different header on the first printed page

1. Activate a header or footer in your worksheet.

2. In the **Options** group, select the **Different First Page** check box.

3. Display the first page of the worksheet and create its header.

To use separate headers and footers for odd and even pages

1. Activate a header or footer in your workbook.

2. In the **Options** group, select the **Different Odd & Even Pages** check box.

3. Display an odd page and create the header for odd pages.

   Or

   Display an even page and create the header for even pages.

To change the vertical size of headers and footers

1. Activate a header or footer in your worksheet.

2. On the **Page Layout** tab of the ribbon, click the **Margins** button, and then click **Custom Margins**.

3. On the **Margins** tab of the **Page Setup** dialog box, change the values in the **Header** and **Footer** spin boxes as desired.

Prepare worksheets for printing

When you are ready to print your workbook, you can change the workbook's properties to ensure that your worksheets display all your information and that printing is centered on the page. In Excel, all these printing functions are gathered together in one place: the Backstage view.

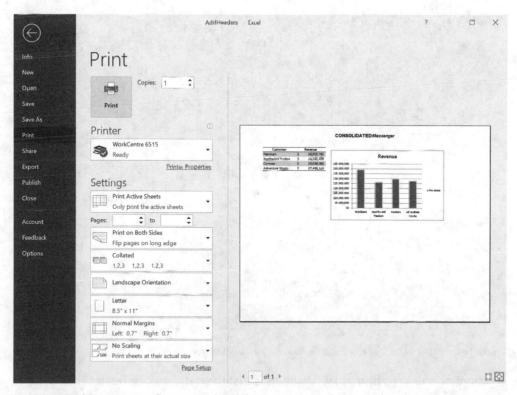

You can control most aspects of your printed worksheet.

11

TIP Press Ctrl+P to preview your worksheet in the Backstage view.

You can change the number of copies to print, the printer to which you will send the file, whether Excel should print the page in landscape or portrait orientation, which paper size to use, which margin settings you want, and whether to scale the worksheet's contents so they fit on a specific number of printed pages.

Fit your worksheet contents to the printed page

Excel comes with three margin settings: Normal, Wide, and Narrow. Excel applies the Normal setting by default, but you can select any of the three options you want, or you can set your own custom margins.

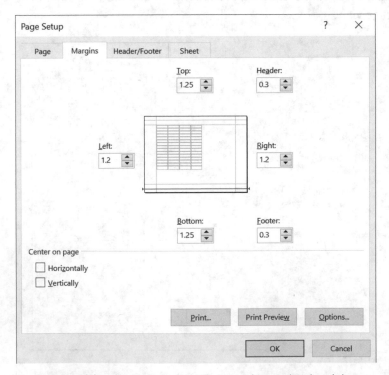

You can control the white space, or margins, around your printed worksheet.

A potential issue with printing worksheets is that the data in worksheets tends to be wider than a standard sheet of paper. If that's the case, you can change the alignment of the rows and columns on the page. When the columns parallel the long edge of a piece of paper, the page is laid out in portrait mode; when the columns parallel the short edge of a piece of paper, it is in landscape mode. Changing between portrait and landscape mode might result in a better fit.

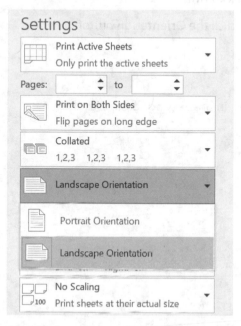

Select landscape or portrait mode for a better fit.

If you can't fit your worksheet on a single page by changing its orientation, you can change its scale. Scaling a worksheet for printing lets you specify the number of printed pages the worksheet will take up. You can scale your worksheet until everything fits on a specified number of printed pages, specify the number of printed pages on which the columns will appear, or specify the number of printed pages on which the rows will appear. For example, if you have a list of data that's 15 columns wide and 100 rows long, you could scale it so the columns all fit on each page of your printout.

When you look at your worksheet in the Backstage view, you can preview what it will look like when printed, including the number of pages on which it will be printed.

> ✓ **TIP** When you display a workbook in the Backstage view, you can view the next printed page by pressing the Page Down key; to move to the previous page, press the Page Up key. You can also use the Previous and Next arrows at the bottom of the Backstage view, enter a page number in the Current Page box, or scroll through the pages by using the vertical scroll bar at the right edge of the Backstage view.

To select landscape or portrait mode for a printed worksheet

1. Display the Backstage view.

2. In the left pane of the Backstage view, click **Print**.

3. On the **Print** page, in the **Settings** area, click the **Orientation** button.

4. Click the orientation you want.

To scale a worksheet for printing

1. On the **Print** page of the Backstage view, in the **Settings** area, click the **Scaling** button.

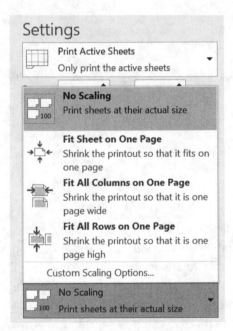

Select a scaling option to print your worksheet on a set number of pages.

2. Click the scaling option you want.

Change page breaks in a worksheet

Another way to affect how your worksheet will appear on the printed page is to change where Excel assigns its page breaks. A page break is the point at which Excel prints all subsequent data on a new sheet of paper. You can make these changes indirectly by modifying a worksheet's margins, but you can also do so directly. You can view a worksheet in Page Break Preview mode by displaying the View tab of the ribbon and clicking the Page Break Preview button. In Page Break Preview mode, the blue lines in the window represent the page breaks.

January

Day	5:00 AM	6:00 AM	7:00 AM	8:00 AM	9:00 AM	10:00 AM	11:00 AM	12:00 PM	1:00 PM	2:00 PM	3:00 PM	4:00 PM	5:00 PM
1	2117	1989	1544	2408	1921	1505	1687	2391	1486	2075	1626	1326	1612
2	1128	1109	1354	1115	2277	1482	1559	2103	2493	1317	1519	1836	1439
3	1228	1350	1662	1758	1892	1710	1709	1889	1495	1405	1513	1493	1997
4	2295	2496	1964	1793	1138	1597	1811	1479	2339	1839	2416	1838	1403
5	1866	1631	1631	1136	1959	2275	2348	1355	1346	1947	2098	1163	1410
6	1234	1536	2348	1208	2109	2382	2487	2464	1733	2086	1261	1989	2338
7	1608	1825	1951	1037	2259	2091	2211	1195	1395	1727	1171	1753	1029
8	1903	2014	1451	1283	2243	1266	1746	2243	1385	1414	1676	1174	1765
9	2275	2360	1392	1511	1947	1639	2018	2468	2247	2493	1827	2261	1861
10	1009	2191	1729	1028	2278	1044	1936	1283	1677	1988	1690	1649	1784
11	1569	1069	1487	1155	2434	2181	1721	2235	1534	1407	1187	1581	2355
12	1773	1782	1224	2401	2426	1514	1526	1086	1478	1943	1028	1988	1892
13	2108	1511	1916	2488	1459	1703	1706	2083	2305	2348	1662	2218	2257
14	1512	2319	2239	1063	1164	2115	1469	1629	2398	1970	1665	1843	1471
15	1003	1283	1874	1512	1238	1993	2390	2040	1366	1422	2344	1144	1011
16	2007	1864	2088	1228	2023	1186	1585	1422	1486	2232	1907	2001	1919
17	1016	2400	1039	1024	1107	2178	1445	1452	1506	1605	1925	2223	1136
18	1794	2291	2156	1966	1650	1899	1931	2124	1166	1630	2178	1185	1915
19	1904	2404	1099	1332	1089	1132	1045	1203	1364	2346	1656	1483	1866
20	2035	2174	1423	2277	1400	2468	1287	2146	1578	1476	2411	1721	2173
21	1288	2521	1171	1884	2292	2437	2465	1936	2138	1043	2265	1660	1949
22	1577	1235	1742	1089	2203	2143	1073	1795	1960	1874	1312	1332	1920
23	1987	1349	2170	1728	2426	1015	1227	1762	2352	1383	2144	1583	2223
24	1868	2459	1380	1390	2270	1336	1886	1541	1774	1911	2079	2269	1688
25	1058	1541	1753	1740	2360	2308	2167	1131	1146	1966	2120	2038	2380
26	2016	2412	1128	1477	1184	2104	1513	1222	1484	1385	2271	1842	2453
27	1640	2180	1904	1048	1531	1541	1858	1744	1605	1280	1937	1013	1817
28	2363	1340	2113	1350	1814	2558	1613	1519	1938	1665	1104	1065	1934
29	2398	1324	1572	2264	1335	2002	1495	1423	2190	2170	2282	1920	1743
30	2225	1178	1633	1148	1640	1872	1581	1431	2024	1423	1972	1674	1700
31	1726	1794	2020	1777	1016	1405	1845	2108	1597	1846	1737	2024	1914

Page 1   Page 2

February

| JanFeb | MarJun |

In Page Break Preview mode, page breaks appear in blue.

If you right-click a cell within the body of a worksheet in Page Break Preview mode and then click Insert Page Break, Excel creates both a vertical page break to the left of the selected cell and a horizontal page break above the selected cell.

11

> ⚠️ **IMPORTANT** If you want to insert a single page break (not both vertical and horizontal page breaks at the same point) in Page Break Preview mode, be sure to click a row header or column header.

You can also move a page break by dragging it to its new position. Excel will change the worksheet's properties so that the area you defined will be printed on a single page, if possible.

To add a page break to a worksheet

1. Click the row or column header where you want to add the page break.

2. On the **Page Layout** tab of the ribbon, in the **Page Setup** group, click the **Breaks** button, and then click **Insert Page Break**.

To remove a page break

1. Click the column header to the right of the page break.

   Or

   Click the row header below the page break.

2. In the **Page Setup** group, click the **Breaks** button, and then click **Remove Page Break**.

To reset all page breaks

1. Click the **Breaks** button, and then click **Reset All Page Breaks**.

Change the page printing order for worksheets

When you view a document in Page Break Preview mode, Excel indicates the order in which the pages will be printed with light gray words on the worksheet pages. (These indicators appear only in Page Break Preview mode; they don't show up when the document is printed.) If you want, you can change the order in which the pages are printed. One reason to change the order in which Excel prints your worksheet pages would be to keep related information on consecutive pages.

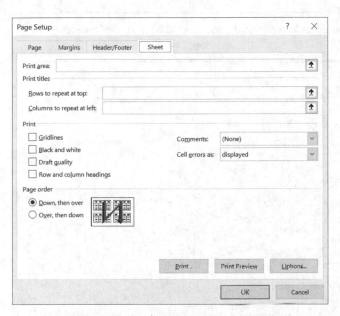

You can change the order in which worksheet pages are printed.

To change the order in which worksheet pages are printed

1. On the **Page Layout** tab, in the **Page Setup** group, click the dialog box launcher at the bottom right corner of the ribbon group.

2. In the **Page Setup** dialog box, click the **Sheet** tab.

3. Select **Down, then over**.

   Or

   Select **Over, then down**.

4. Click **OK**.

Print worksheets

When you're ready to print a worksheet, you can control how Excel prints it. For example, you can choose the printer to which you want to send this job, print multiple copies of the worksheet, and select whether the copies are collated (all pages of a document are printed together) or not (multiple copies of the same page are printed together). You can also print more than one worksheet at a time by selecting the worksheet tabs in the tab bar before you start printing, or you can have Excel print the entire workbook at once.

TIP The worksheets you select for printing do not need to be next to one another in the workbook.

Control your print job from the Print page of Backstage view.

Some worksheets you print might be works in progress, where some of the formulas might display errors due to missing values. You can select how Excel will print any errors in your worksheet: printing it as it normally appears in the worksheet, printing a blank cell in place of the error, or choosing one of two other indicators that are not standard error messages.

To print a worksheet in Excel

1. Display the worksheet you want to print.

2. In the left pane of the Backstage view, click **Print**.

    Or

    Press **Ctrl+P**.

3. Select the options you want to apply to the print job.

4. Click the **Print** button.

To print multiple copies of a worksheet

1. Press **Ctrl+P**.

2. Change the value in the **Copies** box.

3. Click the **Print** button.

To print multiple worksheets

1. Hold down the **Ctrl** key and click the tabs of any worksheets you want to print.

2. Press **Ctrl+P**.

3. Click the **Print** button.

To control how Excel prints worksheet errors

1. On the **Page Layout** tab, in the **Page Setup** group, click the dialog box launcher at the bottom right corner of the ribbon group.

2. In the **Page Setup** dialog box, click the **Sheet** tab.

3. In the **Cell errors as** list, select the option representing how you want errors to be printed.

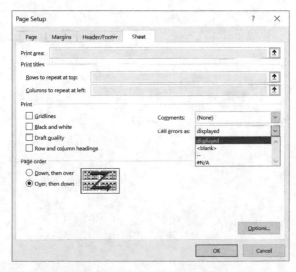

Specify how Excel should print worksheet errors.

4. Click **OK**.

Print parts of worksheets

Excel gives you a great deal of control over what your worksheets look like when you print them, but you also have a lot of control over which parts of your worksheets will be printed. For example, you can choose which pages of a multipage worksheet you want to print. If you want to print a portion of a worksheet instead of the entire worksheet, you can define the area or areas you want to print and use the Center on Page controls on the Margins tab of the Page Setup dialog box to specify how Excel should position the area on the printed page.

 TIP You can include noncontiguous groups of cells in the area to be printed by holding down the Ctrl key as you select the cells.

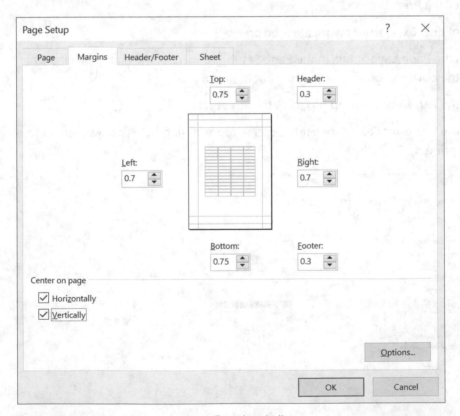

Center printed items on the page horizontally and vertically.

If the contents of a worksheet will take up more than one printed page, you can have Excel repeat one or more rows at the top of the page or columns at the left of the page. Repeating a row with headers makes the data easier to read throughout the printed document, because you and your colleagues won't need to refer to the first page to know which data each row and column contains.

To print specific pages

1. Press **Ctrl+P**.

2. On the **Print** page of the Backstage view, in the first **Pages** box, enter the number of the first page you want to print.

3. In the second **Pages** box, enter the number of the last page you want to print.

To define a print area

1. Select the cells you want to print.

2. On the **Page Layout** tab, in the **Page Setup** group, click **Print Area** to display a menu of print area choices, and then click **Set Print Area**.

> 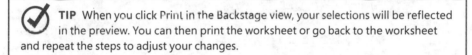 **TIP** When you click Print in the Backstage view, your selections will be reflected in the preview. You can then print the worksheet or go back to the worksheet and repeat the steps to adjust your changes.

To define a multiregion print area

1. Select the first cell region you want to print.

2. Hold down the **Ctrl** key and select any other cells you want to print.

3. On the **Print Area** menu, click **Set Print Area**.

To remove a print area

1. Click any cell in the print area.

2. On the **Print Area** menu, click **Clear Print Area**.

To position printed material on the page

1. In the **Page Setup** group, click the dialog box launcher launcher at the bottom right corner of the ribbon group.

2. In the **Page Setup** dialog box, click the **Margins** tab.

3. Select the **Horizontally** check box to center printing on the page horizontally.

4. Select the **Vertically** check box to center printing on the page vertically.

11

To repeat columns at the left of each printed page

1. In the **Page Setup** group, click **Print Titles**.

2. On the **Sheet** tab of the **Page Setup** dialog box, at the right edge of the **Columns to repeat at left** box, click the **Collapse Dialog** button to collapse the dialog box.

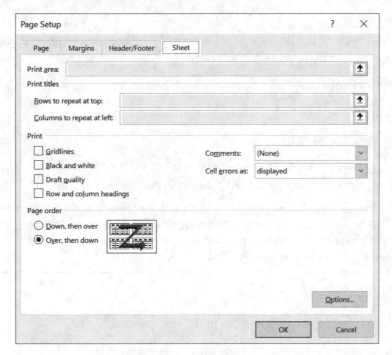

Identify rows or columns to repeat on printed pages.

3. Select the column headers of the columns you want to repeat at the left of the page.

4. Click the **Expand Dialog** button.

5. Click **OK**.

   When you click **Print** in the Backstage view, your selections will be reflected in the preview. You can then print the worksheet or go back to the worksheet and repeat the steps to adjust your changes.

To repeat rows at the top of each printed page

1. Click **Print Titles**.

2. On the **Sheet** tab of the **Page Setup** dialog box, at the right edge of the **Rows to repeat at top** box, click the **Collapse Dialog** button to collapse the dialog box.

3. Select the row headers of any rows you want to repeat at the top of the page.

4. Click the **Expand Dialog** button.

5. Click **OK**.

Print charts

With charts, which are graphic representations of your Excel data, you can communicate a lot of information with a single picture. Depending on your data and the type of chart you make, you can show trends across time, indicate the revenue share for various departments in a company for a month, or project future sales by using trendline analysis. After you create a chart, you can print it to include it in a report or use it in a presentation.

If you embed a chart in a worksheet, the chart will probably obscure some of your data unless you move the chart to a second page in the worksheet. Fortunately, you can print a chart by itself without changing the layout of your worksheet.

Click a chart in your worksheet to print it by itself on a page.

To print a chart

1. Select the chart.

2. Press **Ctrl+P**.

3. Verify that the **Print Selected Chart** option is selected.

4. Click the **Print** button.

Skills review

In this chapter, you learned how to:

- Add headers and footers to printed pages

- Prepare worksheets for printing

- Print worksheets

- Print parts of worksheets

- Print charts

Practice tasks

The practice files for these tasks are located in the Excel2019SBS\Ch11 folder. You can save the results of the tasks in the same folder.

Add headers and footers to printed pages

Open the AddHeaders workbook in Excel, and then perform the following tasks:

1. Enter the text Q1 2019 in the center section of the header, and press **Enter**.

2. Add a code to display the name of the current file, followed by a comma and a space, and then add a control to display the current date.

3. Create separate headers for odd and even pages.

4. In the middle section of the footer, add the ConsolidatedMessenger.png file, and then click any worksheet cell above the footer to view what the image looks like in the footer.

5. Edit the image so it is 80 percent of its original size.

6. Change the margins for both the header and footer so they are 0.5 inches high.

Prepare worksheets for printing

Open the PrepareWorksheets workbook in Excel, and then perform the following tasks:

1. Change the orientation of the **JanFeb** worksheet to **Landscape**.

2. Change the scale of the **JanFeb** worksheet to 80 percent.

3. On the **JanFeb** worksheet, set a horizontal page break above row 38.

4. Set the margins of the **MarJun** worksheet to the **Wide** preset values.

5. For the **MarJun** worksheet, change the page print order to **Over, then down**.

Print worksheets

Open the PrintWorksheets workbook in Excel, and then perform the following tasks:

1. Configure the worksheet so cell errors are displayed as blank cells.

2. Select the **Summary** and **Northwind** sheets and display them on the **Print** page of the Backstage view.

3. If you want, click the **Print** button to print your worksheets on your local printer.

Print parts of worksheets

Open the PrintParts workbook in Excel, and then perform the following tasks:

1. Set the print titles of the worksheet so that columns A and B are repeated at the left edge of each printed page.

2. Change the printer properties so Excel will print only pages 1 and 2 of the worksheet.

3. Scale the worksheet so its columns will fit on one page when printed.

4. Preview what the worksheet will look like when printed.

5. Define a multiregion print area including cells **A1:E8** and **A38:E45**.

6. Center the regions on the printed page.

7. Clear the print area you created.

Print charts

Open the PrintCharts workbook in Excel, and then perform the following tasks:

1. Select the revenue chart.

2. Continue as if you are going to print the revenue chart, and then change the settings on the **Print** page of the Backstage view to print the entire worksheet.

Automate repetitive tasks by using macros

Many tasks you perform in Excel 2019, such as entering data or creating formulas, you do only once. However, there are probably one or two tasks you perform frequently that require a lot of steps to accomplish. To save time, you can create a macro, which is a recorded series of actions, to perform the steps for you. After you have created a macro, you can run, edit, or delete it as needed.

You can make your macros easier to access by creating new buttons on the Quick Access Toolbar and assigning your macros to them. If you run a macro to highlight specific cells in a worksheet every time you show that worksheet to a colleague, you can save time by adding a Quick Access Toolbar button that runs the macro to highlight the cells for you. You can also create macros that run whenever you open the workbook that contains them, and you can add form controls, such as list boxes, to your worksheets to facilitate data entry.

This chapter guides you through procedures related to opening, running, creating, and modifying macros; creating Quick Access Toolbar buttons you can use to run macros with a single mouse click; defining macro security settings; running a macro when a workbook is opened; and inserting form controls into a worksheet.

In this chapter

- Enable and examine macros
- Create and modify macros
- Click a button to run a macro
- Run a macro when you open a workbook
- Insert form controls into a worksheet

Practice files

For this chapter, use the practice files from the Excel2019SBS\Ch12 folder. For practice file download instructions, see the introduction.

Enable and examine macros

Macros are powerful tools that let you automate tasks in Excel 2019, but you must choose to run them by selecting the appropriate security level for your organization. Once you decide to enable and run macros, you can also examine them to see how they work or, if necessary, to edit their code to fix an error or change their behavior.

Set macro security levels in Excel 2019

In versions of Excel prior to Excel 2007, you could define macro security levels to determine which macros, if any, your workbooks would be allowed to run, but there was no workbook type in which all macros were disallowed. Excel 2019 has several file types you can use to control whether a workbook will allow macros to run. The following table summarizes the macro-related file types.

Extension	Description
.xlsx	Regular Excel 2019 workbook; macros are *disabled*
.xlsm	Regular Excel 2019 workbook; macros are *enabled*
.xltx	Excel 2019 template workbook; macros are *disabled*
.xltm	Excel 2019 template workbook; macros are *enabled*

When you open a macro-enabled workbook, the Excel app-level security settings might prevent the workbook from running the macro code. When that happens, Excel displays a security warning on the message bar.

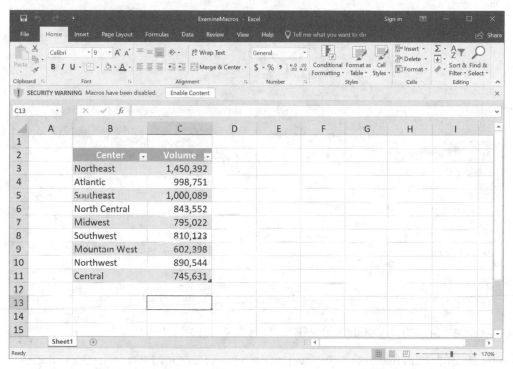

Macro security settings help reduce outside threats.

Clicking the Enable Content button lets the workbook use its macros. Always take the time to verify the workbook's source and consider whether you expected the workbook to contain macros before you enable the content. If you decide not to enable the macros in a workbook, close the message bar without enabling the content. You will still be able to edit the workbook, but macros and other active content will not be available.

12

You can change your app-level security settings to make them more or less restrictive by using the Trust Center dialog box.

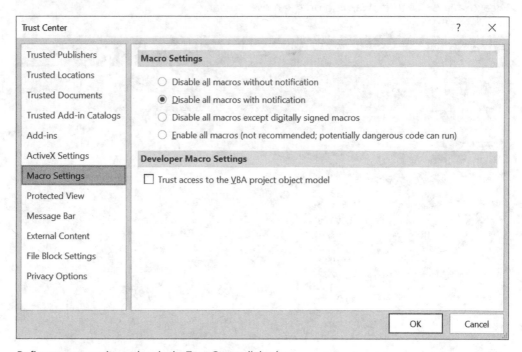

Define macro security settings in the Trust Center dialog box.

The Excel default macro security level is Disable All Macros with Notification, which means that Excel displays a warning on the message bar but allows you to enable the macros manually. Selecting the Disable All Macros Without Notification option does exactly what the label says. If you work in an environment where your workbooks contain macros verified with digital signatures, you could select the Disable All Macros Except Digitally Signed Macros option.

> ⚠ **IMPORTANT** Because it is possible to write macros that act as viruses, potentially causing harm to your computer and spreading copies of themselves to other computers, you should never choose the Enable All Macros security setting, even if you have virus-checking software installed on your computer.

To change macro security settings

1. Display the Backstage view, and then click **Options**.

2. In the **Excel Options** dialog box, click the **Trust Center** category.

3. Click **Trust Center Settings**.

4. Click **Macro Settings**.

5. Select one of the following security levels:

    -   **Disable all macros without notification**

    -   **Disable all macros with notification**

    -   **Disable all macros except digitally signed macros**

    -   **Enable all macros (not recommended; potentially dangerous code can run)**

6. Click **OK** twice.

Examine macros

One great way to get an idea of how macros work is to examine an existing macro. The Macro dialog box displays a list of macros in your workbook by default, but you can also choose to display the macros available in other workbooks. When you display a macro's code, Excel opens it in the Visual Basic Editor.

View and edit macros in the Visual Basic Editor.

TIP You can also open and close the Visual Basic Editor by pressing Alt+F11.

Consider, for example, the code for a macro that selects the cell range C4:C9 and changes the cells' formatting to bold. The first line of the macro identifies the cell range to be selected (in this case, cells C4:C9). After the macro selects the cells, the next line of the macro changes the formatting of the selected cells to bold, which has the same result as clicking a cell and then clicking the Bold button in the Font group on the Home tab.

You can move through a macro one step at a time to observe how the code executes, run the macro to a breakpoint, or run the macro the whole way through.

TIP To execute an instruction, press F8. The highlight moves to the next instruction, and your worksheet then changes to reflect the action that resulted from executing the preceding instruction.

Step through a macro one instruction at a time.

You can run a macro without stopping from within the Macro dialog box. You'll usually run the macro this way; after all, the point of using macros is to save time.

 TIP To open the Macro dialog box by using a keyboard shortcut, press Alt+F8.

To examine a macro

1. On the **View** tab of the ribbon, in the **Macros** group, click the **Macros** button.

2. In the **Macro** dialog box, click the macro you want to examine.

3. Click **Edit**.

4. Make any changes you want to the macro's code.

5. In the Visual Basic Editor, click **File**, and then click **Close and Return to Microsoft Excel**.

To move through a macro one step at a time

1. Click the **Macros** button.

2. In the **Macro** dialog box, click the macro you want to step through.

3. Click **Step Into**.

4. In the Visual Basic Editor, press **F8** to execute the highlighted step.

5. Do one of the following:

    - Repeat step 4 until you have moved through the entire macro.

    - Press **F5** to run the remaining steps without stopping.

    - On the Visual Basic Editor toolbar, click the **Reset** button to stop stepping through the macro.

6. In the Visual Basic Editor, click **File**, and then click **Close and Return to Microsoft Excel**.

12

Create and modify macros

The first step in creating a macro is to plan the process you want to automate. Computers today are quite fast, so adding an extra step during recording won't noticeably slow you down, but leaving out a step means that you will need to re-record your macro.

After you plan your process, you can record your macro by using the tools in the Record Macro dialog box.

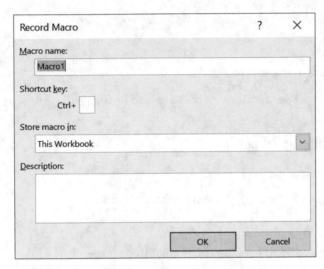

Automate repeatable processes by using the Record Macro dialog box to create a macro.

After you give your macro a name and description, you can record your actions. To modify an existing macro, you can simply delete the macro and re-record it. Or, if you just need to make a quick change, you can open it in the Visual Basic Editor and add to or change the macro's instructions.

To record a macro

1. On the **View** tab, in the **Macros** group, click the **Macros** arrow (not the button), and then click **Record Macro**.

2. In the **Macro name** box, enter a name for your macro.

3. Enter a quick description for your macro in the **Description** box.

4. Click **OK**.

5. Perform the steps you want to record in your macro.

6. Click the **Macros** arrow (not the button), and then click **Stop Recording**.

To edit a macro

1. Click the **Macros** button.

2. In the **Macros** dialog box, click the macro you want to edit.

3. Click **Edit**.

4. Make the changes you want to make to your macro's code.

5. Press **Ctrl+S** to save your changes.

6. In the Visual Basic Editor, click **File**, and then click **Close and Return to Microsoft Excel**.

 TIP To close the Visual Basic Editor and return to the main Excel program window by using a keyboard shortcut, press Alt+Q.

To delete a macro

1. Click the **Macros** button.

2. Click the macro you want to delete.

3. Click **Delete**.

4. In the confirmation dialog box that appears, click **Yes**.

Click a button to run a macro

You can use the ribbon to quickly access the commands built into Excel. However, it can take a few seconds to open the Macro dialog box. When you're in the middle of a presentation, taking even those few seconds can reduce your momentum and force you to regain your audience's attention.

If you want to run a macro without having to display the Macro dialog box, you can do so by adding a button representing the macro to the Quick Access Toolbar. Clicking that button runs the macro immediately, which is very handy when you create a macro for a task you perform frequently.

12

If you want to add more than one macro button to the Quick Access Toolbar, or if you want to change the button that represents your macro on the Quick Access Toolbar, you can select a new button from more than 160 options.

Change the appearance of buttons on your
Quick Access Toolbar.

Finally, you can have Excel run a macro when you click a shape in your workbook. By using this technique, you can create "buttons" that are graphically richer than those available on the Quick Access Toolbar. If you want, you can even create custom button layouts that represent other objects, such as a remote control.

> ⚠️ **IMPORTANT** When you assign a macro to run when you click a shape, don't change the name of the macro that appears in the Assign Macro dialog box. The name that appears refers to the object and what the object should do when it is clicked; changing the macro name breaks that connection and prevents Excel from running the macro.

To add a macro button to the Quick Access Toolbar

1. Right-click any ribbon tab, and then click **Customize Quick Access Toolbar**.

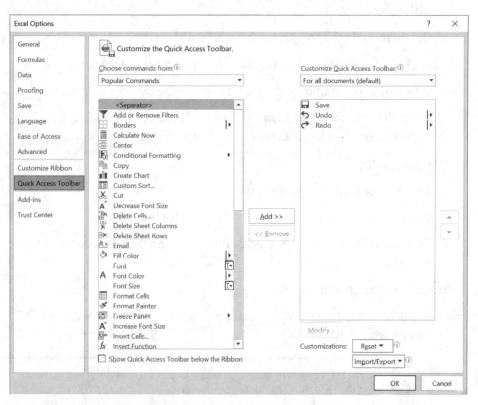

Change the buttons on the Quick Access Toolbar to enhance your usage.

2. In the **Excel Options** dialog box, click the **Choose commands from** arrow, and then click **Macros**.

> ✓ **TIP** If you have more than one workbook open, the macro list will contain macros stored in the other workbooks. To limit the list to macros available in the active workbook, click the Customize Quick Access Toolbar button, and then click For *workbook*.xlsm.

3. Click the macro you want to add, and then click the **Add** button.

4. Click **Modify**.

5. In the **Symbol** pane, click the button image you want.

12

6. In the **Display name** box, enter a new name for the button.

7. Click **OK** twice to close the **Modify Button** dialog box and the **Excel Options** dialog box.

To run a macro assigned to a Quick Access Toolbar button

1. Click the Quick Access Toolbar button to which the macro has been assigned.

To edit the appearance of a macro button on the Quick Access Toolbar

1. On the **Quick Access Toolbar** page of the **Excel Options** dialog box, in the list of commands on the toolbar, click the button you want to modify.

2. Click **Modify**.

3. In the **Symbol** pane, click the button image you want.

4. In the **Display name** box, enter a new name for the button.

5. Click **OK** twice to close the **Modify Button** dialog box and the **Excel Options** dialog box.

To assign a macro to a shape

1. Right-click the shape to which you want to assign a macro, and then click **Assign Macro**.

> **SEE ALSO** For information about how to edit the text displayed within a shape, see Chapter 9, "Create charts and graphics."

2. In the **Assign Macro** dialog box, click the name of the macro you want to run when the shape is clicked.

3. Click **OK**.

To run a macro assigned to a shape

1. Click the shape to which the macro has been assigned.

To edit a shape to which a macro has been assigned

1. Right-click the shape you want to edit.

2. In the shortcut menu, click **Format Shape**.

3. Use the tools in the **Format Shape** task pane to change the shape's formatting.

4. Click the **Close** button to close the **Format Shape** task pane.

Run a macro when you open a workbook

One advantage of writing Excel macros in Visual Basic for Applications (VBA) is that you can have Excel run a macro whenever you open a workbook. For example, if you use a worksheet for presentations, you can create macros that render the contents of selected cells in bold type, italic, or different typefaces to set the data apart from data in neighboring cells. If you close a workbook without removing that formatting, however, the contents of your workbook will still have that formatting applied the next time you open it. Although this change might not be a catastrophe, returning the workbook to its original formatting might take some time to accomplish.

Instead of running a macro manually, or even from a toolbar button or a menu, you can have Excel run a macro whenever you open a workbook. The trick of making that happen is in the name you give the macro. When Excel finds a macro with the name *Auto_Open*, it runs the macro when the workbook to which it is attached is opened.

> **TIP** If you have your macro security set to the Disable All Macros with Notification level, you can click the Options button that appears on the message bar, select the Enable This Content option, and then click OK to allow the *Auto_Open* macro to run.

To run a macro when you open a workbook

1. On the **View** tab, in the **Macros** group, click the **Macros** button.

2. Click the macro you want to run when the workbook is opened.

3. Click **Edit**.

4. Edit the **Sub** *MacroName*() line so it reads **Sub Auto_Open**().

5. Press **Ctrl+S** to save your changes.

6. In the Visual Basic Editor, click **File**, and then click **Close and Return to Microsoft Excel**.

> **TIP** To close the Visual Basic Editor and return to the main Excel program window by using a keyboard shortcut, press Alt+Q.

Or

1. Click the **Macros** arrow (not the button), and then click **Record Macro**.

2. In the **Macro name** box, enter Auto_Open.

12

3. Click **OK**.

4. Record the steps you want Excel to execute when the workbook is opened.

5. Click the **Macros** arrow (not the button), and then click **Stop Recording**.

Insert form controls into a worksheet

When you summarize data in an Excel workbook, you can change the values used in your visualizations in many different ways. Some of those methods include creating filters, sorting your data, or entering new values into a cell to change the result of a formula or filter. You can enhance those capabilities by adding form controls to your worksheets, a process you start by adding the Developer tab to the tabs displayed on the ribbon.

Manage macros, form controls, and other advanced elements by using the Developer tab.

A form control provides additional interactivity that you can use to change your worksheet quickly and visually.

 TIP The form controls described in this chapter mimic controls such as list boxes, check boxes, and option buttons that are available in many Excel dialog boxes.

Two form controls, the list box and the combo box, display a list of values from a cell range you define. The difference between the list box and the combo box is that a list box displays all of its values at the same time, and a combo box has an arrow you can click to display the values from which you can choose.

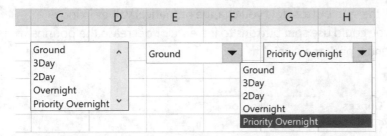

Select values by using list boxes and combo boxes.

After you add a combo box or list box to your worksheet, you can use the settings in the Format Control dialog box to identify the cells that provide values for the control, the cell that displays the control's value, and many other properties.

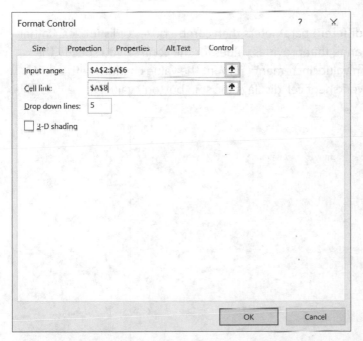

Set form control parameters by using the Format Control dialog box.

> **TIP** The cells that provide values for your list box or combo box don't have to be on the same worksheet as the form control. Putting the values on another worksheet lets you reduce the clutter in the worksheet that contains the form control. Hiding the worksheet that contains the source data also helps prevent users from changing those values.

Another form control, the spin button, lets you change numerical values in increments. For example, you could use spin buttons to increase or decrease the pounds and ounces representing a package's weight.

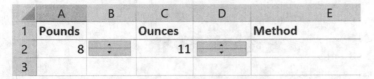

	A	B	C	D	E
1	**Pounds**		**Ounces**		**Method**
2	8		11		
3					

A worksheet with two spin buttons to change cell values.

Spin buttons are effective presentation tools. With a series of mouse clicks, you can change a value up or down in increments you define, illustrating how your worksheet's results change.

Spin buttons use slightly different parameters than combo boxes or list boxes. Rather than identifying the cell range that provides values for the control, you specify the maximum value, minimum value, increment (amount the value changes with each mouse click), and which worksheet cell displays the spin button's value.

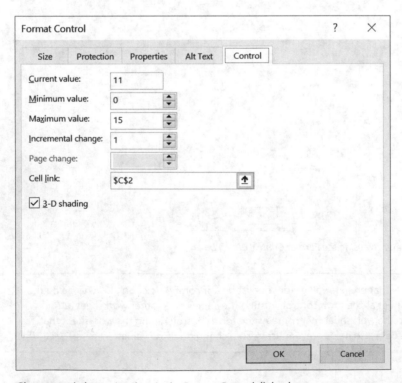

Change a spin button's values in the Format Control dialog box.

> **⚠ IMPORTANT** The maximum, minimum, and increment values must be whole numbers. If you want to use a spin button to change a percentage, for example, you'll need to create a formula in another cell that divides the spin button's value by 100.

The button form control, also referred to as a *command button*, runs a macro when it's clicked. When you add a button to a worksheet, the Assign Macro dialog box appears so you can tell it which macro to run.

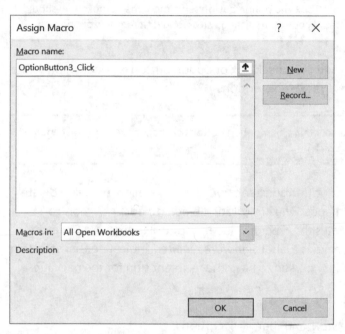

The Assign Macro dialog box for a newly created command button.

The next two form controls, the check box and option button, both let users turn particular options on or off. For example, a package-delivery company could allow customers to waive a signature when a package is dropped off. If the Signature Required option button (the first option button in the group) is selected, the cell displaying the option button's value would contain the number 1. If the Signature Waived option button is selected, the cell would contain the number 2.

12

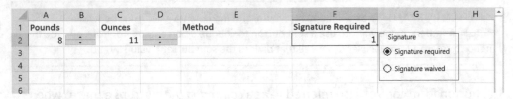

Option button groups let the user select one of several values.

> ✓ **TIP** Even though the check box and option button serve the same purpose, you should consider using both types of controls to distinguish among different sets of options.

You can have a cell display whether a check box or option button is selected, or define a control group that contains the possible options.

> ✓ **TIP** Control groups can contain either option buttons or check boxes, but you can't mix them in the same group.

After you add your controls to your worksheet, you can move, align, edit, and delete them, just as you can other shapes. One important element to edit is the control's caption, or label, which indicates the type of value the control represents. For example, an option button could have the label *Signature required*, indicating that selecting that option requires the delivery person to have the recipient sign for the package.

To add the Developer tab to the ribbon

1. Display the Backstage view, and then click **Options**.

2. In the **Excel Options** dialog box, click **Customize Ribbon**.

3. If necessary, click the **Customize the Ribbon** arrow, and then click **Main Tabs**.

4. In the pane below the list box, select the **Developer** check box.

5. Click **OK**.

To add a list box to a worksheet

1. On the **Developer** tab, in the **Controls** group, click the **Insert** button, and then click the **List Box (Form Control)** icon.

2. In the body of the worksheet, click and drag to draw the list box.

3. Right-click the list box, and then click **Format Control** to display the **Control** tab of the **Format Control** dialog box.

4. Click in the **Input range** box, and then select the cells that will provide the values for the list box.

5. Click in the **Cell link** box, and then click the cell where you want to display the control's value.

6. In the **Selection type** group, select the option button representing the type of selection you want to allow.

7. To display the list box with 3D shading, select the **3-D shading** check box.

8. Click **OK**.

To add a combo box to a worksheet

1. Click the **Insert** button, and then click the **Combo Box (Form Control)** icon.

2. In the body of the worksheet, draw the combo box.

3. Right-click the combo box, and then click **Format Control** to display the **Control** tab of the **Format Control** dialog box.

4. Click in the **Input range** box, and then select the cells that will provide the values for the combo box.

5. Click in the **Cell link** box, and then click the cell where you want to display the control's value.

6. In the **Drop down lines** box, enter the number of items to be displayed when you click the combo box's arrow.

7. To display the list box with 3D shading, select the **3-D shading** check box.

8. Click **OK**.

To add a spin button to a worksheet

1. Click the **Insert** button, and then click the **Spin Button (Form Control)** icon.

2. In the body of the worksheet, draw the spin button.

3. Right-click the spin button, and then click **Format Control** to display the **Control** tab of the **Format Control** dialog box.

12

4. In the **Current value** box, enter the control's initial value.

5. In the **Minimum value** box, enter the smallest value allowed in the spin control.

6. In the **Maximum value** box, enter the largest value allowed in the spin control.

7. In the **Incremental change** box, enter the increment by which the value should increase or decrease with each click.

8. Click in the **Cell link** box, and then click the cell where you want to display the control's value.

9. To display the spin button with 3D shading, select the **3-D shading** check box.

10. Click **OK**.

To add a button to a worksheet

1. Click the **Insert** button, and then click the **Button (Form Control)** icon.

2. In the body of the worksheet, draw the button.

3. In the **Assign Macro** dialog box, click the macro you want to run when the button is clicked.

4. Click **OK**.

To add a check box to a worksheet

1. Click the **Insert** button, and then click the **Check Box (Form Control)** icon.

2. In the body of the worksheet, draw the check box.

3. Right-click the check box, and then click **Format Control** to display the **Control** tab of the **Format Control** dialog box.

4. In the **Value** group, indicate whether the check box should initially be selected, cleared, or mixed.

5. Click in the **Cell link** box, and then click the cell where you want to display the control's value.

6. To display the check box with 3D shading, select the **3-D shading** check box.

7. Click **OK**.

To add an option button to a worksheet

1. Click the **Insert** button, and then click the **Option Button (Form Control)** icon.

2. In the body of the worksheet, draw the option button.

3. Right-click the option button, and then click **Format Control** to display the **Control** tab of the **Format Control** dialog box.

4. In the **Value** group, indicate whether the option button should initially be selected or unselected.

5. Click in the **Cell link** box, and then click the cell where you want to display the control's value.

6. To display the option button with 3D shading, select the **3-D shading** check box.

7. Click **OK**.

To create a group of form controls

1. Click the **Insert** button, and then click the **Group Box (Form Control)** icon.

2. In the body of the worksheet, draw the group box around the items you want to make up your group.

To resize a form control

1. Right-click the control, and then click **Format Control**.

2. Click the **Size** tab.

3. Use the settings available on the **Size** tab to change the control's size.

4. Click **OK**.

Or

1. Select the control, and then drag the handles on the control's edges to change the control's shape.

To edit the text of a form control

1. Right-click the control, and then click **Edit Text**.

2. Edit the control's text in the text box.

3. Click away from the control to stop editing.

To delete a form control

1. Right-click the control, and then click **Cut**.

12

Skills review

In this chapter, you learned how to:

- Enable and examine macros
- Create and modify macros
- Click a button to run a macro
- Run a macro when you open a workbook
- Insert form controls into a worksheet

Practice tasks

The practice files for these tasks are located in the Excel2019SBS\Ch12 folder. You can save the results of the tasks in the same folder.

Enable and examine macros

Open the ExamineMacros workbook in Excel, and then perform the following tasks:

1. If necessary, on the message bar that appears when you open the workbook, click **Enable Content** to enable macros.

2. Open the **Macro** dialog box.

3. Open the **HighlightSouthern** macro for editing.

4. Press **F8** to step through the first three macro steps, and then press **F5** to run the rest of the macro without stopping.

5. Close the Visual Basic Editor and return to Excel.

Create and modify macros

Open the RecordMacros workbook in Excel, and then perform the following tasks:

1. Record a macro that removes bold formatting from cells **C4:C5**. (Leave the values in cells **C6:C7** bold.)

2. Restore bold formatting to cells **C4:C5**, and then run the macro.

3. Restore bold formatting to cells **C4:C5** again, and then edit the macro so it removes bold formatting from cells **C4:C7**.

4. Run the macro you created.

5. Delete the macro.

Run macros when you click a button

Open the AssignMacros workbook in Excel, and then perform the following tasks:

1. Assign the **SavingsHighlight** macro to a button on the Quick Access Toolbar.

2. Change the button icon assigned to the **SavingsHighlight** macro button on the Quick Access Toolbar.

3. Run the **SavingsHighlight** macro.

4. Assign the **EfficiencyHighlight** macro to the **Show Efficiency** shape in the worksheet.

5. Run the **EfficiencyHighlight** macro.

Run a macro when you open a workbook

Open the RunOnOpen workbook in Excel, and then perform the following tasks:

1. Run the **Highlight** macro to display the values in cells **C4**, **C6**, and **C10** in bold.

2. Record a macro named **Auto_Open** that first applies and then removes bold formatting from the cell range **B3:C11**.

3. Re-run the **Highlight** macro to highlight the values in cells **C4**, **C6**, and **C10**.

4. Save the **RunOnOpen** workbook, close it, and then reopen it to run the **Auto_Open** macro.

Insert form controls into a worksheet

Open the InsertFormControls workbook in Excel, and then perform the following tasks:

1. Create a spin button, with the label text **Pounds**, that initially displays the number 0 and lets the user enter a value from 0 to 70 pounds, in increments of 1 pound, into cell **A2**.

2. Create a spin button, with the label text **Ounces**, that initially displays the number 0 and lets the user enter a value from 0 to 16 ounces, in increments of 1 ounce, into cell **B2**.

3. Create a combo box with the label text **Method** that derives its values from cells **A2:A6** on the **ServiceLevels** worksheet and assign its output to cell **C2**.

4. Create two option buttons labeled **Signature Required** and **Signature Waived**. Assign the value of the **Signature Required** option button to cell **D2** and the value of the **Signature Waived** option button to cell **E2**.

5. Create a group that allows either the **Signature Required** or **Signature Waived** option button to be selected, but not both.

Work with other Microsoft Office apps

By itself, Excel 2019 provides a broad range of tools so that you can store, present, and summarize your data. When you use other Microsoft Office 2019 apps, you can extend your capabilities even further. For example, you can include a file created with another Office app in an Excel workbook. If you use Microsoft Word 2019 to write a quick note about why a customer's shipping expenditures decreased significantly in January, you can include the report in your workbook. Similarly, you can include your Excel workbooks in documents created with other Office apps. If you want to copy only part of a workbook, such as a chart, to another Office document, you can also do that.

Excel integrates well with the web. If you know of a web-based resource that would be useful to someone viewing a document, you can create a hyperlink, which is a connection from one place in a document to a file anywhere on a network or on the Internet, as long as the user's computer can reach that location. You can also create hyperlinks to another place in the same file.

This chapter guides you through procedures related to including an Office 2019 document in a workbook, storing an Excel workbook as part of another Office document, creating hyperlinks, and pasting an Excel chart into another document.

In this chapter

- Include Office documents in workbooks and other files
- Create hyperlinks
- Paste charts into documents

Practice files

For this chapter, use the practice files from the Excel2019SBS\Ch13 folder. For practice file download instructions, see the introduction.

Include Office documents in workbooks and other files

One benefit of working with Excel 2019 is that because it is part of Office 2019, you can combine data from Excel and other Office apps to create informative documents and presentations. Just as you do when you combine data from more than one Excel workbook when you combine information from another Office file with an Excel workbook, you can either embed the other Office document into the Excel workbook or create a link between the workbook and the other document.

Updated Summary

Level	Description
Ground	Package transferred by truck or rail carriers from originating location to destination.
3Day	Package transferred by air, truck, or rail as required to guarantee delivery within three business days.
2Day	Package transferred by air, truck, or rail as required to guarantee delivery within two business days.
Overnight	Package transferred by air, truck, or rail as required to guarantee delivery on the next business day.
Priority Overnight	Package transferred by air, truck, or rail as required to guarantee delivery on the next business day before 10 AM.

Embed an Excel workbook in other Office files.

When you link to an Office file from within Excel, any changes made to the Office file will appear in your Excel workbook.

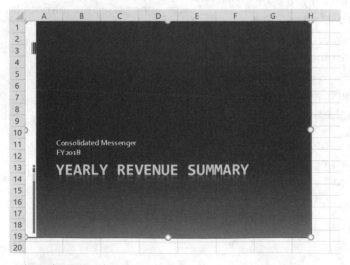

Link to other Office documents from Excel.

Link Office documents to Excel workbooks

There are two advantages to creating a link between your Excel workbook and another file rather than copying the file into your workbook:

- Linking to the other file keeps your Excel workbook small.

- Any changes in the file to which you link are reflected in your Excel workbook.

You create a link between an Excel workbook and another Office document by identifying the file, specifying how to connect to it, and choosing how to display the file within your workbook. After you've defined this connection, you can edit the file by opening it from within Excel or in the app used to create it.

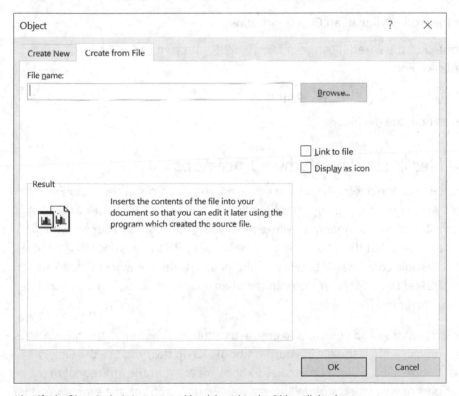

Identify the file to include in your workbook by using the Object dialog box.

 TIP The upper-left corner of the linked or embedded file, or the icon that represents the file, appears in the worksheet's active cell.

13

To create a link to an Office document

1. On the **Insert** tab of the ribbon, in the **Text** group, click **Object** to open the **Object** dialog box.

2. Click the **Create from File** tab.

3. In the **Create from File** page, Click **Browse**.

4. In the **Browse** dialog box, browse to the directory that contains the file you want to insert, select it in the file list, and then click **Insert**.

5. Select the **Link to file** check box.

6. Click **OK** to create a link from your workbook to the presentation.

To edit a file from its link in an Excel workbook

1. Right-click the linked file in your Excel workbook, point to *ObjectType*, and click **Edit**.

2. Edit the file in the other Office app.

3. Save and close the file.

Embed files in Excel and other Office apps

The preceding section described how to link to another file from within your Excel workbook. As mentioned, the advantages of linking to a file are that your workbook remains small, and any changes in the linked file will be reflected in your workbook. The disadvantage is that the linked file must be copied with the workbook or be on a network-accessible computer. If Excel can't find or access the file where the link says it is located, Excel can't display it. You can still open your workbook, but you won't be able to view the linked file's contents.

If file size isn't an issue and you want to ensure that the information in the file is always available, you can embed the file in your workbook. To do this, you use the Object dialog box. Embedding a file in an Excel workbook means that the entirety of that file is saved as part of your workbook. Wherever your workbook goes, the embedded file goes along with it. Note, however, that the embedded version of the file is no longer connected to the original file, so changes in one aren't reflected in the other.

 IMPORTANT To view a linked or embedded file, you must have the app used to create it installed on the computer on which you open the workbook.

If you don't want your workbook to take up much visual space in the file where you embed it, you can have the other app display the workbook as an icon to save space. As with a linked file, you can always edit your workbook in Excel.

Similarly, you can embed, as well as link, an Excel workbook in a file created using another Office application. This is done from the other application's Insert Object dialog box. In this dialog box, if the Link check box is cleared, the Excel workbook will be embedded. If that check box is selected, you will create a link to the Excel workbook instead of embedding it.

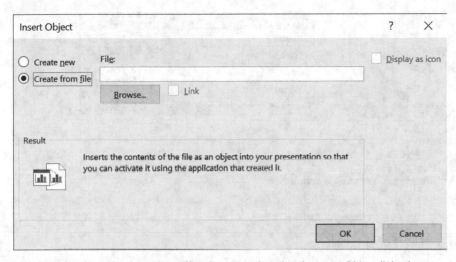

Include an Excel workbook in other Office documents by using the Insert Object dialog box.

To embed an Office document in an Excel workbook

1. On the **Insert** tab, in the **Text** group, click **Object**.

2. In the **Object** dialog box, click the **Create from File** tab.

3. Click **Browse**.

4. Navigate to the folder that contains the file you want to embed, click the file, and then click **Insert**.

5. Click **OK**.

To embed an Excel workbook in a file created using a different Office application

1. In the other Office app, on the **Insert** tab of the ribbon, click **Object**.

2. Click **Create from File**.

3. Click **Browse**.

4. Navigate to the folder that contains the workbook you want to embed and double-click the file's name.

5. Click **OK**.

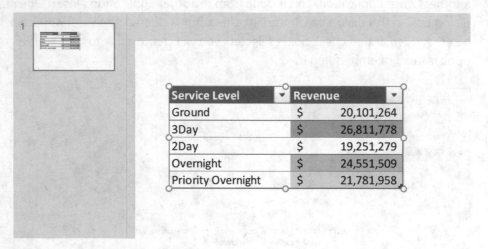

Service Level ▼	Revenue ▼
Ground	$ 20,101,264
3Day	$ 26,811,778
2Day	$ 19,251,279
Overnight	$ 24,551,509
Priority Overnight	$ 21,781,958

Embed Excel files in other Office documents.

Create hyperlinks

One of the characteristics of the web is that documents published on webpages can have references, or hyperlinks, that you can click to display them. In Excel, you can also create hyperlinks that connect to locations in the same document or to other web documents.

A hyperlink functions much like a link between two cells or between two files, but hyperlinks can reach any computer on the Internet, not just those on a corporate network. Hyperlinks that haven't been clicked usually appear as underlined blue text, and hyperlinks that have been clicked appear as underlined purple text, but you can change those settings.

	A	B	C	D
1				
2		**Service Level**	**Revenue**	
3		Ground	$ 20,101,264	
4		3Day	$ 26,811,778	
5		2Day	$ 19,251,279	
6		Overnight	$ 24,551,509	
7		Priority Overnight	$ 21,781,958	
8				
9				
10				
11		Notes		
12				

Add resources to your workbook by using hyperlinks.

You can choose exactly what kind of hyperlink you want to create and specify the text you want to represent it in your workbook.

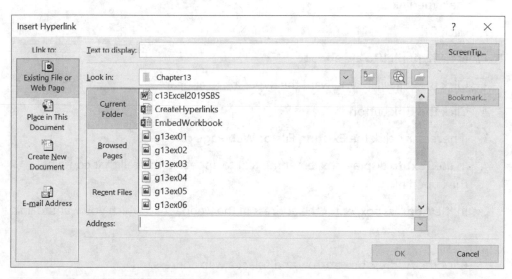

Create a link to an existing file or webpage.

You can choose one of four types of targets, or destinations, for your hyperlink:

- An existing file or webpage

- A place in the current document

- A new document you create on the spot

- An email address

13

Creating a hyperlink that creates an email message when clicked, called a mailto hyperlink, also lets you specify a subject for messages generated by clicking the link. Regardless of the type of hyperlink you create, you can change the text that appears in your worksheet, edit the hyperlink, or remove it at any time.

To create a hyperlink to an existing file

1. Click the cell where you want the hyperlink to appear.

2. On the **Insert** tab of the ribbon, in the **Links** group, click the **Link** button.

3. If necessary, click the **Existing File or Web Page** category.

4. Use the controls in the **Look in** box to locate the file to which you want to create a hyperlink.

5. Select the file name.

6. In the **Text to display** box, enter the text to appear in the cell that contains the hyperlink.

7. Click **OK**.

To create a hyperlink to a webpage

1. Click the cell where you want the hyperlink to appear.

2. Click the **Link** button.

3. If necessary, click the **Existing File or Web Page** category.

4. In the **Text to display** box, enter the text to appear in the cell that contains the hyperlink.

5. In the **Address** box, enter the address of the webpage to which you want to link.

   Or

   Click the **Address** box's arrow and select a web address.

   Or

   Click the **Browsed Pages** button and click a recently visited page to add its address to the hyperlink definition.

6. Click **OK**.

To create a hyperlink to a place in the current file

1. Click the cell where you want the hyperlink to appear.

2. Click the **Link** button.

3. In the **Insert Hyperlink** dialog box, click the **Place in This Document** button.

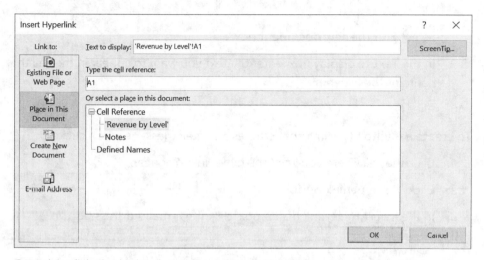

Create hyperlinks that lead to places in the current workbook.

4. Enter the cell reference in the **Type the cell reference** box.

    Or

    Click the link target in the **Or select a place in this document** box.

5. In the **Text to display** box, enter the text you want to appear in the cell that contains the hyperlink.

6. Click **OK**.

To create a hyperlink to a new file

1. Click the cell where you want the hyperlink to appear.

2. Click the **Link** button.

3. In the **Insert Hyperlink** dialog box, click the **Create New Document** button.

4. In the **Name of new document** box, enter a name for the new document.

5. Click the **Change** button.

13

6. In the **Create New Document** dialog box, select the folder where you want to create the document.

7. In the **Save as type** list, select the type of file you want to create, and click **OK**.

8. Select **Edit the new document later**.

   Or

   Select **Edit the new document now**.

9. In the **Text to display** box, enter the text you want to appear in the cell that contains the hyperlink.

10. Click **OK**.

To create a mailto hyperlink that creates an email message when clicked

1. Click the cell where you want the hyperlink to appear.

2. Click the **Hyperlink** button.

3. In the **Insert Hyperlink** dialog box, click the **E-mail Address** button.

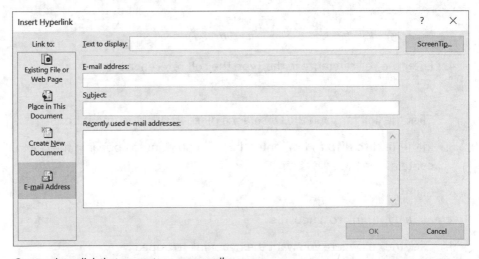

Create a hyperlink that generates a new email message.

4. In the **Text to display** box, enter the text you want to appear in the cell that contains the hyperlink.

5. Enter the target email address in the **E-mail address** box.

   Or

   Select an email address in the **Recently used e-mail addresses** box.

6. Enter a subject for the email message in the **Subject** box.

7. Click **OK**.

To display the target of a hyperlink

1. Click the hyperlink.

To edit a hyperlink

1. Right-click the hyperlink and choose **Edit Hyperlink** from the shortcut menu.

2. Make the changes you want in the **Edit Hyperlink** dialog box.

3. Click **OK**.

To delete a hyperlink

1. Right-click the hyperlink and choose **Remove Hyperlink** from the shortcut menu.

Paste charts into documents

One more way to include objects such as charts from a workbook in another Office document is to copy the object you want to share and then paste it into its new location. You can copy Excel charts directly into Word documents and PowerPoint, in which case the chart updates whenever the data in the source workbook changes. You can also copy an image of the chart. This doesn't create a link to the original data, but it does provide an accurate picture of the chart's appearance when you captured the image.

> ⚠ **IMPORTANT** If you create a link to an Excel chart by pasting the chart into another Office file, the Excel workbook must keep the same relationship with the file as when you linked the chart. If the workbook and other Office file are in the same folder, they must remain in the same folder. If the workbook is on a networked computer, it must remain in its original folder so the link path remains the same.

13

To paste a chart into an Office document, preserving a link to the original workbook

1. In Excel, right-click the chart and click **Copy**.

2. Display the Office file in which you want to paste the chart, and press **Ctrl+V**.

To paste an image of a chart in an Office document

1. In Excel, right-click the chart and click **Copy**.

2. Display the Office file in which you want to paste the chart, and press **Ctrl+V**.

3. Click the **Paste Options** button in the lower-right corner of the pasted chart.

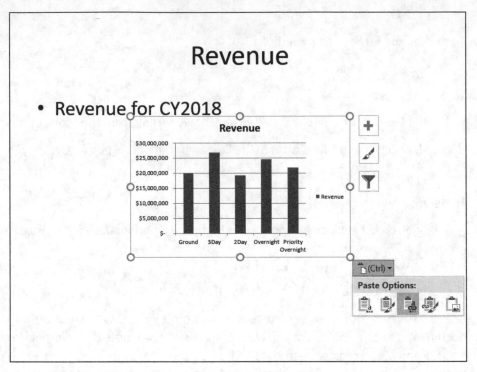

Add links to charts or just copy the chart's current appearance.

4. Click the **Picture** button.

Skills review

In this chapter, you learned how to:

- Include Office documents in workbooks and other files
- Create hyperlinks
- Paste charts into documents

Practice tasks

The practice files for these tasks are located in the Excel2019SBS\Ch13 folder. You can save the results of the tasks in the same folder.

> **IMPORTANT** You must have PowerPoint installed on your system to complete some of the following procedures.

Include Office documents in workbooks and other files

Open the LinkFiles workbook in Excel and the LinkWorkbooks presentation in PowerPoint, and then perform the following tasks:

1. Click cell **B3**.

2. Create a link to the **LinkWorkbooks** PowerPoint presentation.

3. Display the linked file as an icon in your workbook.

4. Open the **LinkWorkbooks** presentation for editing from within Excel, edit the presentation, save your changes, and close the presentation.

5. Switch to the **LinkWorkbooks** presentation and display the second slide.

6. Embed the **EmbedWorkbook** Excel workbook in the practice files folder in the PowerPoint presentation.

7. Edit the embedded file from within PowerPoint and save the presentation.

8. Open the **EmbedWorkbook** workbook in Excel and compare it with your changed file.

Create hyperlinks

Open the CreateHyperlinks workbook in Excel, and then perform the following tasks:

1. On the **Revenue by Level** worksheet, click cell **E2**.

2. Create a hyperlink to the **LevelDescriptions** workbook in the practice files folder.

3. Click cell **B11** and create a hyperlink from the **Notes** text on the **Revenue by Level** worksheet to the **Notes** worksheet.

4. Click cell **C11** and create a mailto hyperlink that sends a message to your email account with the subject **Test from Excel**.

5. Edit the **Text to display** field of the mailto hyperlink to read **Information on service levels**.

6. Delete the hyperlink to the **Notes** worksheet.

Paste charts into documents

Open the LinkCharts workbook in Excel and the ReceiveLinks and LinkWorkbooks presentations in PowerPoint, and then perform the following tasks:

1. Paste the chart from the **LinkCharts** workbook into the **ReceiveLinks** presentation.

2. Paste an image of the chart from the **LinkCharts** workbook into the **LinkWorkbooks** presentation.

Collaborate with colleagues

Many individuals provide input into business decisions. You and your colleagues can enhance the Excel 2019 workbook data you share by adding comments that offer insight into the information the data represents. If the workbook in which those projections and comments are stored is available on a network or an intranet, you can allow more than one user to access the workbook at a time by turning on workbook sharing, and you can track changes.

If you prefer to limit the number of colleagues who can view and edit your workbooks, you can add password protection to a workbook, worksheet, cell range, or even an individual cell. You can also hide formulas used to calculate values. If you work in an environment in which you exchange files frequently, you can use a digital signature to help verify that your workbooks and any macros they contain are from a trusted source. Finally, if you want to display information on a website, you can do so by saving a workbook as a webpage.

This chapter guides you through procedures related to sharing a workbook, saving workbooks for electronic distribution and for the web, managing comments in workbooks, tracking and managing colleagues' changes, protecting workbooks and worksheets, finalizing and authenticating workbooks, importing and exporting XML data, and working with OneDrive and Excel Online.

In this chapter

- Save workbooks for electronic distribution
- Manage comments
- Protect workbooks and worksheets
- Finalize workbooks
- Authenticate workbooks
- Save workbooks for the web
- Import and export XML data
- Work with OneDrive and Excel Online

Practice files

For this chapter, use the practice files from the Excel2019SBS\Ch14 folder. For practice file download instructions, see the introduction.

Save workbooks for electronic distribution

Even though most businesses use Excel, there might be times when you want to distribute a copy of your data in a file other than an Excel workbook. You can create a read-only copy of a workbook for electronic distribution by saving it as a PDF or XML Paper Specification (XPS) file.

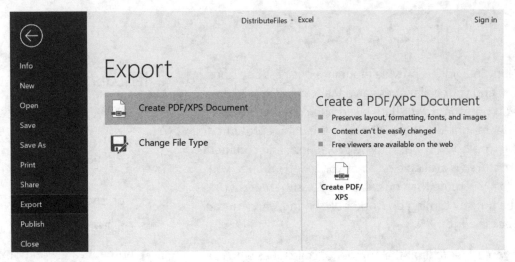

Export a workbook as a PDF or XPS file.

Publishing your workbook as a PDF or XPS document gives your colleagues the information they need to make decisions in an easily readable format that also preserves the integrity of your data.

> 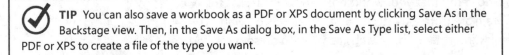 **TIP** You can also save a workbook as a PDF or XPS document by clicking Save As in the Backstage view. Then, in the Save As dialog box, in the Save As Type list, select either PDF or XPS to create a file of the type you want.

To save a workbook as a PDF or XPS file

1. Display the Backstage view, and then click **Export**.

2. Click **Create PDF/XPS Document**.

3. In the **Publish as PDF or XPS** dialog box, in the **File name** box, enter a name for the file.

4. Click the **Save as type** arrow and select the target file type.

5. Use the navigation tools to display the folder in which you want to save the file.

6. Set the output options you want to apply to the file, choosing either to publish it at standard size, which is appropriate for publishing online or printing, or to minimize file size for online-only publishing.

7. Click **Publish**.

Manage comments

Excel makes it easy for you and your colleagues to insert comments in workbook cells, adding insights that go beyond the cell data. When you add a comment to a cell, a flag appears in the cell's upper-right corner. When you point to a cell that contains a comment, the comment appears in a box next to the cell, along with the user name of the user who was logged on to the computer on which the comment was created.

	A	B	C	D	E	F	G
1							
2			**Efficiency Improvement Projections**				
3							
4			**Department**				
5		**Year**	Receiving	**Curtis:** Scanning and machine sorting equipment due to come on line in late 2020.	ng	Loading	Delivery
6		2019	7%		12%	14%	19%
7		2020	10%		7%	5%	5%
8		2021	17%		5%	5%	12%
9							

An Excel worksheet with a comment in cell C8.

> ⚠ **IMPORTANT** The name attributed to a comment might not be the same as the name of the person who actually created it. Access controls, such as those that require users to enter account names and passwords when they access a computer, can help you track who made a comment or change.

Normally, Excel displays a cell's comment only when you point to the cell. You can change that behavior to display an individual comment or to show all comments within a worksheet. If you want to edit a comment, you can do so. You can also delete a comment from your workbook.

14

Manage comments by using the tools on the Review tab of the ribbon.

 IMPORTANT When someone other than the original user edits a comment, that person's input is marked with the new user's name and is added to the original comment.

You can control whether a cell displays just the comment indicator or the indicator and the comment itself. Also, if you've just begun to review a worksheet, you can display all of the comments on the sheet or move through them one at a time.

To add a comment to a cell

1. Click the cell where you want to add a comment.

2. On the **Review** tab of the ribbon, in the **Comments** group, click **New Comment**.

   Or

   Right-click the cell, and then click **Insert Comment**.

3. In the comment box that appears, enter a comment.

4. Click away from the cell to close the comment box.

To display a comment

1. Point to the cell that contains the comment.

To show or hide a comment

1. Click the cell that contains the comment.

2. In the **Comments** group, click **Show/Hide Comment**.

   Or

   Right-click the cell, and then click **Show/Hide Comments**.

To edit a comment

1. Click the cell that contains the comment.

2. In the **Comments** group, click **Edit Comment**.

Or

Right-click the cell, and then click **Edit Comment**.

3. In the comment box that appears, edit the text of the comment.

4. Click away from the cell to close the comment box.

To delete a comment

1. Click the cell that contains the comment.

2. In the **Comments** group, click **Delete**.

Or

Right-click the cell, and then click **Delete Comment**.

To change how Excel indicates that a cell contains a comment

1. Display the Backstage view, and then click **Options**.

2. In the **Excel Options** dialog box, click **Advanced**.

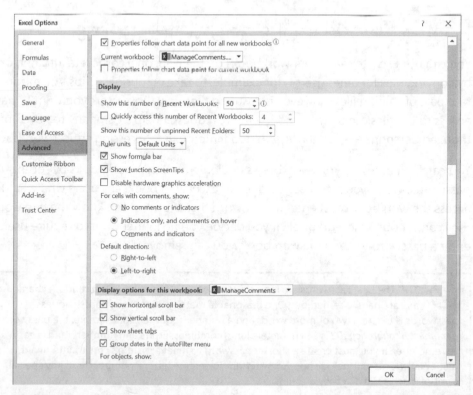

Manage how Excel displays comments.

3. In the **Display** section of the **Advanced** page, select one of the three available comment display options:

    - **No comments or indicators**

    - **Indicators only, and comments on hover**

    - **Comments and indicators**

To display or hide all comments

1. On the **Review** tab of the ribbon, in the **Comments** group, click **Show All Comments**.

To move through worksheet comments

1. In the **Comments** group, do either of the following:

    - Click **Previous** to display the previous comment.

    - Click **Next** to display the next comment.

Protect workbooks and worksheets

You can use Excel to share your workbooks on the web, on a corporate intranet, or by copying files for other users—for example, to take on business trips. An important part of sharing files, however, is ensuring that only those users you want to have access to the files can open or modify them. It doesn't help a company to have unauthorized personnel—even those with good intentions—accessing critical workbooks.

You can limit access to your workbooks or elements within workbooks by setting passwords. When you set a password for an Excel workbook, any users who want to access the workbook must enter its password first. If users don't know the password, they cannot open the workbook. If you decide you no longer want to require users to enter a password to open the workbook, you can remove it.

> **TIP** The best passwords are long strings of random characters, but random characters are hard to remember. One reasonable method of creating hard-to-guess passwords is to string two or more words and a number together. For example, the password *genuinestarcalibration302* is 24 characters long, combines letters and numbers, and is easy to remember. If you must create a shorter password to meet a system's constraints, avoid dictionary words and include uppercase letters, lowercase letters, numbers, and any special symbols such as ! or # if they are allowed.

Encrypt a workbook by setting a password to open the file.

If you want to allow anyone to open a workbook but want to prevent unauthorized users from editing a worksheet within that workbook, you can protect the individual worksheet. You can also set a password that a user must type in before protection can be turned off and choose which elements of the worksheet a user can change while protection is turned on. You do this from the Protect Sheet dialog box.

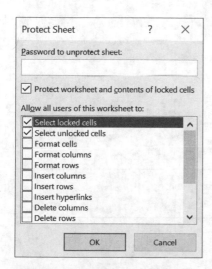

Limit the worksheet elements that a user can edit without a password.

14

The check box at the top of the list of allowed actions in the Protect Sheet dialog box mentions locked cells. A locked cell is a cell that can't be changed when worksheet protection is turned on.

You can lock or unlock a cell by changing the cell's formatting. You do this in the Format Cells dialog box. When worksheet protection is turned on, selecting the Locked check box in the dialog box prevents unauthorized users from changing the contents or formatting of the locked cell, whereas selecting the Hidden check box hides the formulas in the cell.

You might want to hide the formula in a cell if you draw sensitive data, such as customer contact information, from another workbook and don't want casual users to see the name of the workbook in a formula. This is also possible using the Format Cells dialog box.

Finally, you can password-protect a cell range. For example, you might want to let users enter values in most worksheet cells but also want to protect the cells with formulas that perform calculations based on those values.

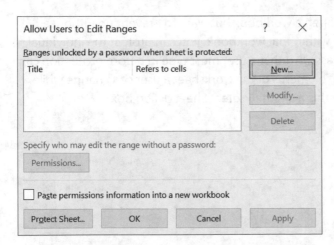

Define ranges users can edit after a worksheet is protected.

 TIP Remember that a range of cells can mean just one cell!

To require a password to open a workbook

1. Display the Backstage view, and then click **Info**.

2. Click **Protect Workbook**, and then click **Encrypt with Password**.

3. In the **Encrypt Document** dialog box, enter a password for the file.

4. Click **OK**.

5. In the **Confirm Password** dialog box, re-enter the password, and then click **OK**.

To remove a password from a workbook

1. Open the password-protected workbook.

2. On the **Info** page of the Backstage view, click **Protect Workbook**, and then click **Encrypt with Password**.

3. In the **Encrypt Document** dialog box, delete the existing password.

4. Click **OK**.

To require a password to change workbook structure

1. On the **Review** tab of the ribbon, in the **Protect** group, click **Protect Workbook**.

2. In the **Protect Structure and Windows** dialog box, enter a password for the workbook.

3. Click **OK**.

4. In the **Confirm Password** dialog box, re-enter the password.

5. Click **OK**.

To remove a password that protects a workbook's structure

1. Click **Protect Workbook**.

2. In the **Unprotect Workbook** dialog box, enter the workbook's password.

3. Click **OK**.

To protect a worksheet by setting a password

1. In the **Protect** group, click **Protect Sheet**.

2. In the **Protect Sheet** dialog box, enter a password in the **Password to unprotect sheet** box.

3. Select the check boxes next to the actions you want to allow users to perform.

14

4. Click **OK**.

5. In the **Confirm Password** dialog box, re-enter the password.

6. Click **OK**.

To remove a worksheet password

1. In the **Protect** group, click **Unprotect Sheet**.

2. In the **Unprotect Sheet** dialog box, enter the worksheet's password.

3. Click **OK**.

To lock a cell to prevent editing

1. Right-click the cell you want to lock, and then click **Format Cells**.

2. In the **Format Cells** dialog box, click the **Protection** tab.

Prevent cell editing and hide formulas when you protect a sheet.

3. Select the **Locked** check box.

4. Click **OK**.

To hide cell formulas

1. Right-click the cell you want to lock, and then click **Format Cells**.

2. Click the **Protection** tab.

3. Select the **Hidden** check box.

4. Click **OK**.

> **IMPORTANT** You must protect your worksheet for the Locked and Hidden settings to take effect.

To restrict editing of a cell range by using a password

1. In the **Protect** group, click **Allow Edit Ranges**.

2. In the **Allow Users to Edit Ranges** dialog box, click **New**.

3. In the **New Range** dialog box, in the **Title** box, enter a title for the range.

4. Click in the **Refers to cells** box and select the cell range you want to affect.

5. In the **Range password** box, enter the password for the range.

6. Click **OK**.

7. In the **Confirm Password** dialog box, re-enter the password.

8. Click **OK**.

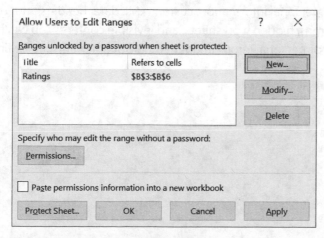

Define cell ranges users are allowed to edit.

14

9. Repeat steps 2 through 8 to protect another cell range.

10. Click **OK**.

 IMPORTANT You must protect your worksheet for the range password settings to take effect.

To remove a cell range password

1. Click **Allow Edit Ranges**.

2. In the **Allow Users to Edit Ranges** dialog box, click the range you want to edit.

3. Click **Delete**.

4. Click **OK**.

Finalize workbooks

Distributing a workbook to other users carries many risks—including the possibility that the workbook might contain information you don't want to share with users outside your organization. With Excel, you can inspect a workbook for information you might not want to distribute to other people and create a read-only final version that prevents other people from making changes to the workbook content.

By using the Document Inspector, you can quickly locate comments and annotations, document properties and personal information, custom XML data, headers and footers, hidden rows and columns, hidden worksheets, and invisible content. You can then easily remove any hidden or personal information that the Document Inspector finds.

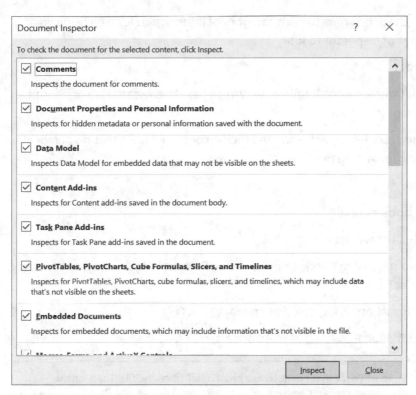

Check for personally identifiable information by using the Document Inspector.

The Document Inspector checks your document for every category of information selected in the list. When the Document Inspector displays its results, you can select which pieces of personally identifiable information you want to remove.

When you're done making changes to a workbook, you can mark it as final. Marking a workbook as final sets the status property to Final and disables data entry and editing commands. If you later decide that you want to make more changes, you can do so, save your changes, and mark the worksheet final again.

To remove personally identifiable information from a workbook

1. Press **Ctrl+S** to save the workbook.

2. Display the Backstage view and, if necessary, click **Info**.

3. Click **Check for Issues**, and then click **Inspect Document**.

 TIP If you didn't save your workbook earlier, Excel will prompt you to do so now.

4. Select the check box next to each category of information for which you want the **Document Inspector** to look.

5. Click **Inspect**.

6. In the results list, click the **Remove All** button next to any category of information you want to remove.

7. If necessary, click **Reinspect**, and then click **Inspect** to ensure that no personal information remains in the file.

8. Click **Close**.

To mark a workbook as final

1. Press **Ctrl+S** to save the workbook.

2. On the **Info** page of the Backstage view, click **Protect Workbook**, and then click **Mark as Final**.

3. In the confirmation dialog box that appears, click **OK**.

4. In the informational dialog box that appears, click **OK**.

 TIP To edit a file that has been marked as final, open the file. Then, on the message bar, click Edit Anyway.

Authenticate workbooks

When exchanging files over a network, especially the Internet, you need to be sure of the origin of the files you're working with to avoid viruses or falsified data. One way an organization can achieve this is to authenticate every workbook by using a digital signature. A digital signature is a character string created by combining a user's unique digital certificate with the contents of the workbook, which apps such as Excel can recognize and use to verify the identity of the user who signed the file. A good analogy for a digital signature is a wax seal, which was used for thousands of years to verify the integrity and origin of a document.

The technical details of and procedure for managing digital certificates are beyond the scope of this book, but your network administrator should be able to create or obtain a digital certificate for you. You can also directly purchase a digital signature from a third party; these signatures can usually be renewed annually for a small fee. For the purposes of this book, you can use the *selfcert.exe* Microsoft Office accessory app to generate a certificate with which to perform this topic's practice task at the end of this chapter. This type of certificate is useful for certifying a document as part of a demonstration, but other users might not accept it as a valid certificate.

 TIP When you click Add a Digital Signature in the Protect Workbook list on the Info page of the Backstage view, Excel checks your computer for usable digital certificates. If it can't find one, Excel displays a dialog box indicating that you can buy a digital signature from a third-party provider. You won't be able to add a digital signature to a file until you acquire a digital certificate, either by generating a test certificate using the included selfcert.exe app or by purchasing one through a third-party vendor.

If you have several certificates from which to choose, and the certificate you want doesn't appear when you attempt to sign your file, you can change the chosen certificate and start the signing process again.

⚠️ **IMPORTANT** Editing a workbook that has a digital signature invalidates the signature. To verify the file, you must sign it again.

To display available third-party vendors of digital certificates

1. Display the Backstage view and, if necessary, click **Info**.

2. Click **Protect Workbook**.

3. Click **Add a Digital Signature**.

 TIP If your workbook is not saved in a file format that supports digital signatures, such as .xlsx, Excel will prompt you to save it accordingly.

4. In the **Get a Digital ID** dialog box, click **Yes**.

Or

1. Go to *https://support.office.com* in your web browser.

2. Enter **Digital ID** in the search box.

3. Click **Get a digital ID**.

14

To create a test certificate by using selfcert.exe

1. In File Explorer, open the **C:\Program Files (x86)\Microsoft Office\root\Office16** folder and double-click **selfcert.exe**.

2. In the **Create Digital Signature** dialog box, enter a name for your certificate.

3. Click **OK**.

4. In the confirmation dialog box that appears, click **OK**.

To authenticate a workbook by using a digital signature

1. Press **Ctrl+S** to save the workbook.

2. On the **Info** page of the Backstage view, click **Protect Workbook**, and then click **Add a Digital Signature**.

3. In the **Sign** dialog box, click the **Commitment Type** arrow and select the role you played in creating and approving the document.

4. In the **Purpose for signing this document** box, enter a reason for signing the file.

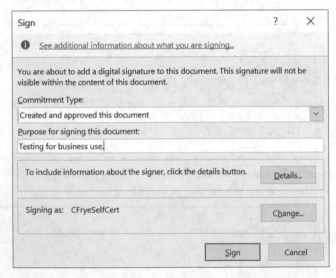

Authenticate a workbook by signing it with a digital certificate.

5. If necessary, click **Change** and use the tools in the **Windows Security** dialog box to select a digital certificate.

6. Click **Sign**.

Save workbooks for the web

You can use Excel to save your workbooks as web documents so that you and your colleagues can view workbooks over the Internet or on an organization's intranet. For a document to be viewable on the web, it must be saved as an HTML file. HTML files, which end with either the *.htm* or the *.html* extension, include tags that tell a web browser such as Microsoft Edge how to display the contents of the file.

For example, you might want to set the data labels in a workbook apart from the rest of the data by having the labels displayed with bold text. The coding in an HTML file that indicates text to be displayed as bold text is ..., where the ellipsis between the tags is replaced by the text to be displayed. So, the following HTML fragment would be displayed as **Excel** in a webpage:

```
<b>Excel</b>
```

> **TIP** If the only sheet in your workbook that contains data is the one displayed when you save the workbook as a webpage, Excel saves only that worksheet as a webpage.

After you save an Excel workbook as a set of HTML documents, you can open it in your web browser. It's also possible to save a workbook as a web file that retains a link to the original workbook. That way, whenever someone updates the workbook, Excel updates the web files to reflect the new content.

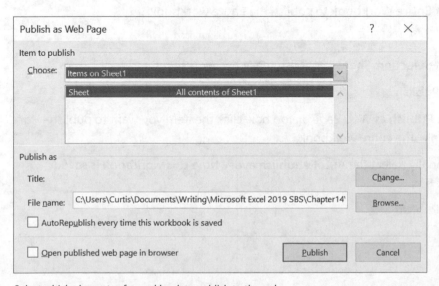

Select which elements of a workbook to publish to the web.

You can select which elements of your workbook to publish to the web in the Publish as Web Page dialog box. Clicking the Choose arrow displays a list of publishable items, including options to publish the entire workbook, items on specific sheets, or a range of cells. You can also specify which text appears on the webpage's title bar.

To save a workbook as a web file

1. Display the Backstage view, and then click **Save As**.

2. Click **Browse**.

3. In the **Save As** dialog box, click the **Save as type** arrow, and then click **Web Page**.

4. If necessary, in the **File name** box, edit the name of the file.

5. Click **Save**.

6. If necessary, in the dialog box that appears, click **Yes** to acknowledge that some features might be lost when you save the workbook as a webpage.

To publish a workbook to the web

1. Display the Backstage view, and then click **Save As**.

2. Click **Browse**.

3. In the **Save As** dialog box, click the **Save as type** arrow, and then click **Web Page**.

4. If necessary, in the **File name** box, edit the name of the file.

5. Select **Entire Workbook** to publish the entire workbook.

   Or

   Select **Selection: Sheet** to publish the active worksheet.

6. Click **Publish**.

7. In the **Publish as Web Page** dialog box, click the item you want to publish—for example, the entire workbook.

8. Optionally, select the **AutoRepublish every time this workbook is saved** check box.

9. Click **Publish**.

Import and export XML data

HTML lets you determine how a document will be displayed in a web browser—for example, by telling Internet Explorer to display certain text in bold type or to start a new paragraph. However, HTML doesn't tell you anything about the meaning of data in a document. Internet Explorer might "know" it should display a set of data in a table, but it wouldn't "know" that the data represented an Excel worksheet.

You can add metadata, or data about data, to web documents by using Extensible Markup Language (XML). Although a full discussion of XML is beyond the scope of this book, the following bit of XML code shows how you might identify two sets of three values (Month, Category, and Exceptions) by using XML:

```
<?xml version="1.0" encoding="UTF-8" standalone="yes"?> <ns2:exceptions xmlns:ns2=
"http://www.w3schools.com"> <exception> <Month>January</Month> <Category>2Day</
Category> <Exceptions>14</Exceptions> </exception> <exception> <Month>January</Month>
<Category>3Day</Category> <Exceptions>3</Exceptions> </exception> </ns2:exceptions>
```

XML is meant to be a universal language, allowing data to move freely from one app to another. Excel might display those two sets of exceptions data as rows of data in an Excel worksheet.

	A	B	C	D
1	**Month**	**Category**	**Exceptions**	
2	January	2Day	14	
3	January	3Day	3	
4				

Data imported from an XML file can be displayed in an Excel worksheet.

Other apps could display or process the XML file's contents in other ways, but you wouldn't have to change the underlying XML file. All the work is done by the other apps' programmers.

To work with XML data in Excel, you must use the controls on the Developer ribbon tab, which you can display by using the ribbon customization commands available in the Excel Options dialog box.

14

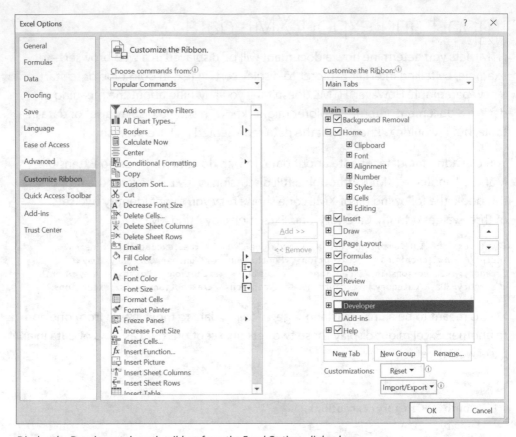

Display the Developer tab on the ribbon from the Excel Options dialog box.

You can bring XML data into Excel either by opening a workbook saved in a compatible XML format or by importing the data from a text file. XML data is organized according to a specified schema or structure. If the schema file isn't available, you can have Excel look at the structure of the imported data and create one for you. If you export a worksheet to an XML file, you can have Excel create a schema for that operation, too.

> **✓ TIP** If you have imported an XML file but believe that the original XML data file has changed, click the Refresh Data button in the XML group on the Developer tab to update your worksheet.

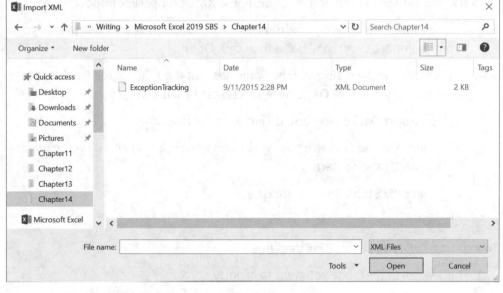

Select an XML source file by using the Import XML dialog box.

To save a workbook as an XML file

1. Display the Backstage view, and then click **Save As**.

2. Click **Browse**.

3. In the **Save As** dialog box, click the **Save as type** arrow, and then click one of the following file types:

   - **XML Data**

   - **XML Spreadsheet 2003**

   - **Strict Open XML Spreadsheet**

4. If necessary, in the **File name** box, edit the name of the file.

5. Click **Save**.

To import an XML data file into a workbook

1. If necessary, use the tools in the **Excel Options** dialog box to add the **Developer** tab to the ribbon.

> **SEE ALSO** For more information on displaying an existing ribbon tab, see "Customize the ribbon" in Chapter 1.

14

2. On the **Developer** tab of the ribbon, in the **XML** group, click **Import**.

3. In the **Import XML** dialog box, navigate to the folder that contains the file you want to import, click the file, and then click **Open**.

4. If necessary, in the dialog box that indicates that the XML source file does not refer to a schema, click **OK** to have Excel create a schema for you.

5. In the **Import Data** dialog box, do either of the following:

   • Select **XML table in existing worksheet** and click the cell where you want the XML table to start.

   • Select **XML table in new worksheet**.

6. Click **OK**.

To export a cell range as an XML data file

1. Click a cell in the range you want to export.

2. In the **XML** group, click **Export**.

3. In the **Export XML** dialog box, navigate to the folder where you want to export the XML data.

4. In the **File name** box, enter a name for the file.

5. Click **Export**.

Work with OneDrive and Excel Online

As information workers become increasingly mobile, they need to be able to access their data from anywhere and have a single version of a file to which they can turn. Excel 2019 is integrated with OneDrive, a Microsoft cloud service that stores your files remotely and provides you with access to them over the Internet.

 IMPORTANT You can find OneDrive online at *www.onedrive.com*. You will need a Microsoft account to use OneDrive.

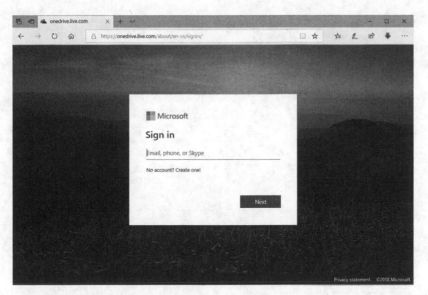

Sign in to OneDrive at www.onedrive.com.

When you sign in to OneDrive, you'll see the main directory of your OneDrive account, which you can navigate to reach your files.

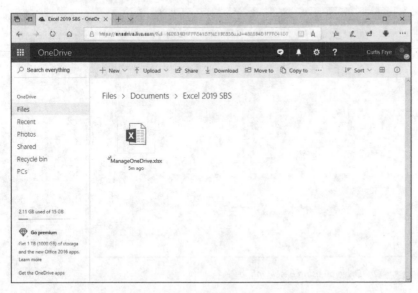

OneDrive manages files and folders like File Explorer.

You can manage files by using the built-in interface, performing familiar tasks such as opening, creating, uploading, downloading, and copying files. You can also navigate the file structure, moving between folders and creating or deleting them as needed.

14

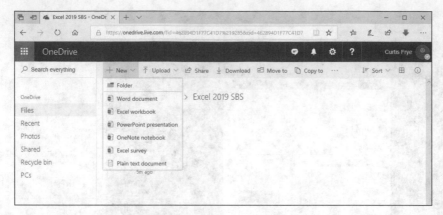

Create new folders and documents by using the OneDrive New menu.

Clicking the New button also displays links to create a folder, Word document, Excel workbook, PowerPoint presentation, OneNote notebook, Excel survey, or plain text document. When you create a new Excel workbook from this menu, Excel Online starts and you can begin adding data to the new workbook.

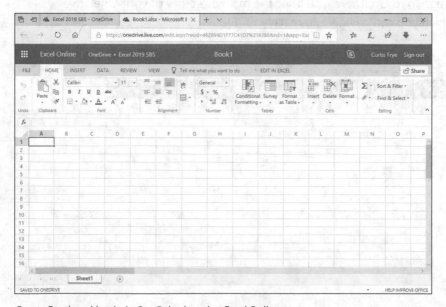

Create Excel workbooks in OneDrive by using Excel Online.

 TIP Excel Online saves your workbook every time you edit a cell, so there's no Save button on the Quick Access Toolbar.

Excel Online provides a rich set of capabilities you can use to create new workbooks and edit workbooks you created in the desktop edition of the app. If you find you need some features that aren't available in Excel Online, you can always open the file in the Excel 2019 desktop app.

> ⚠️ **IMPORTANT** You might see a series of dialog boxes asking you to sign back in to your Microsoft account and to provide other information. These queries are normal and expected.

If you want to collaborate with colleagues who also have OneDrive accounts, you can share your Excel workbook with them online. You can choose how to share your workbook, either by allowing your colleagues to edit the file or just view it, or you can require them to access the file from a Microsoft account or just over the web.

To sign in to OneDrive

1. In your web browser, go to *www.onedrive.com*.

2. Click **Sign in**.

3. Enter your account name (usually an email address) and press **Enter**.

4. Enter your password and press **Enter**.

To upload a file or folder to OneDrive

1. In OneDrive, click the **Upload** button on the toolbar.

2. In the **Open** dialog box, select the file or folder you want to upload.

3. Click **Open**.

To download a file from OneDrive

1. Point to the icon representing the file you want to download and select the round check box that appears in the upper-right corner of the icon.

2. On the menu bar, click **Download** to download the file to your computer's Downloads folder.

To create a new Excel workbook in OneDrive

1. Open your OneDrive account in your web browser.

2. Click **New**, and then click **Excel workbook**.

14

To open an Excel workbook stored in OneDrive in the desktop edition of Excel

1. Open your OneDrive account in your web browser.

2. Click the file you want to work with to open it in Excel Online.

> **TIP** Depending on your computer's settings, the order and appearance of dialog boxes and messages might differ slightly from what is described here.

3. Click **Open in Excel**.

4. In the **External Protocol Request** dialog box, click **Launch Application**.

5. In the alert dialog box that appears, click **Yes**.

6. If necessary, in the **Sign in** dialog box, enter your email address and password and click **Sign in**.

7. When you're done working with the file in Excel, close Excel and any remaining dialog boxes from Excel Online.

To collaborate with colleagues by using Excel Online

1. Open a workbook in Excel Online.

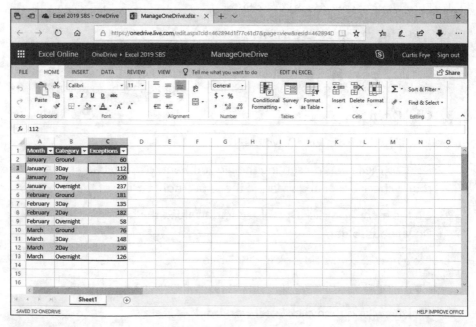

Share a workbook by using Excel Online.

2. In the upper-right corner of the screen, click **Share**.

3. In the **Share** dialog box, in the **To** box, enter the email addresses of individuals with whom you want to share the workbook.

   To add multiple addresses, enter the first address and press the **Tab** key.

4. If you want to include a note, enter it into the **Add a quick note** box.

5. To change sharing characteristics, click **Recipients can edit** and then do any of the following:

   - Click **Recipients can only view**.

   - Click the **Recipients don't need a Microsoft account** box, and then click **Recipients need to sign in with a Microsoft account**.

6. Click **Share**.

7. In the confirmation dialog box that appears, click **Close**.

Skills review

In this chapter, you learned how to:

- Save workbooks for electronic distribution

- Manage comments

- Protect workbooks and worksheets

- Finalize workbooks

- Authenticate workbooks

- Save workbooks for the web

- Import and export XML data

- Work with OneDrive and Excel Online

14

Practice tasks

The practice files for these tasks are located in the Excel2019SBS\Ch14 folder. You can save the results of the tasks in the same folder.

Save workbooks for electronic distribution

Open the DistributeFiles workbook in Excel, and then perform the following tasks:

1. Display the **Sheet1** worksheet of the workbook and export it as a **PDF** file.

2. Export the entire workbook as an **XPS** file.

Manage comments

Open the ManageComments workbook in Excel, and then perform the following tasks:

1. Add comments to four or five cells.

2. Edit one of the comments to invite a colleague to provide input for that value.

3. Move through the comments, going forward and backward through the list.

4. Change the workbook so it displays all comments.

5. Delete a comment.

Add protection to workbooks and worksheets

Open the ProtectWorkbooks workbook in Excel, and then perform the following tasks:

1. By using the controls on the **Info** page of the Backstage view, encrypt the workbook with a password.

2. On the **Performance** worksheet, click cell **B8** and format the cell so its contents are locked and hidden.

3. By using the controls on the **Review** tab, protect the active worksheet with a password after clearing the **Select locked cells** and **Select unlocked cells** check boxes in the dialog box.

4. On the **Weights** worksheet, select cells **A3:B6** and define a protected range named **AllWeights**.

5. Protect the **Weights** worksheet by requiring users to enter a password to edit it.

Finalize workbooks

Open the FinalizeWorkbooks workbook in Excel, and then perform the following tasks:

1. Inspect the workbook by using the Document Inspector.

2. Remove any personally identifiable information from the file.

3. Use the tools on the **Info** page of the Backstage view to mark the file as final.

4. Close the workbook.

5. Reopen the workbook and click the **Edit Anyway** button on the message bar to work with the file.

6. Save any changes and close the workbook.

Authenticate workbooks

Open the AuthenticateWorkbooks workbook in Excel, and then perform the following tasks:

1. Acquire or create a digital certificate.

2. Sign the workbook and give the reason for signing it as Testing procedure for later use in business.

Save workbooks for the web

Open the SaveForWeb workbook in Excel, and then perform the following tasks:

1. Display the **Sheet1** worksheet in the workbook, and then save that worksheet as a web file named **ShipmentSummaryWeb**.

2. Close the web file and, if necessary, reopen the **SaveForWeb** workbook.

3. Display **Sheet2** of the workbook, and then publish the PivotTable on **Sheet2** to the web.

4. Set the workbook to autorepublish the web file every time the original workbook changes.

5. Select the **Open published web page in browser** check box, and then publish the file.

Import and export XML data

Open the ImportXMLData workbook in Excel, and then perform the following tasks:

1. Import data from the **ExceptionTracking.xml** file in the Excel2019SBS\Ch14 folder.

2. Export the data you just imported to a new file named ExportXML.xml.

3. Save your workbook in one of the XML-based formats available in the **Save As** dialog box.

Work with OneDrive and Excel Online

Open the ManageOneDrive workbook in Excel, and then perform the following tasks:

1. If necessary, create a new OneDrive account.

2. Sign in to a OneDrive account.

3. Upload the **ManageOneDrive** workbook to your OneDrive account.

4. Open the **ManageOneDrive** file in Excel Online.

5. Open the file in the desktop edition of Excel.

6. Add a row of data showing **April** exceptions in the Ground category totaling 45 incidents.

7. Save your work, and then close your files.

Part 4

Perform advanced analysis

Perform business intelligence analysis

Organizations of all kinds generate and collect data from operations, sales, and customers. As the volume of data grows, so does the importance of generating useful insights into your operations from that data. Excel supports business intelligence analysis, which is the practice of examining data to improve business performance.

Analytical tools such as formulas, data tables, and PivotTables all provide valuable insights into your data, but their applications can be limited in size and scope. Excel 2019 includes many advanced data analysis capabilities that were previously exclusive to enterprise customers. One technology underlying the new tools is the Excel Data Model, which you can use to create relationships among Excel tables in your workbooks. Add to this the ability to import and analyze large data sets by using Power Query and Power Pivot, and Excel 2019 puts significant data analysis capabilities at your fingertips.

This chapter guides you through procedures related to enabling the Data Analysis add-ins and adding tables to the Data Model, defining relationships between tables, analyzing data by using Power Pivot, viewing data by using timelines, and bringing in external data by using Power Query.

> ⚠ **IMPORTANT** The tools and techniques described in this chapter will be available to you only after you enable the Data Analysis add-ins.

In this chapter

- Define a Data Model
- Define relationships between tables
- Analyze data by using Power Pivot
- View data by using timelines
- Bring in external data by using Power Query

Practice files

For this chapter, use the practice files from the Excel2019SBS\Ch15 folder. For practice file download instructions, see the introduction.

Define a Data Model

Excel 2019 includes a collection of Data Analysis add-ins you can use to perform advanced analysis on your data. These tools build on the Excel Data Model, which manages Excel tables, query tables, and other data sources, as part of a coherent whole, rather than individual tables.

After you enable the Data Analysis add-ins, you can add data sources to the Data Model, display the Data Model, and return to your main Excel workbook.

To enable the Data Analysis add-ins

1. Display the Backstage view, and then click **Options**.

2. In the **Excel Options** dialog box, click **Data**.

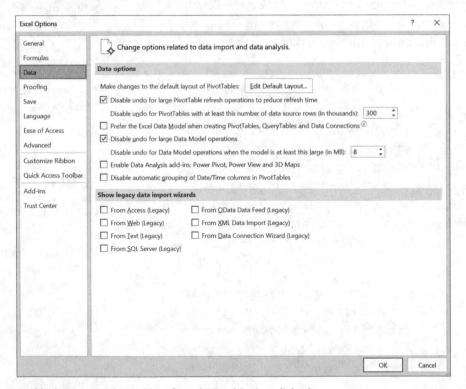

Enable the Data Analysis add-ins from the Excel Options dialog box.

3. In the **Data options** group, select the **Enable Data Analysis add-ins: Power Pivot, Power View and 3D Maps** check box.

4. Click **OK**.

To add an Excel table to the Data Model

1. If necessary, enable the Data Analysis add-ins.

2. Click any cell in the Excel table.

3. On the **Power Pivot** tab, in the **Tables** group, click **Add to Data Model** to add the Excel table and display it in the **Power Pivot** window.

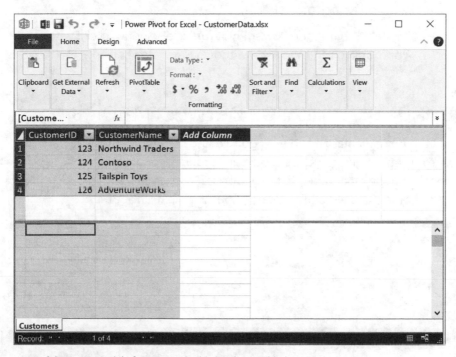

View of the Data Model after an Excel table has been added.

To set a preference to add data to the Data Model

1. Open the **Excel Options** dialog box, and then click **Advanced**.

2. In the **Data** group, select the **Prefer the Data Model when creating PivotTables, QueryTables, and Data Connections** check box.

3. Click **OK**.

To display the Data Model

1. On the **Data** tab, in the **Data Tools** group, click **Manage Data Model**.

   Or

   On the **Power Pivot** tab, in the **Data Model** group, click **Manage**.

15

2. In the **Power Pivot for Excel** window, on the tab bar, click the sheet tab of the worksheet you want to display.

To return to the Excel workbook

1. Perform either of these actions:

   - In the **Power Pivot for Excel** window, click the **Close** button to close Power Pivot and return to Excel.

   - On the title bar of the **Power Pivot for Excel** window, click **Switch to Workbook** to return to Excel without closing Power Pivot.

Define relationships between tables

One of the fundamental principles of good database design is to store data about specific business objects, such as customers, products, or orders, in a table by itself, separate from the other tables in the database. For example, you might store data about customers in one table and data about shipments in another.

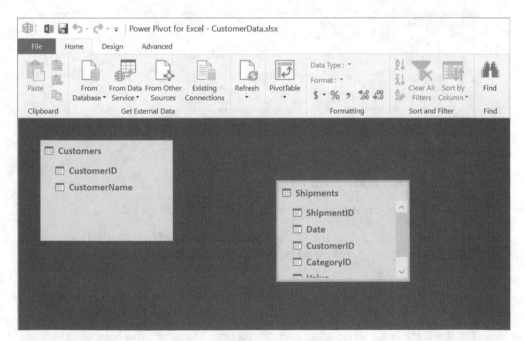

Display relationships between tables by using Diagram View.

Each table has one column, or field, that contains a unique value for each row. This type of column, called a key, makes it possible to distinguish a row from every other row. For example, a table listing customers could have a *CustomerID* field as its key, with the same field appearing in a table named *Orders*, which tracks the date, time, value, and identity of the customer who placed each order.

> **TIP** The best keys are arbitrary numerical values. If you try to store information in a key field, you will likely run into issues of duplication that make processing your data harder, not easier.

You can create connections between tables by identifying fields they have in common. For example, consider a *Customers* table that has two fields—*CustomerID* and *CustomerName*—and an *Orders* table that has three fields—*OrderID*, *CustomerID*, and *OrderPrice*. The *CustomerID* field appears in both tables, so it can be used to establish a link, or relationship.

> **IMPORTANT** You must add Excel tables to the Data Model to define relationships between them.

In the *Customers* table, each *CustomerID* field value occurs exactly once, so that column is called a primary key. The *CustomerID* field also occurs in the *Orders* table, but because it's possible for a customer to place more than one order, the *CustomerID* field's values can repeat. When a key field appears in another table in which it doesn't distinguish each row from every other row, it's called a foreign key.

When you create a relationship, you link the primary key field from one table to the corresponding foreign key field in another table. Although it's easier to spot the fields if they have the same name, such as *CustomerID*, they don't have to have the same name; they just need to contain the same data.

15

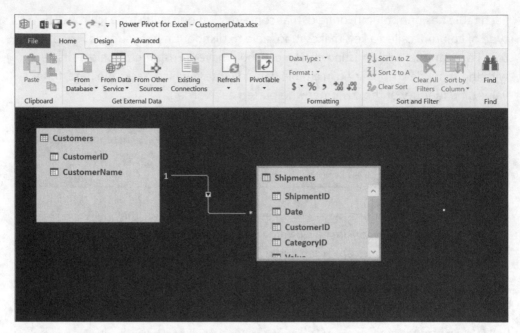

Diagram View of a Data Model with a relationship between two tables.

After you define a relationship in the Data Model, you can create PivotTables that use data from both Excel tables. You can also edit or delete relationships if necessary.

To display the Data Model in Diagram View

1. If necessary, on the **Data** tab, in the **Data Tools** group, click **Manage Data Model**.

2. In the **Power Pivot for Excel** window, on the **Home** tab, in the **View** group, click **Diagram View**.

To display the Data Model in Data View

1. If necessary, click **Manage Data Model**.

2. In the **Power Pivot for Excel** window, in the **View** group, click **Data View**.

To define a relationship between tables

1. If necessary, click **Manage Data Model**.

2. In the **Power Pivot for Excel** window, in the **View** group, click **Diagram View**.

3. In the **Diagram View** window, drag the field from the source table to the corresponding field in the table that includes the source field's values.

4. When the pointer changes to a curved arrow, release the mouse button to create the relationship.

Or

1. In Power Pivot, on the **Design** tab of the ribbon, in the **Relationships** group, click **Create Relationship**.

2. In the **Create Relationship** dialog box, click the **Table 1** arrow, and then click the table in which the field you want to link is the table's primary key field.

3. In the **Columns** list on the left, click the field you want to link to the other table.

4. Click the **Table 2** arrow, and then click the table in which the field you want to link is a foreign key field.

5. In the **Columns** list on the right, click the field that corresponds to the primary key field from the source table.

6. Click **OK**.

To view the Excel table that provides data to a linked table in the Data Model

1. In Power Pivot, click **Diagram View**.

2. In the viewing pane, click the table you want to view.

3. On the **Linked Table** tab of the ribbon, click **Go to Excel Table**.

To edit an existing relationship

1. In Power Pivot, on the **Design** tab, click **Manage Relationships**.

2. In the **Manage Relationships** dialog box, click the relationship you want to edit.

3. Click **Edit**.

15

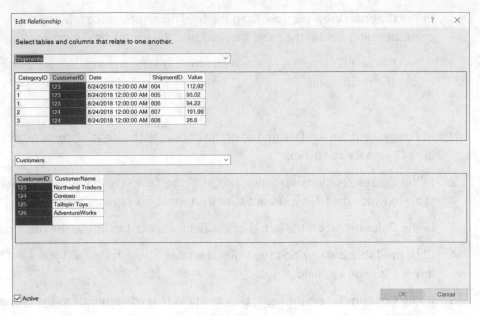

Edit relationships between tables in the Data Model.

4. In the **Edit Relationship** dialog box, change the tables and fields that form the relationship.

5. Click **OK**.

To delete a relationship

1. In Power Pivot, click **Manage Relationships**.

2. In the **Manage Relationships** dialog box, click the relationship you want to delete.

3. Click **Delete**.

4. In the confirmation dialog box that appears, click **OK**.

5. Click **Close**.

Analyze data by using Power Pivot

When the Excel product team changed the underlying file format of Excel 2007 from XLS to XLSX, they let users store much more data on each worksheet. Rather than limiting each worksheet to 65,536 rows, you can now store up to 1,048,576 rows of data. In 2007, that larger number of rows seemed more than adequate for most Excel users.

It still is, but the powerful business intelligence analysis tools built into Excel led users to import large data sets and to find ways to combine data collections that spanned multiple worksheets.

Originally introduced as an add-in for Excel 2010, Power Pivot is a tool you can use to work with any amount of data, as long as the total file size is less than 2 gigabytes (GB) and takes up less than 4 GB of memory. For such large data collections, you'll usually work with summaries of your data, though you can focus on specific aspects of the data by sorting and filtering.

 SEE ALSO For more information about creating filters, see "Limit data that appears on your screen" in Chapter 5, "Manage worksheet data."

When you bring a data collection into Power Pivot, Excel attempts to identify the data type of each column. The app is usually accurate, but some data types can cause confusion. For example, Excel will occasionally identify currency or accounting data columns as containing regular numbers that include decimal values. If this type of mistake happens, you can always change the column's data type.

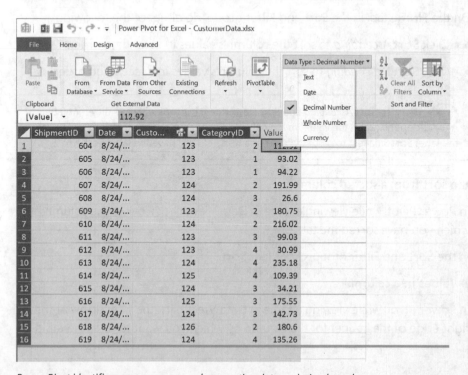

Power Pivot identifies some currency and accounting data as decimal numbers.

IMPORTANT When you change the data type of a column, it might affect the column values' precision and the results of calculations performed using the data.

Most large data sets contain raw data, such as sales amounts, and rely on the visualization or summary software program to calculate values such as sales tax, commissions, or profit. To add this type of summary to your Power Pivot data, you can define a calculated column. The formula syntax for creating a calculated column is very similar to creating a formula that refers to an Excel table column, so you already have the skills to create them.

As with columns in Excel tables, you can rename and delete Power Pivot columns, but the real analytical power of Power Pivot comes from creating PivotTables from the large Power Pivot data sets. Creating a PivotTable from 10,000 rows of data is useful; creating a PivotTable from 10,000,000 rows can provide incredible insight.

To sort values in a column in ascending or descending order

1. In Power Pivot, while viewing a table in Data View, click a cell in the column by which you want to sort the table.

2. On the **Home** tab, in the **Sort and Filter** group, do either of the following:

   - Click **Sort** *Ascending* to sort the column's values in ascending order.

   - Click **Sort** *Descending* to sort the column's values in descending order.

> **TIP** The Sort *Ascending* and Sort *Descending* buttons will have different labels depending on the values in the column. For example, a number field will have the label Sort Smallest to Largest, whereas a text field will have the label Sort A to Z.

To clear a sort from a sorted column

1. In Power Pivot, while viewing a table in Data View, click a cell in the column by which you have sorted the table.

2. In the **Sort and Filter** group, click **Clear Sort**.

To filter values in a column

1. In Power Pivot, while viewing a table in Data View, click the filter arrow at the right edge of the header for the column by which you want to filter the table.

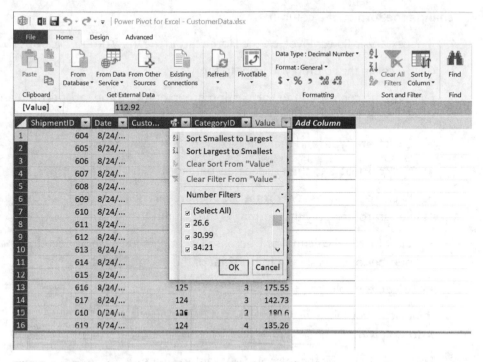

Filter Power Pivot columns by creating rules or selecting specific values.

2. In the filter list, perform either of the following actions:

   - Click *DataType* **Filters**, click the type of filter rule you want to create, create the rule, and click **OK**.

   - Select and clear the check boxes to show or hide individual values.

3. Click **OK**.

To clear filters applied to a Power Pivot sheet

1. In Power Pivot, on the **Home** tab, in the **Sort and Filter** group, click **Clear All Filters**.

Or

1. Click the filter arrow of the column from which you want to remove the filter.

2. In the filter list, click **Clear Filter from** *"FieldName"*.

3. Click **OK**.

15

To change the format of a column

1. If necessary, in Power Pivot, on the **Home** tab, in the **View** group, click **Data View**.

2. Click a cell in the column you want to format.

3. By using the controls in the **Formatting** group of the **Home** tab, perform any of the following actions:

   - Click **Data Type**, and then click a new data type in the list.

   - Click **Format**, and then click a new data format in the list.

   - Click **Apply Currency Format**, **Apply Percentage Format**, or **Thousands Separator** to apply that format to the column.

   - Click **Increase Decimal** or **Decrease Decimal** to increase or decrease the number of digits shown to the right of the decimal point.

To add a calculated column

1. In Power Pivot, while viewing a table in Data View, click the top cell in the **Add Column** column.

2. Enter = followed by the formula you want to create.

   Add fields to the formula by entering [and then selecting the field that contains the values you want to use in your formula.

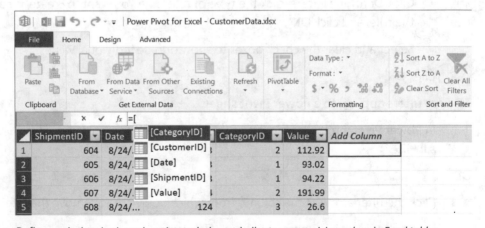

Define a calculated column by using techniques similar to summarizing values in Excel tables.

3. Press **Enter**.

To rename a column

1. In Power Pivot, while viewing a table in Data View, double-click the header cell of the column you want to rename.

2. Enter the new column name.

3. Press **Enter**.

To delete a column

1. In Power Pivot, while viewing a table in Data View, right-click the header cell of the column you want to delete.

2. Click **Delete Columns**.

To create a PivotTable from Power Pivot data

1. In Power Pivot, on the **Home** tab, click **PivotTable**.

2. In the **Create PivotTable** dialog box, click **New Worksheet**.

3. Click **OK**.

> **TIP** Excel creates a PivotTable by using all available data in the Data Model, not just the table that was displayed when you created the PivotTable.

View data by using timelines

Business data often records events at a specific point in time, whether a sale to an individual customer on a specific day or net profit for a quarter or a year. If your data contains a time-based value, such as the day of a sale, you can analyze that data by creating a timeline.

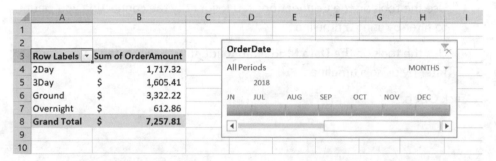

Use timelines to filter PivotTable data based on time increments.

15

> **TIP** Timelines and slicers are built on the same design philosophy: providing a visual indication of the elements included and excluded by a filter. What slicers do for category data, timelines do for chronological data.

A timeline provides a graphical interface you can use to filter a PivotTable. For table columns that contain individual date values, such as 8/2/2018, the timeline box will recognize those dates and let you filter by year, quarter, month, or day.

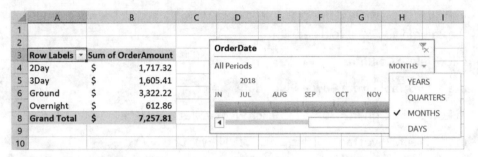

Change the time increment by which you filter data by using a timeline.

You can use the elements within a timeline to select individual increments, such as days or months, or ranges of those same values. As with other objects, such as charts, you can change the appearance of your timeline, resize it, change its appearance, hide or display elements, and delete it when it's no longer required.

To create a timeline

1. Click a cell in an Excel table that is based on a connection to an external data source or that is part of the workbook's Data Model.

2. On the **Insert** tab, in the **Filters** group, click **Timeline**.

3. In the **Existing Connections** dialog box, do either of the following:

   - Use the tools on the **Connections** tab to identify the connection you want to filter by using a timeline.

   - Use the tools on the **Data Model** tab to identify the Excel table you want to filter by using a timeline.

4. Click **Open**.

5. In the **Insert Timelines** dialog box, select the check box next to the field by which you want to filter.

6. Click **OK**.

To filter a PivotTable by using a timeline

1. Create a timeline based on an Excel table that has been used to create a PivotTable.

2. Click **Time Level** in the upper-right area of the timeline, and then click the time level you want to use (such as months, quarters, or days).

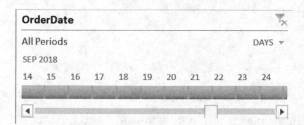

Select the increment by which you want to filter in your timeline.

3. In the scrolling time display, do any of the following:

   - Click the increment you want to display.

   - Select multiple increments by holding down the **Ctrl** key and clicking the increments you want to display.

   - Select a range of increments by clicking the first increment in the range and then, while holding down the **Shift** key, clicking the last increment in the range of dates you want to display.

To clear a timeline filter

1. In the timeline, click the **Clear Filter** button at the right end of the title bar.

To change the appearance of a timeline

1. Click the timeline.

2. On the **Options** tool tab of the ribbon, in the **Timeline Styles** gallery, click the style you want to apply.

15

To resize a timeline

1. Click the timeline.

2. Drag any of the handles on the timeline to change its size, as follows:

   - Drag a handle in the middle of the top or bottom edge to make the timeline shorter or taller.

   - Drag a handle in the middle of the left or right edge to make the timeline wider or narrower.

   - Drag a handle in the corner of the timeline to change its shape both horizontally and vertically.

Or

1. Click the timeline.

2. On the **Options** tool tab, in the **Size** group, do either (or both) of the following:

   - In the **Height** box, enter a new height for the timeline, and then press **Enter**.

   - In the **Width** box, enter a new width for the timeline, and then press **Enter**.

To hide or display timeline elements

1. Click the timeline.

2. On the **Options** tool tab, in the **Show** group, select or clear any of these check boxes:

   - **Header**

   - **Selection Label**

   - **Scrollbar**

   - **Time Level**

To change a timeline caption

1. Click the timeline.

2. On the **Options** tool tab, in the **Timeline** group, in the **Timeline Caption** box, enter a new caption for the timeline.

3. Press **Enter**.

To delete a timeline

1. Right-click the timeline, and then click **Remove Timeline**.

Bring in external data by using Power Query

Excel includes a wide range of analytical tools you can use to generate useful insights from your data. Excel 2019 includes Power Query, a versatile tool you can use to manage external data sources effectively. Unlike in previous versions of Excel, in which you needed to install Power Query as a separate add-in, Power Query is built into Excel 2019.

 TIP You don't need to enable the Data Analysis add-ins to use Power Query, but they work best together.

You can create data connections to many different sources:

- **Files** These include Excel workbooks, CSV files, XML files, and text files.

- **Databases** These include Microsoft SQL Server, Access, SQL Server Analysis Services, Oracle, IBM DB2, MySQL, PostgreSQL, Sybase, and Teradata.

- **Microsoft Azure** These include Azure SQL Database, Azure Marketplace, Azure HDInsight, Azure Blob Storage, and Azure Table Storage.

- **Other sources** These include the web, Microsoft SharePoint lists, Hadoop files (HDFS), Facebook, Salesforce, and other sources with available Open Database Connectivity (ODBC) drivers.

Creating a query involves identifying the type of data source to which you want to connect, selecting the software from among that type's choices, and providing any necessary credentials to access the data source. Some systems require you to log on to an account to access your data, for example.

After you define your data connection, you can specify which elements of the data source you want to import. Many Excel files and databases contain multiple tables, so you can select which of them to bring in.

15

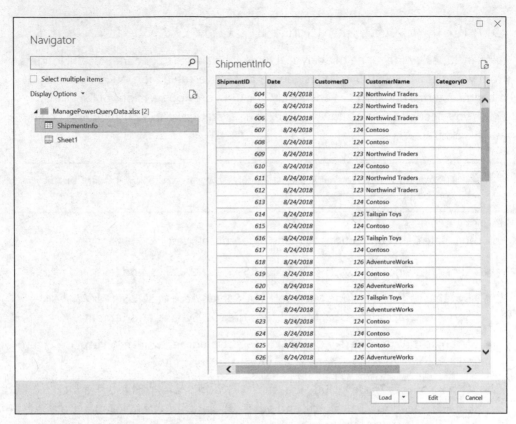

Select the file element you want to use as your query data source.

After your query data appears in an Excel table, you can work with it as you would any other data. You can unlock more powerful tools by turning on the Data Analysis add-ins and adding the Excel table to the Data Model. When the Excel table is part of the Data Model, you can define relationships between it and other tables to enhance your analysis.

Some data sources are poorly designed and don't include an index field, which contains a unique value for each row. If that's the case, you can add an index, starting at the value of your choice and increasing in the increment you want, to provide the tool you need to create relationships between tables.

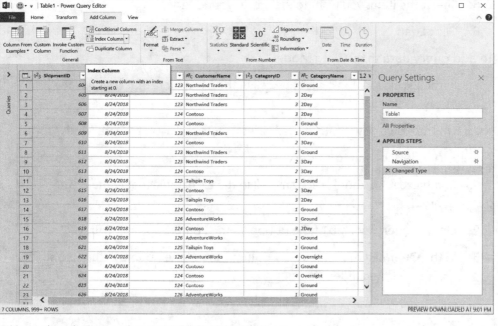

Add an index column so each row contains a unique value.

As with other Excel workbook objects, you can edit your queries after you create them. You can select which columns to include in or exclude from your results, change the query's name, edit or undo a change, and even delete your query to generate the result you want.

To create a query

1. In the Excel workbook, on the **Data** tab of the ribbon, in the **Get & Transform** group, click **New Query**.

2. Use the tools on the list to identify the data source to which you want to connect.

3. In the **Import Data** dialog box, click the data source you want to query, and then click **Open**.

4. In the **Navigator**, click the data source you want to query.

   Or

   Select the **Select multiple items** check box, and then click the data sources you want to query.

15

5. Select the items you want to include in your query.

6. Click **Load**.

To add query data to the Data Model

1. In the Excel workbook, click any cell in the Excel table that contains the query data.

2. On the **Power Pivot** tab, in the **Tables** group, click **Add to Data Model**.

To add an index column to a query

1. In the Excel workbook, click any cell in the Excel table that contains the query data.

2. On the **Query** tool tab of the ribbon, in the **Edit** group, click **Edit**.

3. In the **Query Editor**, on the **Add Column** tab of the ribbon, in the **General** group, click **Add Index Column**.

   Or

   Click the **Add Index Column** arrow (not the button), and then use the tools in the list to define the starting point for your index.

4. In the **Query Editor**, on the **Home** tab of the ribbon, in the **Close** group, click **Close & Load**.

To choose columns to include in your query results

1. In the Excel workbook, click any cell in the Excel table that contains the query data.

2. On the **Query** tool tab, click **Edit**.

3. In the **Query Editor**, on the **Home** tab, in the **Manage Columns** group, click **Choose Columns**.

4. In the **Choose Columns** task pane, select the check boxes next to the columns you want to keep in your query results.

5. Click **OK**.

To remove a column from your query results

1. Open the query in the **Query Editor**.

2. Click a cell in the column you want to remove.

3. In the **Manage Columns** group, click **Remove Columns**.

To change the data type of a column

1. Open the query in the **Query Editor**.

2. Click a cell in the column you want to edit.

3. On the **Home** tab, in the **Transform** group, click **Data Type**, and then click the new data type for the column.

To change the name of a query

1. Display the query in the **Query Editor**.

2. If necessary, on the **View** tab of the ribbon, in the **Show** group, click **Query Settings** to display the **Query Settings** task pane.

3. In the **Query Settings** task pane, in the **Name** box, enter a new name for the query.

Use the Query Settings task pane to rename and edit queries.

To undo a change to a query

1. Display the query in the **Query Editor**.

2. If necessary, click **Query Settings** to display the **Query Settings** task pane.

3. In the **Applied Steps** list, point to the change you want to delete, and then click the delete icon that appears to the left of the change.

4. If necessary, in the **Delete Step** confirmation dialog box, click **Delete** to finish deleting the change.

To edit a change to a query

1. Display the query in the **Query Editor**.

2. If necessary, click **Query Settings** to display the **Query Settings** task pane.

3. In the **Applied Steps** list, point to the change you want to edit, and then click the action icon (it looks like a gear or cog) that appears to the right of the change.

4. In the dialog box that appears, edit the properties of the change.

5. Click **OK**.

To close a query and return to Excel

1. In the **Query Editor**, on the **Home** tab, in the **Close** group, click **Close & Load**.

2. If necessary, in the dialog box that appears, click **Keep** to keep your changes.

To delete a query

1. In the Excel workbook, click any cell in the Excel table that contains the query data.

2. On the **Query** tool tab, in the **Edit** group, click **Delete**.

3. In the **Delete Query** dialog box that appears, click **Delete**.

Skills review

In this chapter, you learned how to:

- Define a Data Model
- Define relationships between tables
- Analyze data by using Power Pivot
- View data by using timelines
- Bring in external data by using Power Query

Practice tasks

The practice files for these tasks are located in the Excel2019SBS\Ch15 folder. You can save the results of the tasks in the same folder.

Define a Data Model

Open the DefineModel workbook in Excel, and then perform the following tasks:

1. Open the **Excel Options** dialog box.

2. Enable the **Data Analysis** add-ins.

3. Close the **Excel Options** dialog box.

4. Add the **Customers** and **Shipments** tables to the Data Model.

Define relationships between tables

Open the DefineRelationships workbook in Excel, and then perform the following tasks:

1. If necessary, add the two Excel tables in the workbook to the Data Model.

2. Display the Data Model in Diagram View.

3. Create relationships between the following pairs of tables:

   - **Customers** and **Shipments** based on **CustomerID**

   - **Categories** and **Shipments** based on **CategoryID**

4. Close the Data Model and return to the main workbook.

Analyze data by using Power Pivot

Open the AnalyzePowerPivotData workbook in Excel, and then perform the following tasks:

1. Display the Data Model in Data View.

2. On the **Home** tab of the ribbon, click **PivotTable**.

3. Create a **PivotTable** that displays the customers' names as the row headers and the total value of their shipments in the **Values** area.

4. Change the data type of the **Value** field to **Currency**.

5. Add a calculated column that adds a 3-percent surcharge to each shipment to account for increased fuel costs.

View data by using timelines

Open the ViewUsingTimelines workbook in Excel, and then perform the following tasks:

1. Click any cell in the PivotTable in the **Summary** worksheet.

2. Create a timeline that lets you filter the PivotTable by using the values in the **OrderDate** field.

3. Using the timeline, filter the PivotTable to display the **Sum of OrderAmount** for **November 2018**, then for **November** and **December 2018**, and for the third quarter of the year.

4. Change the timeline's appearance so it has a yellow and black theme.

5. Clear the filter, and then delete the timeline.

Bring in external data by using Power Query

Open the CreateQuery workbook in Excel, and then perform the following tasks:

1. Using the tools on the **Data** tab of the ribbon, use Power Query to import the table named **ShipmentInfo** from the **ManagePowerQueryData** workbook.

2. Add the query's results to the Data Model.

3. Remove the **CustomerID** and **CategoryID** fields from the query's results.

4. Change the name of the query.

5. Save your work and return to the main Excel workbook.

Create forecasts and visualizations

The business intelligence tools built into Excel 2019 greatly extend the app's analytical and visualization capabilities. For example, although you have always been able to forecast future data based on current trends, you can now use an advanced technique called exponential smoothing to give greater weight to recent values instead of considering all historical data in the same light.

You can also use the Excel Data Model to create forecast worksheets, measures, key performance indicators (KPIs), and 3D maps to visualize your data. Forecast worksheets use exponential smoothing formulas to project future values in a visual display. Measures and KPIs summarize and evaluate business data against goals you set. Finally, 3D maps represent your data geographically, using maps to show static values and how your data changes over time.

This chapter guides you through procedures related to creating forecast worksheets, forecasting data by using formulas that define and manage measures, defining and displaying KPIs, and creating 3D maps.

> ⚠ **IMPORTANT** To complete some of the tasks in this chapter, you will need to enable the Data Analysis add-ins.

In this chapter

- Create forecast worksheets
- Define and manage measures
- Define and display key performance indicators
- Create 3D maps

Practice files

For this chapter, use the practice files from the Excel2019SBS\Ch16 folder. For practice file download instructions, see the introduction.

Create forecast worksheets

Excel 2019 extends your ability to analyze business data by creating forecasts. Analyzing trends in Excel isn't new; you've been able to guess at future values based on historical data for quite some time. For example, you can create a linear forecast by using the *FORECAST.LINEAR()* function, which has the syntax *FORECAST.LINEAR(x, known_ys, known_xs)*. The *known_xs* argument contains a range of independent variables, such as years, and the *known_ys* describe dependent variables, such as package volumes for a specified year. The *FORECAST.LINEAR()* function takes those historical values and projects the package volume for future year *x* if current trends continue.

A quick way to extend a data series is to select the cells that contain your historical data and then drag the fill handle down to extend the series. Excel analyzes the pattern of the available values and adds new values based on that analysis.

 IMPORTANT The values used to create your forecast worksheet must be evenly spaced, such as every day, every seven days, or the first day of each month or year.

The standard exponential smoothing function, *FORECAST.ETS()*, returns the forecasted value for a specific future target date by using an exponential smoothing algorithm. This function has the syntax *FORECAST.ETS(target_date, values, timeline, [seasonality], [data_completion], [aggregation])*. The arguments used by this function are as follows:

- *target_date (required)* The date for which you want to predict a value, expressed as either a date/time value or a number. The *target_date* value must come after the last data point in the timeline.

- *values (required)* Refers to the historical values Excel uses to create a forecast.

- *timeline (required)* Refers to the dates or times Excel uses to establish the order of the *values* data. The dates in the *timeline* range must have a consistent step between them, which can't be zero.

- *seasonality (optional)* A number value indicating the presence, absence, or length of a season in the data set. A value of *1* has Excel detect seasonality automatically, *0* indicates no seasonality, and positive whole numbers up to *8,760* (the number of hours in a year) indicate to the algorithm to use patterns of this length as the seasonality period.

- *data_completion (optional)* *FORECAST.ETS()* allows, and can adjust for, up to 30 percent of missing data in a time series. A value of *0* directs the algorithm to account for missing points as zeros, whereas the default value of *1* accounts for missing points by computing them as the average of the neighboring points.

- *aggregation (optional)* This argument tells *FORECAST.ETS()* how to aggregate multiple points that have the same time stamp. The default value of *0* directs the algorithm to use *AVERAGE*. Other options available in the AutoComplete list are *SUM*, *COUNT*, *COUNTA*, *MIN*, *MAX*, and *MEDIAN*.

FORECAST.ETS.SEASONALITY() follows exactly the same syntax as *FORECAST.ETS()*, but it returns the length of the seasonal period the algorithm detects. As with *FORECAST.ETS()*, the maximum seasonal period is 8,760 units.

You will often use *FORECAST.ETS.SEASONALITY()* and *FORECAST.ETS()* together, or *FORECAST.ETS()* by itself. The output of *FORECAST.ETS.SEASONALITY()* isn't very useful without a forecast.

The final function, *FORECAST.ETS.CONFINT()*, returns a confidence interval for the forecast value at the specified target date. The confidence interval is the value by which the actual value will differ from the forecast, plus or minus a certain value that Excel calculates, which is a specified percentage of the time. The function has the following syntax: *FORECAST.ETS.CONFINT(target_date, values, timeline, [confidence_level], [seasonality], [data_completion], [aggregation])*.

 TIP Smaller *confidence_level* values allow for smaller confidence intervals because the actual result doesn't have to be within the confidence interval as often. Larger *confidence_level* values require a larger interval to account for the greater probability of unlikely results.

The new argument, *confidence_level*, is an optional argument that lets you specify how certain you want the estimate to be. For example, a *confidence_level* value of 80 percent would require the actual value to be within the confidence interval (plus or minus a certain value that Excel calculates) 80 percent of the time.

 TIP The default *confidence_level* value is 95 percent.

16

Excel 2019 also includes the capability to create a forecast worksheet, which uses the *FORECAST.ETS()* function to create a line or column chart showing a forecast when given historical data. The forecast worksheet provides a striking visual summary of the exponential smoothing forecast. In addition to creating the forecast, you can control the start date, set seasonality, and determine how to handle missing or duplicate values.

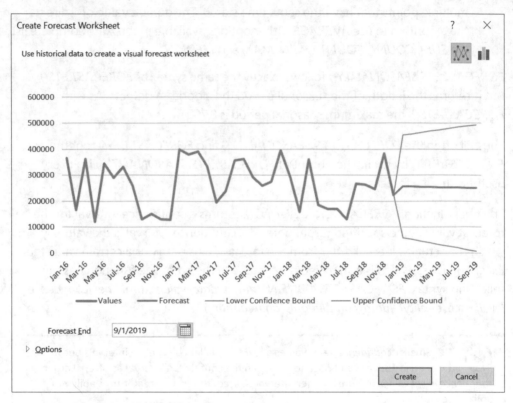

Forecast worksheets show projections for future values.

To create a linear forecast by using a formula

1. Create a list of data that contains pairs of independent variables (*known_xs*) and dependent variables (*known_ys*).

2. In a separate cell, enter a future value of *x*.

3. In another cell, create a formula with the following syntax:

   FORECAST.LINEAR(*x, known_ys, known_xs*)

4. Press **Enter**.

To create a simple forecast by using the fill handle

1. Select the cells that contain the historical data.

2. Drag the fill handle down the number of cells that represents the number of periods by which you want to extend the trend.

To create a forecast worksheet

1. Click any cell in an Excel table that contains a column with date or time data and another column with numerical results.

2. On the **Data** tab of the ribbon, in the **Forecast** group, click the **Forecast Sheet** button.

3. In the upper-right corner of the **Create Forecast Worksheet** dialog box, do one of the following:

   • Click the **Create a line chart** button to create a line chart.

   • Click the **Create a column chart** button to create a column chart.

4. Click the **Forecast End** calendar to specify an end for the forecast.

5. Click **Create**.

To create a forecast worksheet with advanced options

1. Click any cell in an Excel table that contains a column with date or time data and another column with numerical results.

2. Click **Forecast Sheet**.

3. In the **Create Forecast Worksheet** dialog box, set the chart type and forecast end, and then click **Options** to expand the dialog box.

16

Set advanced options and manage data used to create a forecast worksheet.

4. Using the tools in the **Options** area of the **Create Forecast Worksheet** dialog box, do any of the following:

   - Identify the cell range that contains the timeline values.

   - Identify the cell range that contains the numerical values.

   - Set a new forecast start date.

   - Change the confidence interval.

   - Set seasonality manually or automatically.

   - Include or exclude forecast statistics.

   - Select a method for filling in missing values.

   - Select a method for aggregating multiple values for the same time period.

5. Click **Create**.

To calculate a forecast value by using exponential smoothing

1. Create a list of data that contains pairs of independent variables (*timeline*) and dependent variables (*values*).

2. In a separate cell, enter a future date (*target_date*).

3. In another cell, create a formula with the following syntax:

   FORECAST.ETS(*target_date, values, timeline, [seasonality], [data_completion], [aggregation]*)

4. Press **Enter**.

To calculate the confidence interval for a forecast by using exponential smoothing

1. Create a list of data that contains pairs of independent variables (*timeline*) and dependent variables (*values*).

2. In a separate cell, enter a future date (*target_date*).

3. In another cell, create a formula with the following syntax:

   FORECAST.ETS.CONFINT(*target_date, values, timeline, [confidence_level], [seasonality], [data_completion], [aggregation]*)

4. Press **Enter**.

To calculate the length of a seasonally repetitive pattern in time series data

1. Create a list of data that contains pairs of independent variables (*timeline*) and dependent variables (*values*).

2. In a separate cell, enter a future date (*target_date*).

3. In another cell, create a formula with the following syntax:

   FORECAST.ETS.SEASONALITY(*target_date, values, timeline, [seasonality], [data_completion], [aggregation]*)

4. Press **Enter**.

16

Define and manage measures

You can use Power Pivot to analyze huge data collections that include millions or even hundreds of millions of rows of values. Although the details are important, it's also valuable to examine your data in aggregate. This type of aggregate summary, such as the average of values in a column, is called a measure.

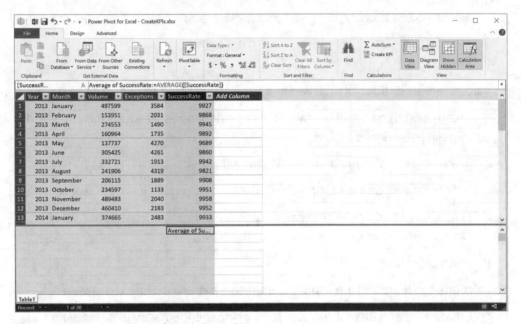

Measures summarize columns of data in Power Pivot.

 SEE ALSO For more information about using Power Pivot to analyze data, see "Analyze data by using Power Pivot" in Chapter 15, "Perform business intelligence analysis."

There are two main ways to define a measure in Power Pivot. The first is to use a version of AutoSum, which calculates a sum, average, median, or other summary of a Power Pivot column. The other method is to create a calculated column manually. Regardless of the technique you use to create your measure, you can always edit it or delete it if necessary.

To create a measure by using AutoSum

1. Open a workbook in which you have added at least one Excel table to the Excel Data Model.

2. On the **Power Pivot** tab of the ribbon, in the **Data Model** group, click **Manage** to display the Power Pivot for Excel window.

3. If necessary, in Power Pivot, on the **Home** tab of the ribbon, in the **View** group, click the **Calculation Area** button to display the Calculation Area of the grid.

4. In the Calculation Area, click the first cell below the column on which you want to base your measure.

5. On the **Home** tab, in the **Calculations** group, do either of the following:

   - Click the **AutoSum** button to create a measure by using the *SUM* function.

   - Click the **AutoSum** arrow, and then click the function you want in the list.

To create a calculated column

1. In the **Power Pivot for Excel** window, display an Excel table that is part of the Data Model.

2. Click the first blank cell in the **Add Column** column.

3. Enter = followed by the formula.

> **TIP** To refer to fields in the Excel table, enclose the name in square brackets—for example, *[Exceptions]*.

To edit a measure

1. Open a workbook in which you have added at least one measure to the Data Model.

2. If necessary, in Power Pivot, click the **Calculation Area** button to display the Calculation Area of the grid.

3. Click the cell that contains the measure.

4. In the formula bar, change the text of the measure's formula.

5. Press **Enter**.

16

To delete a measure

1. Open a workbook in which you have added at least one measure to the Data Model.

2. If necessary, in Power Pivot, click the **Calculation Area** button to display the Calculation Area of the grid.

3. Click the cell that contains the measure, and then press **Delete**.

4. In the **Confirm** dialog box, click **Delete from Model**.

Define and display key performance indicators

Businesses of all sizes can evaluate their results by using measures, which convey overall business performance by summarizing operations data. The next step in this analysis is to compare results from a specific part of the business, whether for a department or for the entire company's overall performance for a month, to determine whether the company is meeting its goals.

One popular way to measure business performance is by using key performance indicators (KPIs). A KPI is a measure that the company's officials have determined reflects the underlying health and efficiency of the organization. A shipping company might set KPIs for maintaining a low level of package handling errors, or a charitable organization could set a KPI for returning as much of its donation income as possible to their clients through service and direct support.

KPIs are most often implemented through a dashboard that summarizes organizational performance. In Excel 2019, you add KPIs to your workbooks by creating PivotTables based on data stored in the Data Model.

	A	B	C	D	E
1					
2					
3		Row Labels ▾	Sum of SuccessRate	Average of SuccessRate Status	
4		⊟ 2016			
5		January	9927 ●		
6		February	9868 ●		
7		March	9945 ●		
8		April	9892 ●		
9		May	9689 ●		
10		June	9860 ●		
11		July	9942 ●		
12		August	9821 ●		
13		September	9908 ●		
14		October	9951 ●		
15		November	9958 ●		
16		December	9952 ●		

A PivotTable that includes a KPI created in Power Pivot.

In some cases, high values are good, whereas in other cases low values are preferred.
For example, reducing package-handling errors and maximizing operating profit
would represent success for a shipping company. Or, a manufacturing firm might
want to reduce variance in the items they fabricate for their customers. In that case,
variance from the target value in either direction, high or low, would indicate a fault in
the process.

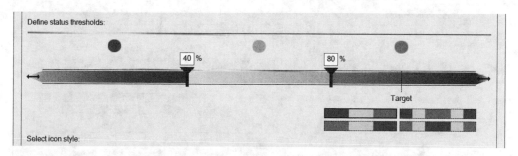

Select the pattern used to evaluate data in a KPI.

After you create a KPI, you can edit or delete it as required to meet your organization's needs.

16

To create a KPI

1. Open a workbook in which you have added at least one measure to the Data Model.

2. If necessary, in Power Pivot, on the **Home** tab, in the **View** group, click the **Calculation Area** button to display the Calculation Area of the grid.

3. In the Calculation Area, right-click the cell that contains the measure you want to use as the basis for your KPI, and then click **Create KPI**.

4. In the **Key Performance Indicator (KPI)** dialog box, click **Measure** and select the measure to use as the comparison for the KPI.

   Or

   Click **Absolute Value** and enter the target value in the box to the right of the label.

5. In the **Target** group, click the pattern that represents the distribution of good, neutral, and bad values in the data set.

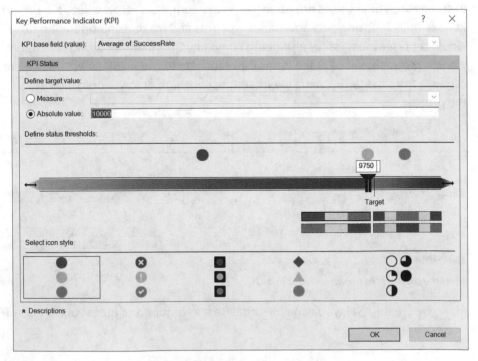

Create KPIs to summarize your organization's performance.

6. In the **Define status thresholds** area, drag the sliders to indicate where the bad, neutral, and good zones start.

   Or

   Click in the box above a slider and enter a value that defines where the zone starts.

7. Click the icon set you want to apply to the KPI.

8. Click **OK**.

To use a KPI in a PivotTable

1. On the **Data** tab, in the **Data Tools** group, click **Manage Data Model**.

2. In the **Power Pivot for Excel** window, on the **Home** tab, click the **PivotTable** button (not the arrow).

3. In the **Create PivotTable** dialog box, click **New Worksheet**, and then click **OK**.

4. If necessary, in the **PivotTable Fields** task pane, click the name of the Excel table that contains your data.

5. Add fields to the **Rows** and **Columns** areas to organize your data, and then add the field that contains the data to the **Values** area.

6. At the bottom of the field list, expand the field name of the measure you used to create your KPI.

7. Drag the **Status** field to the **Values** area.

To edit a KPI

1. Open a workbook in which you have added at least one KPI to the Data Model.

2. If necessary, in Power Pivot, on the **Home** tab, in the **View** group, click the **Calculation Area** button to display the Calculation Area of the grid.

3. In the Calculation Area, right-click the cell that contains the measure you are using as the basis for your KPI, and then click **Edit KPI Settings**.

4. Use the controls in the **Key Performance Indicator (KPI)** dialog box to change the KPI's settings.

5. Click **OK**.

16

To delete a KPI

1. Open a workbook in which you have added at least one KPI to the Data Model.

2. If necessary, display the Calculation Area of the grid.

3. In the Calculation Area, right-click the cell that contains the measure you are using as the basis for your KPI, and then click **Delete KPI**.

4. In the **Confirm** dialog box, click **Delete from Model**.

Create 3D maps

Much of the business data you collect will refer to geographic entities such as countries, regions, cities, or states. In Excel 2019, you can plot your data on 3D maps by using the built-in Power Map facilities.

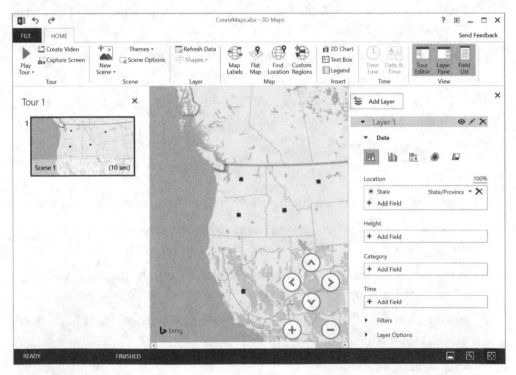

Summarize data by using a 3D map.

After you add an Excel table to the Data Model, you can summarize its data geographically. All you need to do is click a cell in the Excel table and indicate that you want to create a 3D map. Excel examines your data source and, if it recognizes geographic entities such as cities, countries, regions, and so on, it adds the corresponding field to the map's layout.

> **TIP** If you haven't clicked a cell in an Excel table that contains data you can use to create a map, Excel doesn't add a geographic data field to the Location area of the Layers task pane.

With the 3D map in place, you can add data fields to its layout, supplement the display by adding a 2D line or column chart of the data, or change the fields used in the visualization. If you have multiple geographic data levels available, such as country or region, state, and city, you can change the level of analysis before closing your map and returning to the main Excel workbook.

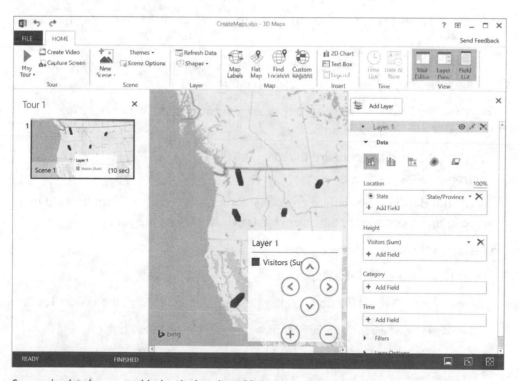

Summarize data by geographical entity by using a 3D map.

16

> **TIP** After you close the 3D Maps window, Excel adds a text box to the worksheet from which the 3D map draws its data, indicating that the workbook has 3D Maps tours available.

One real strength of 3D maps in Excel 2019 is the ability to create tours, which are animations of the data summarized in your map. If your data has a date or time component, such as years, months, and days (or specific dates), you can create an animation that shows how the data changes over time.

 IMPORTANT The field you add to the Time box must be formatted by using a Date or Time data type.

After you create your map, you can copy an image of the screen to the Clipboard, save the animation as a video, edit the map, or delete the map.

To create a 3D map

1. Click a cell in the Excel table that contains the data you want to map.

2. On the **Insert** tab of the ribbon, in the **Tours** group, click the **3D Map** button (not the arrow).

3. In the **3D Maps** window, on the **Home** tab of the ribbon, in the **View** group, click **Field List** to display the **Field List** pane.

4. Drag the field that contains geographic information, such as states, from the **Field List** to the **Location** box.

5. Drag the field that contains the summary data from the **Field List** to the **Height** box.

6. If your data contains a third component, such as a company, drag the field that contains this category data from the **Field List** to the **Category** box.

To return to the main Excel workbook

1. Perform either of these steps:

   • In the **3D Maps** window, display the Backstage view, and then click **Close**.

   • On the title bar of the **3D Maps** window, click the **Close** button.

To launch a 3D map

1. On the **Insert** tab of the ribbon, in the **Tours** group, click the **3D Map** button (not the arrow).

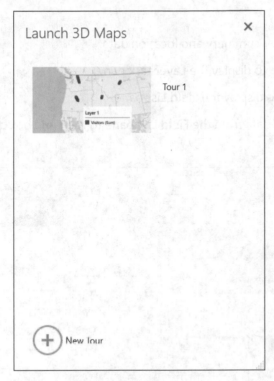

Select an existing 3D map to launch.

2. In the **Launch 3D Maps** dialog box, click the tour you want to launch.

To summarize mapped data by using a 2D chart

1. Launch the 3D map you want to summarize.

2. On the **Home** tab, in the **Insert** group, click **2D Chart**.

3. If necessary, point to the chart, click the **Change the chart type** button in the upper-right corner of the chart, and then click a new chart type.

To change the geographical type of a visualization

1. Launch the 3D map you want to edit.

2. In the **View** group, click **Layer Pane** to display the **Layer** task pane.

3. Also, if necessary, click **Field List** to display the **Field List** pane.

4. In the **Location** box, click the geographical type.

5. In the list that appears, click the new level at which you want to summarize the data.

16

To animate your data over time

1. Create a 3D map that includes summary and location data.

2. If necessary, click **Layer Pane** to display the **Layer** task pane.

3. If necessary, click **Field List** to display the **Field List** pane.

4. Drag a field containing time data from the **Field List** pane to the **Time** box of the **Layer** task pane.

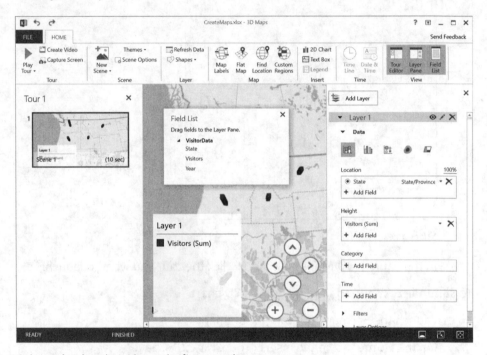

Animate data by using a time series from your data set.

5. On the **Home** tab, in the **Tour** group, click **Play Tour**.

To filter 3D map data

1. Launch the 3D map you want to edit.

2. If necessary, click **Layer Pane** to display the **Layer** task pane.

3. In the **Layer** task pane, click **Filters**, click **Add Filter**, and then click the field by which you want to filter your map.

Apply a filter to focus on specific data in your map.

4. Use the controls in the **Filters** area of the **Layer** task pane to create your filter.

5. Click **Apply Filter**.

To remove a 3D map filter

1. Display the 3D map from which you want to remove the filter.

2. In the **Layer** task pane, display the available filters.

3. Point to the filter you want to remove, and then click **Delete Filter**.

To capture a screenshot of a 3D map

1. Display the 3D map whose image you want to capture.

2. On the **Home** tab, in the **Tour** group, click **Capture Screen** to copy an image of the map to the Clipboard.

3. Open the document in which you want to paste the image of the map.

4. Press **Ctrl+V** (or use the appropriate paste command for the app you opened) to paste the map image into the open document.

To play a 3D map tour as a video

1. Display a 3D map tour that has a time component.

2. On the **Home** tab, in the **Tour** group, click **Play Tour**.

3. When the tour finishes playing, point to the bottom of the screen to display the control bar, and then click the **Go Back to Edit View** button.

16

To save a 3D map video

1. Display a 3D map tour that has a time component.

2. In the **Tour** group, click **Create Video**.

3. In the **Create Video** dialog box, click the button that represents the video quality and resolution you want.

4. Click **Create**.

5. In the **Save Movie** dialog box, navigate to the folder where you want to save the video.

6. In the **File name** box, enter a name for the video.

7. Click **Save**.

To delete a 3D map

1. In an Excel workbook that contains 3D maps, on the **Insert** tab, click the **3D Map** button (not the arrow).

2. In the **Launch 3D Maps** dialog box, point to the 3D map tour you want to delete, and click the **Delete this Tour** button in the upper-right corner of the tour.

3. In the **Delete Tour** dialog box, click **Yes** to confirm that you want to delete the tour.

4. Close the **Launch 3D Maps** dialog box.

Skills review

In this chapter, you learned how to:

- Create forecast worksheets

- Define and manage measures

- Define and display key performance indicators

- Create 3D maps

Practice tasks

The practice files for these tasks are located in the Excel2019SBS\Ch16 folder. You can save the results of the tasks in the same folder.

Create forecast worksheets

Open the CreateForecastSheets workbook in Excel, and then perform the following tasks:

1. In cell **I5**, create a formula that uses exponential smoothing to forecast the value for **January 2019** (found in cell **I3**) based on the values in the **MonthYear** and **Volume** columns in the Excel table.

2. Using the same inputs, calculate the 95-percent confidence interval (the default value) for your forecast.

3. In cell **I9**, calculate the length of the season implied by the data used in the previous two formulas.

4. Create a forecast worksheet by using the data in the **MonthlyVolume** table on **Sheet1**.

5. If necessary, edit the forecast worksheet so its **Timeline Range** is cells **D1:D37** and the **Values Range** is cells **E1:E37**.

6. Change the forecast worksheet's **Confidence Interval** to 90 percent.

Define and manage measures

Open the DefineMeasures workbook in Excel, and then perform the following tasks:

1. Display the Data Model.

2. Create a measure for the **Exceptions** field that finds the sum of the **Exceptions** values.

3. Create a measure for the **SuccessRate** field that finds the sum of the **SuccessRate** values.

4. Delete the measure that finds the sum of the **Exceptions** values.

5. Edit the measure that finds the sum of the **SuccessRate** values so that it finds the average of those values.

Define and display KPIs

Open the CreateKPIs workbook in Excel, and then perform the following tasks:

1. Open PowerPivot and display the Data Model.

2. Create a KPI named **Status** based on the **Average of SuccessRate** measure with the following characteristics:

   - An absolute value of 9925

   - A green lower limit of 9900

   - A yellow lower limit of 9825

   - The black-bordered traffic-light icon set

3. While still within Power Pivot, create a PivotTable on a new worksheet.

4. In the **PivotTable Fields** task pane, add the **Year** and **Month** columns to the **Rows** area, and then the **Success Rate** and **Status** fields to the **Values** area.

Create 3D maps

Open the CreateMaps workbook in Excel, and then perform the following tasks:

1. Create a 3D map based on the data in the **VisitorData** Excel table. Show the visitors by state.

2. Add the **Year** field to the **Time** area, and then play the tour.

3. Create and save a video based on the tour you created.

4. Add a 2D chart that summarizes your data in a clustered column chart.

Appendix

Keyboard shortcuts

Following is a comprehensive list of shortcuts derived from Excel 2019 Help. Some shortcuts might not be available in every edition of Excel 2019.

Ctrl-combination shortcut keys

Key	Description
Ctrl+Shift+)	Unhides any hidden columns within the selection.
Ctrl+Shift+(	Unhides any hidden rows within the selection.
Ctrl+Shift+&	Applies the outline border to the selected cells.
Ctrl+Shift+_	Removes the outline border from the selected cells.
Ctrl+Shift+~	Applies the General format.
Ctrl+Shift+$	Applies the Currency format with two decimal places (negative numbers in parentheses).
Ctrl+Shift+%	Applies the Percentage format with no decimal places.
Ctrl+Shift+^	Applies the Scientific format with two decimal places.
Ctrl+Shift+#	Applies the Date format with the day, month, and year.
Ctrl+Shift+@	Applies the Time format with the hour and minute, and A.M. or P.M.
Ctrl+Shift+!	Applies the Number format with two decimal places, the thousands separator, and a minus sign (-) for negative values.
Ctrl+Shift+*	Selects the current region around the active cell (the data area enclosed by blank rows and blank columns). In a PivotTable, selects the entire PivotTable report.
Ctrl+;	Enters the current date.
Ctrl+Shift+:	Enters the current time.
Ctrl+Shift+"	Copies the value from the cell above the active cell into the selected cell or the formula bar.

Key	Description
Ctrl+'	Copies a formula from the cell above the active cell into the cell or the formula bar.
Ctrl+Plus (+)	Opens the Insert dialog box to insert blank cells, rows, or columns.
Ctrl+Minus (-)	Opens the Delete dialog box to delete the selected cells, rows, or columns.
Ctrl+1	Opens the Format Cells dialog box.
Ctrl+2	Switches to apply or remove bold formatting. (Ctrl+B does the same thing.)
Ctrl+3	Switches to apply or remove italic formatting. (Ctrl+I does the same thing.)
Ctrl+4	Switches to apply or remove underlining. (Ctrl+U does the same thing.)
Ctrl+5	Switches to apply or remove strikethrough.
Ctrl+6	Switches between hiding and displaying objects.
Ctrl+8	Switches to display or hide the outline symbols.
Ctrl+9	Hides the selected rows.
Ctrl+0	Hides the selected columns.
Ctrl+A	Selects the entire worksheet. If the worksheet contains data, Ctrl+A selects the current region. Pressing Ctrl+A a second time selects the entire worksheet. When the cursor is to the right of a function name in a formula, this shortcut opens the Function Arguments dialog box.
Ctrl+Shift+A	Inserts the argument names and parentheses when the cursor is to the right of a function name in a formula.
Ctrl+B	Switches to apply or remove bold formatting. (Ctrl+2 does the same thing.)
Ctrl+C	Copies the selected cells.
Ctrl+D	Uses the Fill Down command to copy the contents and format of the topmost cell of a selected range into the cells below.
Ctrl+F	Opens the Find And Replace dialog box, with the Find tab active. (Shift+F5 also displays this page, whereas Shift+F4 repeats the last Find action.)

Key	Description
Ctrl+Shift+F	Opens the Format Cells dialog box with the Font tab active.
Ctrl+G	Opens the Go To dialog box. (F5 also opens this dialog box.)
Ctrl+H	Opens the Find And Replace dialog box, with the Replace tab active.
Ctrl+I	Switches to apply or remove italic formatting. (Ctrl+3 does the same thing.)
Ctrl+K	Opens the Insert Hyperlink dialog box for new hyperlinks or the Edit Hyperlink dialog box for selected existing hyperlinks.
Ctrl+L	Opens the Create Table dialog box.
Ctrl+N	Creates a new, blank workbook.
Ctrl+O	Displays the Open page of the Backstage view to open or find a file.
Ctrl+Shift+O	Selects all cells that contain comments.
Ctrl+P	Displays the Print page of the Backstage view.
Ctrl+Shift+P	Opens the Format Cells dialog box with the Font tab active.
Ctrl+Q	Displays the Quick Analysis Lens.
Ctrl+R	Uses the Fill Right command to copy the contents and format of the leftmost cell of a selected range into the cells to the right.
Ctrl+S	Saves the active file with its current file name, location, and file format.
Ctrl+T	Opens the Create Table dialog box.
Ctrl+U	Switches to apply or remove underlining. (Ctrl+4 does the same thing.)
Ctrl+Shift+U	Switches between expanding and collapsing the formula bar.
Ctrl+V	Inserts the contents of the Clipboard at the cursor and replaces any selection. Available only after you have cut or copied an object, text, or cell contents on a worksheet or in another app.
Ctrl+Alt+V	Opens the Paste Special dialog box. Available only after you have cut or copied an object, text, or cell contents on a worksheet or in another app.
Ctrl+W	Closes the selected workbook window.
Ctrl+X	Cuts the selected cells.

Key	Description
Ctrl+Y	Repeats the last command or action, if possible.
Ctrl+Z	Uses the Undo command to reverse the last command or to delete the last entry that you entered.

 TIP The Ctrl combinations Ctrl+J and Ctrl+M are currently unassigned to any shortcuts.

Function keys

Key	Description
F1	Opens the Excel Help window.
Ctrl+F1	Displays or hides the ribbon.
Alt+F1	Creates an embedded chart of the data in the current range.
Alt+Shift+F1	Inserts a new worksheet.
F2	Opens the active cell for editing and positions the cursor at the end of the cell contents. Moves the cursor into the formula bar when editing in a cell is turned off.
Ctrl+F2	Displays the Print Preview area on the Print page of the Backstage view.
Shift+F2	Adds a cell comment or opens an existing comment for editing.
F3	Opens the Paste Name dialog box. Available only if there are existing names in the workbook.
Shift+F3	Opens the Insert Function dialog box.
F4	Repeats the last command or action, if possible.
Ctrl+F4	Closes the selected workbook window.
Shift+F4	Repeats the last Find action.
Alt+F4	Closes Excel.
F5	Opens the Go To dialog box.
Ctrl+F5	Restores the window size of the selected workbook window.

Key	Description
Shift+F5	Opens the Find And Replace dialog box, with the Find tab active. (Ctrl+Shift+F also displays this page.)
F6	Switches between the worksheet, ribbon, task pane, and Zoom controls. In a worksheet that has been split, includes the split panes when switching between panes and the ribbon area.
Ctrl+F6	Switches to the next workbook window when more than one workbook window is open.
Shift+F6	Switches between the worksheet, Zoom controls, task pane, and ribbon.
F7	Opens the Spelling dialog box to check spelling in the active worksheet or selected range.
Ctrl+F7	Performs the Move command on the workbook window when it is not maximized. Use the arrow keys to move the window, and when finished, press Enter or Esc to cancel.
F8	Turns extend mode on or off. In extend mode, Extended Selection appears in the status line, and the arrow keys extend the selection.
Ctrl+F8	Performs the Size command (on the Control menu for the workbook window) when a workbook is not maximized.
Alt+F8	Opens the Macro dialog box to create, run, edit, or delete a macro.
Shift+F8	Turns on the functionality with which you can add a non-adjacent cell or range to a selection of cells by using the arrow keys or selecting additional cells by using the mouse. If using the arrow keys, click a cell in the next range you want to add to your selection.
F9	Calculates all worksheets in all open workbooks.
Ctrl+F9	Minimizes a workbook window to an icon.
Shift+F9	Calculates the active worksheet.
Ctrl+Alt+F9	Calculates all worksheets in all open workbooks, regardless of whether they have changed since the last calculation.
Ctrl+Alt+Shift+F9	Rechecks dependent formulas, and then calculates all cells in all open workbooks, including cells not marked as needing to be calculated.
F10	Turns key tips on or off, which allows keyboard control of the ribbon. (Pressing Alt does the same thing.)

Key	Description
Ctrl+F10	Maximizes or restores the selected workbook window.
Shift+F10	Displays the shortcut menu for a selected item.
Alt+Shift+F10	Displays the menu or message for an error-checking button.
F11	Creates a chart of the data in the current range in a separate chart sheet.
Alt+F11	Opens the Microsoft Visual Basic Editor, in which you can create a macro by using Visual Basic for Applications (VBA).
Shift+F11	Inserts a new worksheet.
F12	Opens the Save As dialog box.

Other useful shortcut keys

Key	Description
Arrow key	When a worksheet cell is selected, moves one cell up, down, left, or right in a worksheet, depending on which key you click.
Ctrl+Arrow key	Moves in the direction of the arrow key to the edge of the current data region (a range of cells that contains data and that is bounded by empty cells or datasheet borders) in a worksheet.
Shift+Arrow key	Extends the selection of cells by one cell in the direction of the arrow key.
Ctrl+Shift+ Arrow key	Extends the selection of cells in the direction of the arrow key to the last nonblank cell in the same column or row as the active cell, or if the next cell is blank, extends the selection to the next nonblank cell.
Left Arrow or Right Arrow	Selects the tab to the left or right when the ribbon is selected. When a submenu is open or selected, switches between the main menu and the submenu. When a worksheet cell is selected, moves you to the next cell in that direction.
Down Arrow or Up Arrow	Selects the next or previous command when a menu or submenu is open. When a ribbon tab is selected, navigates up or down the tab group. When a worksheet cell is selected, moves to the next cell in that direction. In a dialog box, moves between options in an open drop-down list, or between options in a group of options.

Key	Description
Down Arrow or Alt+Down Arrow	Opens a selected drop-down list.
Backspace	Deletes one character to the left in the formula bar. Clears the contents of the active cell. In cell-editing mode, deletes the character to the left of the cursor.
Delete	Removes the cell contents (data and formulas) from selected cells without affecting cell formats or comments. In cell-editing mode, deletes the character to the right of the cursor.
End	Turns End mode on. In End mode, you can press an arrow key to move to the next nonblank cell in the same column or row as the active cell in the direction of the arrow key. If the cells are blank, pressing End followed by an arrow key moves to the last cell in the row or column in the direction of the arrow key. End also selects the last command on the menu when a menu or submenu is visible.
Ctrl+End	Moves to the last cell on a worksheet: the cell in the lowest used row of the rightmost used column (in other words, the lower-right corner). If the cursor is in the formula bar, moves the cursor to the end of the text.
Ctrl+Shift+End	Extends the selection of cells to the last used cell on the worksheet (the lower-right corner). If the cursor is in the formula bar, selects all text in the formula bar from the cursor position to the end. (This does not affect the height of the formula bar.)
Enter	Completes a cell entry from the cell or the formula bar and selects the cell below (by default). In a data form, moves to the first field in the next record. Opens a selected menu (press F10 to activate the menu bar) or performs the action for a selected command. In a dialog box, performs the action for the default command button in the dialog box (the button with the bold outline, often the OK button).
Alt+Enter	Starts a new line in the same cell.
Ctrl+Enter	Fills the selected cell range with the current entry.
Shift+Enter	Completes a cell entry and selects the cell above.
Esc	Cancels an entry in the cell or formula bar. Closes an open menu or submenu, dialog box, or message window. Also switches from full-screen mode (when this mode has been applied) to normal screen mode (with the ribbon and status bar displayed).

Key	Description
Home	Moves to the beginning of a row in a worksheet. Moves to the cell in the upper-left corner of the window when Scroll Lock is turned on. Selects the first command on the menu when a menu or submenu is visible.
Ctrl+Home	Moves to the beginning of a worksheet.
Ctrl+Shift+Home	Extends the selection of cells to the beginning of the worksheet.
Page Down	Moves one screen down in a worksheet.
Alt+Page Down	Moves one screen to the right in a worksheet.
Ctrl+Page Down	Moves to the next sheet in a workbook.
Ctrl+Shift+Page Down	Selects the current and next sheets in a workbook.
Page Up	Moves one screen up in a worksheet.
Alt+Page Up	Moves one screen to the left in a worksheet.
Ctrl+Page Up	Moves to the previous sheet in a workbook.
Ctrl+Shift+Page Up	Selects the current and previous sheets in a workbook.
Spacebar	In a dialog box, performs the action for the selected button, or selects or clears a check box.
Ctrl+Spacebar	Selects an entire column in a worksheet.
Shift+Spacebar	Selects an entire row in a worksheet.
Ctrl+Shift+Spacebar	Selects the entire worksheet. If the worksheet contains data, selects the current region. Pressing Ctrl+Shift+Spacebar a second time selects the current region and its summary rows. Pressing Ctrl+Shift+Spacebar a third time selects the entire worksheet. When an object is selected, selects all objects on a worksheet.
Alt+Spacebar	Displays the Control menu for the Excel window.
Tab	Moves one cell to the right in a worksheet. Moves between unlocked cells in a protected worksheet. Moves to the next option or option group in a dialog box.
Shift+Tab	Moves to the previous cell in a worksheet or the previous option in a dialog box.
Ctrl+Tab	Switches to the next tab in a dialog box.
Ctrl+Shift+Tab	Switches to the previous tab in a dialog box.

Glossary

3-D reference A pattern for referring to the workbook, worksheet, and cell from which a value should be read.

absolute reference A cell reference, such as =$B$3, that doesn't change when you copy a formula containing the reference to another cell. See also *relative reference*.

active cell The cell that is currently selected and open for editing.

add-in A supplemental app that can be used to extend Excel.

alignment The manner in which a cell's contents are arranged within that cell (for example, centered).

arguments The specific data a function requires to calculate a value.

aspect ratio The relationship between a graphic's height and its width.

auditing The process of examining a worksheet for errors.

AutoCalculate The Excel functionality that displays summary calculations on the status bar for a selected cell range.

AutoComplete The Excel functionality that completes data entry for a cell based on similar values in other cells in the same column.

AutoFill The Excel functionality that extends a series of values based on the contents of a single cell.

AutoFilter An Excel tool you can use to create filters.

AutoRepublish The Excel technology that maintains a link between a web document and the worksheet on which the web document is based, and updates the web document whenever the original worksheet is saved.

Backstage view A view that gathers workbook-management tasks into a single location. You access Backstage view by clicking the File tab.

bin A value range used to summarize frequencies in a histogram chart. See also *histogram*.

box-and-whisker A chart type that visualizes average, median, minimum, and maximum values for one or more data series.

browser An app with which users view web documents.

button A worksheet control that can be configured to run a macro when clicked.

cell The box at the intersection of a row and a column.

cell range A group of cells.

cell reference The letter and number combination, such as C16, that identifies the row and column intersection of a cell.

cell style A built-in format that can be applied to a cell.

chart A visual summary of worksheet data, also called a *graph*.

check box A worksheet control, depicted as a square, that can be selected or cleared to turn an option on or off.

circular reference A formula that contains a reference either to itself or to a cell that uses the formula's result.

color scale A type of conditional format that changes the color of a cell's fill to reflect the value in the cell. See also *conditional format*.

column Cells that are on the same vertical line in a worksheet.

combo box A worksheet control that lets users enter or select a value from a defined list.

combo chart A chart that combines two visualization styles into a single graphic.

conditional format A format that is applied only when cell contents meet certain criteria.

conditional formula A formula that calculates a value by using one of two or more different expressions, depending on whether a third expression is true or false.

confidence interval The range of values within which future values will fall a specified percentage of the time (for example, "plus or minus 3 percent with 95-percent confidence").

control group A set of check boxes or option buttons within which only one control can be selected at a time.

data bar A horizontal line within a cell that indicates the relative magnitude of the cell's value.

data consolidation Summarizing data from a set of similar cell ranges.

data table A defined cell range that applies a set of alternative input values to a single formula.

delimiter A character in a text file that separates values from each other.

dependent A cell with a formula that uses the value from a particular cell. See also *precedent*.

digital certificate A file that contains a unique string of characters that can be combined with another file, such as an Excel workbook, to create a verifiable signature for that file.

digital signature A mathematical construct, created by combining a file and a digital certificate, that verifies the authorship and contents of a file.

distribute To share a file with other users.

Document Inspector A utility with which you can inspect an Excel workbook for personal information, tracked changes, and other sensitive data.

embed To save a file as part of another file, as opposed to linking one file to another. See also *link*.

error code A brief message that appears in a worksheet cell, describing a problem with a formula or a function.

Excel table An Excel object with which you can store and refer to data based on the name of the table and the names of its columns and rows.

exponential smoothing The process of creating a forecast by giving recent values in a data series more weight than older values.

field A column of data used to create a PivotTable.

fill handle The square at the lower-right corner of a cell that can be dragged to indicate other cells that should hold values in the series defined by the active cell.

FillSeries The Excel functionality that allows you to create a data series by defining the starting value, the rule for calculating the next value, and the length of the series.

filter A rule that Excel uses to determine which worksheet rows to display.

footer An area of the worksheet that appears below the contents of the worksheet grid when you print the worksheet or view it in Layout view.

foreign key A value in a data list or Excel table that uniquely identifies a row in another table. See also *primary key*.

format A predefined set of characteristics that can be applied to cell contents.

formula An expression used to calculate a value.

Formula AutoComplete The Excel functionality with which you can enter a formula quickly by selecting functions, named ranges, and table references that appear when you begin to type the formula into a cell.

formula bar The area just above the worksheet grid that displays the active cell's formula and within which you can edit the formula.

function A predefined formula.

Goal Seek An analysis tool that finds the value for a selected cell that would produce a specified result from a calculation.

graph A visual summary of worksheet data, also called a *chart*.

header An area of the worksheet that appears above the contents of the worksheet grid when you print the worksheet or view it in Layout view.

histogram A chart type that represents the distribution of values by counting the number of occurrences within specified ranges. See also *bin*; *Pareto*.

HTML A document-formatting system that tells a web browser such as Microsoft Edge how to display the contents of a file.

hyperlink A reference to a file on the web.

Hypertext Markup Language (HTML) See *HTML*.

icon set A conditional format that uses distinct visual indicators to designate how a value compares to a set of criteria.

key performance indicator (KPI) A metric by which an organization is deemed to be meeting, exceeding, or falling short of its goals. See also *measure*.

landscape mode A display and printing mode whereby columns run parallel to the short edge of a sheet of paper.

link 1) A formula that has a cell show the value from another cell. 2) A connection to an external data source. See also *embed*.

list box A worksheet control in which you select a value from a specified set of values.

live preview A feature of Excel that displays the result of an operation, such as pasting data or applying a cell style, without implementing the change until you complete the operation.

locked cell A cell that cannot be modified if its worksheet is protected.

macro A series of recorded automated actions that can be replayed.

mailto hyperlink A special type of hyperlink with which a user creates an email message to a particular email address.

map A correspondence between an XML schema and an Excel worksheet.

measure A summary of data, such as an average or sum, stored in a PowerPivot worksheet column. See also *key performance indicator (KPI)*.

Merge And Center An operation that combines a contiguous group of cells into a single cell. Selecting a merged cell and clicking the Merge And Center button splits the merged cells into the original group of separate cells.

named range A group of related cells defined by a single name.

OneDrive An online service, accessed through a Microsoft account, with which a user can store data in the cloud.

option button A worksheet control, depicted as a circle, that can be selected or cleared to turn an option on or off.

Pareto A type of chart that combines a histogram with a line chart to show the progressive contribution of categories to a whole. See also *histogram*.

Paste Options A button that appears after you paste an item from the Clipboard into your workbook, and that provides options for how the item appears in the workbook.

Pick From List The Excel functionality that you can use to enter a value into a cell by choosing the value from the set of values already entered into cells in the same column.

pivot To reorganize the contents of a PivotTable.

PivotChart A chart, which can be linked to a PivotTable, that can be reorganized dynamically to emphasize different aspects of the underlying data.

PivotTable A dynamic worksheet that can be reorganized by a user.

portrait mode A display and printing mode whereby columns run parallel to the long edge of a sheet of paper.

precedent A cell that is used in a formula. See also *dependent*.

primary key A field or group of fields with values that distinguish a row of data from all other rows. See also *foreign key*.

property A file detail, such as an author name or project code, that helps identify the file.

Quick Access Toolbar A customizable toolbar that contains a set of commands that are independent of the tab on the ribbon that is currently displayed.

Quick Analysis Lens A selection of tools with which a user can summarize data quickly by using formulas and charts.

range A group of related cells.

recommended chart A chart, designed by the Excel app, that summarizes a selected data range.

recommended PivotTable A PivotTable, designed by the Excel app, that summarizes a selected data range.

refresh To update the contents of one document when the contents of another document are changed.

relationship A link between two tables, based on a common field, that allows the contents of the tables to be combined.

relative reference A cell reference in a formula, such as =B3, that refers to a cell that is a specific distance away from the cell that contains the formula. For example, if the formula =B3 were in cell C3, copying the formula to cell C4 would cause the formula to change to =B4. See also *absolute reference*.

ribbon The tab-based user interface introduced in Microsoft Office 2007.

row Cells that are on the same horizontal line in a worksheet.

scale The percentage of actual size at which a worksheet is printed or displayed.

scenario An alternative data set with which you view the impact of specific changes on your worksheet.

schema A defined structure an app can use to interpret the contents of an XML file.

search filter A filter in which you enter a string of characters to instruct Excel to display every value within an Excel table, data set, or PivotTable that contains that character string.

selection filter A mechanism for selecting the specific values to be displayed in a data list, Excel table, or PivotTable.

sharing Making a workbook available for more than one user to open and modify simultaneously.

sheet tab The indicator for selecting a worksheet, located at the bottom of the workbook window.

Slicer An Excel tool with which you can filter an Excel table, data list, or PivotTable while indicating which items are displayed and which are hidden.

Solver An Excel add-in that finds the optimal value for one cell by varying the results of other cells.

sort To reorder the contents of a worksheet based on a criterion.

sparkline A compact chart that summarizes data visually within a single worksheet cell.

spin button A worksheet control that lets users increase or decrease a value by clicking up or down arrows on the control, respectively.

subtotal A partial total for related data in a worksheet.

sunburst A chart, shaped as a circle, that depicts the magnitude of values within a data set by using a combination of color, size, and position.

template A workbook used as a pattern for creating other workbooks.

theme A predefined format that can be applied to a worksheet.

timeline A worksheet control that lets users filter the contents of a PivotTable based on time increments.

Top 10 filter A filter by which a user can specify the top or bottom number of items, or top or bottom percentage of items, to display in a worksheet.

tracer arrow An arrow that indicates the formulas to which a cell contributes its value (a dependent arrow) or the cells from which a formula derives its value (a precedent arrow).

treemap A square chart that depicts the magnitude of values within a data set by using a combination of color, size, and position.

trendline A projection of future data (such as sales) based on past performance.

validation rule A test that data must pass to be entered into a cell without generating a warning message.

watch The display of a cell's contents in a separate window even when the cell is not visible in the Excel workbook.

waterfall A chart that uses columns to depict increases and decreases of a value over time based on transactional data.

what-if analysis Analysis of the contents of a worksheet to determine the impact that specific changes have on your calculations.

workbook The basic Excel document, consisting of one or more worksheets.

worksheet A page in an Excel workbook.

x-axis The horizontal axis of a chart, which usually depicts category or time data.

XML The Extensible Markup Language, through which users can identify the structure, elements, and semantic meaning of data in a text file.

y-axis The vertical axis of a chart, which usually depicts value data.

Index

D

E

Plug into learning at

microsoftpressstore.com

The Microsoft Press Store by Pearson offers:

- Free U.S. shipping

- Buy an eBook, get three formats – Includes PDF, EPUB, and MOBI to use with your computer, tablet, and mobile devices

- Print & eBook Best Value Packs

- eBook Deal of the Week – Save up to 50% on featured title

- Newsletter – Be the first to hear about new releases, announcements, special offers, and more

- Register your book – Find companion files, errata, and product updates, plus receive a special coupon* to save on your next purchase

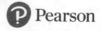 Pearson